ALSO BY PRUE LEITH
FROM CLIPPER LARGE PRINT

Choral Society
A Serving of Scandal
The Gardener

Relish

My Life on a Plate

Prue Leith

W F HOWES LTD

This large print edition published in 2013 by
W F Howes Ltd
Unit 4, Rearsby Business Park, Gaddesby Lane,
Rearsby, Leicester LE7 4YH

1 3 5 7 9 10 8 6 4 2

First published in the United Kingdom in 2012
by Quercus

Lines from the poem 'This be the Verse' by Philip
Larkin are taken from *The Complete Poems of Philip
Larkin*, published by Faber & Faber, London 2012

A CIP catalogue record for this book is available
from the British Library

ISBN 978 1 47123 979 3

Typeset by Palimpsest Book Production Limited,
Falkirk, Stirlingshire
Printed and bound by
CPI Group (UK) Ltd, Croydon, CR0 4YY

They fuck you up, your mum and dad.
They may not mean to, but they do.

Philip Larkin

In memory of my mum and dad,
who absolutely didn't.

CONTENTS

PREFACE

My brother Jamie calls me Mersey Mouth because, he says, I've a mouth as wide as the Mersey tunnel, am hopelessly indiscreet, and will make a story out of anything. My husband used to kick me under the table to shut me up.

So, first, a warning: I've taken the view that a memoir consists of events as the author remembers them: true, half-true or corrupted by years of retelling.

At first, writing a memoir seemed easier than writing a novel, where you must invent. And, I thought, it could be gratifyingly egotistical, all about me. But then, thinking harder, I realised that what I like about writing *is* the inventing. Now I'd be racking my memory rather than my imagination. And wouldn't it be boring to spend two years re-telling a life already lived?

In fact, I've enjoyed it. Indeed, too much. I've had to chop a lot out – mostly my involvement with government committees and quangos, with campaigns, commissions and reports. I'm deeply interested in the governance of companies, in education, food policy, art and design, but I can be very tedious on my soapbox so there is more about my personal life and my career in food than there is about the rest. Nevertheless, I've been unable to resist some memories of the fat-cat life of a company director, or the rewarding – but unrewarded – life of a charity boss. Readers can skip, after all.

Fifteen years ago I heard the lecturer on a screen-writing course pronounce that all good writing stemmed from an unhappy childhood – if you hadn't had one, forget it, you'd never make a writer. At lunchtime I tackled him. 'I had a *very* happy childhood. And I've managed to get two novels published.'

'Well, either you write bad novels or you are in denial about your childhood. If you are any good, believe me, it was unhappy.'

It still riles me. Why should unhappiness be the only route to good writing? Or 'misery memoirs' the only ones worth reading?

So here goes, with a very happy childhood.

CHAPTER 1

A SOUTH AFRICAN CHILDHOOD

'No lions in the Game Reserve'

While my mother was giving birth to my brother in her bedroom with the help of a midwife, I was on the kitchen table having an abscess in my ear lanced by our family doctor. My mother had insisted on this arrangement because she didn't want me, aged six, in one hospital while she was in another.

When I came round, I knew I should ask if I had a baby brother or sister, but instead I asked for a banana. Kate (our housekeeper-cum-everything who had been our father's nanny) promised I could have one later, and led me into my mother's bedroom.

My first sight of Jamie did not accord with the build-up of a delightful baby born and bred especially to be my infant playmate. The sight of my mother's nipple leaking onto his sleeping cheek disgusted me. Also he was very small and I was not allowed to wake him up.

But I was soon proudly lugging him round like a doll. He was so delicious we called him Butterball.

I adored him, and adore him still. But jealousy must have been buried somewhere: when he was nearly two and I was eight, I stood by his cot with Mum, stroking his back, and my strokes suddenly turned into pats and the pats into vicious slaps. I ran from the room, crying and baffled by the strength of my hatred. I thought my mother would come after me, furious. But she picked me up and kissed my teary face.

'Sometimes I hate him,' I wept. 'I'll end up murdering him.'

'Nonsense,' she said, handing me one of Dad's big white hankies, 'don't be such a drama queen. You love him to bits.'

At that time I worshipped my elder brother, David, two years my senior and president of the Tree Climbing Club, an all-boys affair. After a deal of badgering, I was granted honorary boyhood. I promptly climbed higher than any of them, which should have given me the presidency, but did not.

I was an honorary boy for a lot of my childhood. In David's wake I went to Cubs rather than Brownies and I played football on our lawn with the local lads. When I turned eleven my mother mysteriously decreed that I change out of my school gymslip into trousers to play.

We lived a privileged, white-South African life, and in spite of my mother (a well-known actress) being considered dangerously liberal we children were unaware of the horrors of apartheid. Mum campaigned against the laws segregating black and white actors and forbidding mixed-race audiences. She demonstrated with the women's anti-apartheid movement, the Black Sash, once coming home covered in egg yolk from a vigil on the City Hall steps.

Yet it did not seem strange or wrong to me that venerable black men would step into the gutter to make way for a bunch of chattering white kids. I thought nothing of sitting in the front of a bus while our nanny, Emma, sat at the back; that she looked after us six days a week while her aging mother took care of Emma's own children hundreds of miles away, or that Emma, along with most servants working in the reserved-for-whites areas of Johannesburg, only saw her family once a year for two weeks. I took it for granted that she was there to look after me, like an extra mother.

Most white South Africans are screwed up about race to some degree. I retain an awareness of colour that my English friends and my cosmopolitan children just don't have. My brother David tells a tale that perfectly illustrates this: when he first arrived in London, he had only a ten-shilling note to last him until his student allowance arrived a few days later. He took a taxi from Victoria station to his digs. The fare was one shilling and sixpence, but the taxi driver, who was black, said he had no change. David let him keep the whole ten bob. He would never have been so generous, or so nervous of being thought racist, if he wasn't South African.

We had a three-acre garden in the smart northern suburbs of Johannesburg, with tennis court and pool. We spent our time outdoors, free of grown-up interference. My Wendy house was an empty corrugated-iron tank with holes cut in it for door and window. We built a tree house, climbed on (and got thrown off) the donkeys that wandered unhobbled down the street, spied on 'next door', shelled peas with the cook on the back step, and hung round the servants while they did the laundry, cooked, cleaned or gardened. Best of all was being allowed into their dark, warm-smelling quarters behind the garages.

Occasionally there were outings to the zoo to ride on the elephants. Huge excitement. We sat facing out on long benches hung on the flanks of the swaying beasts as they lumbered patiently along the zoo paths. It was both frightening, like a tipping roller coaster, and wonderful to be so high, to see the other animals from our majestic vantage point. Of course animal rights or something has put a stop to such innocent pleasures, something I really don't understand. I bet the elephants preferred a walk in the park with a pack of kids up top, than standing all day in a small field as they do now.

Sometimes we'd hire a row-boat on the zoo lake. Or picnic at one of the Modderfontein dams, wild places where we could swim without seeing a soul. The whole district of Modderfontein (Mud Spring in Afrikaans) was owned by African Explosives and Chemical Industries, for which my father worked. There were the dynamite factory, office and residential areas on huge tracts of veld, the whole fenced off, gated and guarded. We would be saluted through by the smiling guards at the gatehouse.

On VJ Day (Victory over Japan) in 1945, the whole family, except old Kate and baby Jamie, who were sitting in the shade, walked across a narrow pedestrian bridge over a dam weir. The bridge had a handrail on one side only, so crossing was exciting. Dad was behind me, and my brother David, then seven, in front. Suddenly I knew that David, ever dreamy and his head full of something irrelevant, was going to turn round to ask Dad some daft question like how many inches there were in a mile, and step off the bridge. He did.

I don't remember him falling. Just him stepping off, and then lying, very small, far below on the concrete. Dad climbed rapidly round me, shouting at me to go to Kate, and he and Mum ran along the bridge and scrambled down the steep bank.

David's white shirt was billowing slightly and I thought he was moving. But he was unconscious, with a piece of reinforcing iron piercing his lower jaw. He came round at the cottage hospital almost immediately with nothing more serious than concussion and a very sore jaw. He was home two days later.

★   ★   ★

In 1946, Dad was sent to work for African Explosives' parent company, ICI, in England for three years, and we all went too.

At first we lived in a little house in Wembley. David and I, sent to play with baby Jamie in the garden, would start well enough with his favourite game: you draped a muslin nappy over his head and said, 'Where's Jamie? Where's Jamie?' And then pulled it off, exclaiming, '*There's* Jamie, *there's* Jamie!' while he hooted and giggled with delight. But, horrible children that we were, we would leave him sitting on the rug, nappy over his head, plaintively calling, 'Where's Jamie? Where's Jamie?' while we scarpered off to play without him and Kate remonstrated from the kitchen window.

Soon we were sharing a house in Blomfield Road by the Regent's Canal with the actress Nan Munro. Nan was my mother's great friend and theatrical partner. She had taken her three children to South Africa when war broke out and she and Mum had formed the Munro-Inglis Company (Mum's professional name was Margaret Inglis), which thrived until Nan went back to England after the war.

Nan's daughter Angela became my best friend and room-mate. I remember her stepfather, Rayne, carrying us children about on his shoulders and labelling our drawers 'Angela's vests, Prue's socks,' etc in a vain attempt to make two seven-year-olds keep their room tidy.

We used to watch the heavy horses plodding

along the canal tow path hauling the barges piled with coal. The once-grand houses were mostly divided into flats, some had been bombed to rubble and the area was hardly smart. But even then people called it Little Venice and Christopher Fry, the playwright, had a sign on his gate, 'Beware of the Doge'.

A group of German POWs, still captive two years after the war had ended, were digging a trench in the Edgware Road when we walked past. I was clutching both families' sweet ration, a big bag of toffees. Mum told me to offer the poor prisoners a sweet. I held out the bag to one of them, and he took the whole bag. My imminent protest was quickly stalled by Mum, with 'Don't be silly, darling. Those poor men have suffered more than we will ever know. It's only a bag of sweets.'

One day, David, then nine, was carrying our precious week's ration of six eggs (one for each child in the household) in a paper bag. One of them must have been cracked and leaked, because suddenly all six eggs were smashed on the entrance hall floor. I remember the stricken horror on David's face and the sweetness on my mother's as she tried to make him believe it did not matter. I felt it did matter. A lot.

Living with the Krugers was wonderful. Five of us children were close in age, and we got on well. I do remember some protests when it was my mother's turn to produce the family Nativity play and the Leiths got all the juicy parts. I was the

Virgin Mary, Jamie an overlarge infant Jesus, and David the Angel Gabriel with huge glamorous wings. But poor David got little satisfaction out of his archangel role. He had to stand on a radiator under the window, behind the curtains, which eventually opened to allow Mary to behold him and the Annunciation to proceed. Only later did David reveal blistered feet. The radiator had been on and David, being David, had said nothing.

Angela and I were sent to the same boarding school, a girls-only prep near Brighton that was very keen on outdoor eurhythmics, hockey, and nature study by way of freezing 'rambles' through the woods.

The big treat was a Sunday exeat. One or other of our parents would sometimes take Ange and me for Sunday lunch at the Birch Hotel in Haywards Heath. One Sunday my father was mortified by my indignant voice, an early indication of a bossy nature, 'Daddy, you may eat your pudding with a fork, or with a spoon *and* a fork, but never *ever* with a spoon by itself!' He looked round the tables of tweed-suited parents all eating their puddings correctly and realised the depth of his transgression. From then on 'Never do for the Birch' was a family saying, trotted out at any social blunder.

My most painful memory of that school was writing 'Silly Fool' on the blackboard and having the whole school kept in over break while the headmistress pressed the culprit to own up. I sat,

10

immobile with shame and fear, and said nothing. The guilt of this haunted me for years. Finally, when I was twelve, in my religious phase and wanting to wipe my slate clean with God, I wrote to the headmistress and confessed. While I was at it I also owned up to carving 'Nicky Hall' (a girl I had a crush on but now cannot remember at all) into the panelling in the girls' loo. I don't remember getting any absolution.

I do remember the misery of chilblains, an agony modern children have no conception of, and being told by the matron that it served me right for warming my frozen hands on the radiators. And I remember being sick into the hydrangeas after eating a whole pot of Marmite with my finger instead of handing it in for the breakfast table.

We returned to South Africa in 1949 when I was nine. We were to travel back on the *Cape Town Castle*. ICI, grateful for my father's three-year stint, treated him and my mother to the presidential state cabin. Mum was beside herself with excitement. Then, two weeks before we were to sail, Dad had a phone call from the head of the Union Castle Steamship company, asking if he would mind dropping by.

Dad reported the conversation:

'Mr Leith, this is a very delicate situation, and I hope you won't mind, but we have a problem . . .'

'You want me to give up my cabin for someone more important.'

'Well, yes, I am afraid . . .'

'Look. I *am* sorry, but the answer is no. There is only one man in the country that I would stand aside for, and that's Sir Winston Churchill.'

'Mr Leith, you have just lost your cabin.'

Dad used to tell a tale of feeling an arm round his stoutish shoulders and turning to confront Churchill, who hastily released his grasp and stepped back, saying, 'So sorry, I thought you were my wife.'

And in the Bay of Biscay when almost everyone was felled by sea sickness, three-year-old Jamie and I were alone in the breakfast room when Churchill came in. He surveyed the empty room and sat down with us. Jamie suddenly stood up, bowed and said, 'Excuse me, sir,' and turned to throw up in a potted plant.

Once back at my old school in Johannesburg, I wanted to curry favour with my new classmates so I claimed to know Enid Blyton personally. This of course led to demands for her autograph, and one deception rapidly led to more. I forged her signature thirty times in my school exercise book, cut each signature out and distributed them. Needless to say the lined paper gave me away at once.

One day I didn't want to go to school so pleaded a tummy ache. My performance must have been convincing because I was kept in bed, but I was alarmed when the doctor appeared. Now too deep in the lie to retreat, I yelped at every prod and to every question answered, yes it hurt. Next thing I was in hospital having my appendix out.

The surgeon gave it to me – a little white worm – in a jar of formaldehyde. One suppertime David and I added it to Kate's spaghetti, although we did rescue it before she ate it. Maybe we wanted to repeat the trick on someone else . . .

Home was much nicer than school. I spent holidays drooling over horses at the local stables or pretending my bike, Rattlecrank, was a horse. I laid out a cross-country course of ditches, small ramps and even logs, which I would pedal over fast while lifting the front wheel off the ground. Then I'd lean forward to whisper encouragement to my steed.

I genuinely couldn't understand why I should not marry a horse. I had read about an Englishwoman who had married her dog, and that made sense to me. When my father pointed out that my offspring would be centaurs, I saw nothing wrong with that. I also determined that when I grew up I would invent perfumes that would smell of horses. Or petrol, the next best smell.

I wasn't much of a rider though. When I was about ten I was competing in a gymkhana with my hired pony Cherry. We were first in the ring, but Cherry skidded to a stop at the first jump. I wheeled her round and tried again. Twice. And then the bell rang and that was that. My loyal mother, watching, cringed with shame when I lost my temper and whacked poor Cherry with my riding crop as we ignominiously cantered out of the ring.

One holiday I was sent to stay on an Afrikaans farm – the theory being that it would improve my Afrikaans, which, since we all talked English, it didn't. But I fell in love with a bay pony called Laddie.

My relentless campaign to own Laddie finally wore my parents down, whereupon all the consequences they had feared and I had denied, came to pass. Laddie's tack cost more than he did; vet's bills and livery bills arrived thick and fast. And now I pestered to go to the farm every holiday, or pleaded for Laddie to come to Johannesburg.

And of course, as soon as Laddie was in Johannesburg, stabled a few miles away, I wanted him at home, but my parents baulked at building him a stable in the back garden. So I built a barricade on the back *stoep* (veranda) and secretly installed him behind it. I don't know how I thought I could keep his presence secret, but anyway his sojourn was short-lived. On the first night he barged his way through my flimsy fencing and disappeared. Half-mad with anxiety, I searched the suburban streets for miles around. Eventually I found him in a field of mares three miles away and the other side of a dual-carriageway.

There were other animals: various dogs, multiple cats and a succession of white mice. David had an aviary full of budgies and parakeets on the terrace, and once briefly owned a magnificent

14

eagle owl. And I had two bush babies who lived in my bedroom, refusing to be caught at night and leaping from cupboard top to curtain rail and back again.

David was still my hero. He was sweet-natured and absent-minded, but when challenged showed steely determination. I admired his bravery, but even then I found him strangely different from extrovert me and sunny Jamie. In his first term at his secondary school he was asked by a prefect to box for his house. In spite of never having boxed before, he agreed. By far the lightest lad in his class, he was punched round the ring for round after round while my poor mother watched. He eventually won on points.

As a teenager, he and his friend Mike went bird-nesting at Modderfontein and were attacked by a swarm of African bees. Mike, with three hundred stings, collapsed, so David, covered in stings himself and pursued by the swarm, ran several miles to the hospital, refused treatment and persuaded a complete stranger to drive him back to collect Mike, who was by now unconscious.

Another time, David and his friend Robin nicked the friend's aunt's car and drove it into a lamp-post, putting out all the lights in the district, and ending up in hospital.

'But why did you let Robin drive, when he can't?' I wanted to know.

'Because it was only fair. It was his aunt's car, not mine.'

Having an elder brother, especially a slightly mad one, was a feather in my cap. When David and a bunch of classmates stole into my boarding school at night to sink the great school bell in the deep-end of the swimming pool, I basked in reflected glory.

My brothers' school terms and mine did not always coincide, so I was sometimes packed off for a holiday to my Cape relatives. My Leith grandparents lived in a little bungalow outside Simonstown, and they let me do much as I liked. I would run down the road past all the other bungalows, step illegally over the railway tracks (heart thumping in terror of being mown down by a train even though I could see both ways and *knew* there was no train). Then I would slide down the embankment to the unkempt shingle beach on which my grandparents had a painted beach hut. I would pretend it was my house and that I lived there all alone.

I was fascinated by Gran's beautiful Regency table. There were little compartments for money and pens, and drawers that swung out sideways on hinges. I was told it had been the rent-table belonging to Lord Charles Somerset, Governor of the first British Cape Settlement of 1820. The whole table top swivelled so that when the factor put a rent-book down, or the tenant put his money down, no hand need touch.

When Granny Leith died, I was astonished to find she'd left the table to me. It arrived in a huge crate at my little mews cottage in Paddington. I have it still, by far the most valuable piece of furniture I possess. And it still has the mark of a pair of Victorian embroidery scissors that must have once rusted onto the top, the mark then polished over for nearly 200 years.

More exciting, though, was staying with my Uncle Jack, my mother's brother, and Aunt Judy. Jack never dished out compliments but he was always interested in us children and we all adored him, as do all today's current crop of grand-children, great-grandchildren, nieces and nephews.

At the age of eleven (nascent puberty I suppose) my adoration for my quiet, slim, fit, handsome and tanned uncle became heart-stopping love. Once, staying with him and Judy at their holiday house in Hermanus. I slept on the top bunk on the *stoep*, trying desperately to stay awake so I could demand a kiss goodnight. The most I ever achieved was an affectionate ruffle of my hair.

Jack was always as good as his word. At breakfast one day he announced we were leaving for the beach at eleven o'clock and anyone who wasn't in the car by then would be left behind. William, his second youngest, then about eight, was duly abandoned as he ran after us down the drive, wailing.

One holiday, knowing I was mad about horses, Jack and Judy borrowed a farmer's carthorse for me. I was used to the riding school discipline of wearing a hard hat and proper boots, being closely watched and held on a leading rein. But Jack just told me the horse and tack were in the shed, and let me get on with it. The horse was huge and I had to climb up a water butt to mount him, but somehow I managed, and was mighty pleased with myself.

Once we climbed Table Mountain and camped in a cave. Jack made a fire and we *braai'd* (barbecued) our lamb chops and then, cosy in sleeping bags, drifted off to sleep listening to the utter silence. But there was a downpour in the night and our shelter turned out to be more river-tunnel than cave. We woke, cold and wet, to find that our breakfast eggs and bacon had been eaten by meerkats.

When I was fifteen, I was sent to help Judy with her fifth boy, Paul, who became my godson. Judy was a doctor but had an impressively no-nonsense attitude to health and safety. She was unperturbed when I found the baby, then just crawling, eating the flies that had drowned in the cat's milk on the kitchen floor. 'It won't kill him,' she said, casually scooping him up and depositing him on the veranda, where he promptly made for the dog's dinner.

Jack was climbing Table Mountain in his eighties and still goes camping with my brother Jamie in Namibia. As I write, he is a fit ninety-three and I'm still half in love with him.

Looking back on the people I've admired all my life, I realise that I've had a steady penchant for older men. One of my early secret passions was for Rayne, Nan's young husband. We'd left their house in 1949 to return to South Africa and I did not see him again until I was about twelve, when he came to South Africa to do research for his book *Goodbye Dolly Gray*, a history of the Boer War. He stayed with us while he toured battlefields and trawled through archives. He gave me a pound, in two crisp ten-shilling notes, equivalent to twenty weeks of pocket money. (We were given a penny for every year of our age so I'd have been on a shilling a week then.)

Years later I found tucked into my school Bible a cringe-making slip of paper. On it was written, in my round schoolgirl hand, *'Happiness hangs by a hair, but not in the love, mercy and comfort of God' Rayne Kruger*

I obviously had made the banal quote up, and must have felt that a real live author would give it authenticity. Little did I know that Rayne was as heathen as my father.

Dad was a relaxed atheist. He regarded believers as slightly batty, even amusing, like people who believe in fairies. When, at twelve or so, I was in love with religion, he would tease me. I lacked any sense of humour and attributed none to God, so when Dad once greeted me after Sunday communion with 'Been up to cannibalism again, have you?' I was deeply upset at the blasphemy. And when he left the door open and I protested in a smart-ass phrase from school, 'Were you born in a barn, Dad?' he replied, 'Yes, of course. Don't you remember? In Bethlehem.'

I spent a lot of time on my knees trying to save his soul.

Like most comfortably off white South Africans, we would go to the Game Reserve – the Kruger National Park – on family holidays. In the postwar decade it was not the sophisticated experience it is today with air-conditioned vehicles and, for the wealthy, private camps with open jeeps and radio contact to suss out where the animals are.

I hated being sandwiched between my brothers in the back of a hot car; unable to open the window for the dust; dawn sun in our eyes; animals invisible in the grass or indistinguishable from logs and boulders. Mum would turn round to check on us: 'David, put that book down. You are meant to be looking for the animals,' she'd bark, or 'Prue, wake up. We've not brought you all this way to sleep.'

But we loved the camps. Safely fenced from the wild, we were allowed to run about, make friends, swim in the pool. We'd have an evening *braai* outside our thatched *rondavel* (a circular building modelled on traditional African tribal houses), and listen to the hippos grunting like giants snoring. We'd lie on our backs, staring at the night sky and very soon we'd see falling stars. I loved the frisson of fear at the visceral roar of lions at night, tempered by the warm knowledge of safety fences and guards. And Daddy next door.

Today I love the bush. I set a good deal of my

second novel, *Sisters*, in it, but I'm still terrified of lions. My most recurrent nightmare is one of being chased by a lion. As an adult I've been on expensive bush holidays when you drive (or walk or ride) close to these creatures. I feel sick with fear, and all I want is to get away.

This dread could stem from a silly joke. On one of these early family holidays, we had to get out of the Landrover and walk with the game warden down a narrow path to a hippo pool. I was about ten, and could not decide where safety lay: next to my father bringing up the rear, or next to the warden in front with a gun. I opted for the gun and stuck to its owner like a shadow. Only when we were out of the bushes and standing at the edge of the pool did I begin to relax. At which point Dad crept up behind me, gave a low growl and bit my elbow.

It took me a long time to find it funny.

We seldom saw lions in those days. Indeed, I can still sing a song we invented on the long drive home after one holiday:

> *No lions in the Game Reserve*
> *We saw some kudu and a big baboon*
> *Impala and a warthog and*
> *A bird like a loon*
> *A rat and a bat and a*
> *Big crocodile*
> *Giraffe, wildebeest*
> *And ants by the mile . . .*
> *But no lions in the Game Reserve*

But once we saw a kill right up close that none of us ever forgot. A herd of impala were running beside the road when a lioness suddenly shot out of the bushes in pursuit. Her pouncing leap seemed to take her ten feet forward and five feet into the air as she brought down a buck by its hindquarters. It struggled until she got her jaws in its neck. She held it still while she roared for her cubs to join the feast. It was hot, her family did not come, and after a while she seemed to doze off in the sun. Suddenly the buck made a bid for freedom and she sprang after it, bringing it down again. This happened twice more, a cat playing with a mouse. Finally, tired of the game, she bent her prey's head back and we could clearly hear the crack as its neck snapped.

After more cub-calling, hunger got the better of the lioness and she ripped the impala's throat open and drank from the presumably still-pumping artery. We heard the rip, as of canvas, as she tore the skin, and then the lap-lap of her drinking.

She roared repeatedly. Eventually, I suppose an hour after she'd brought her prey down, a big male strolled up, cubs in tow. And then they tore the impala to pieces and had dinner.

We were never spanked, our parents governing by the withdrawal of approval. We had buckets of affection, praise and attention, but if we behaved badly they could turn down the glow a little – or a lot. We'd work hard to get back into the light.

One evening at supper, aged about nine and showing off newly learned playground language, I called my father a bloody fool. He picked me up and carried me to my bedroom as I furiously kicked his shins with the steel-tips of school shoes. He dumped me on the bed, saying I must stay there until I apologised. After a while my mother called through the door, 'Prue, are you sorry yet?'

'No, I wish Daddy was dead.' She went away. Every time she returned with the same question I said the same thing, first angrily, then sulkily, finally in floods of tears and apology.

We had three acres to play in and as long as we came when called, no one worried much what we got up to. David invented a good game: we used the gardener's huge fruit-tree sprayer to shower water on passing cars from behind our garden wall. If you timed it right, and the car was open-topped, you could drench the occupants. Once we gleefully soaked a long line of wedding cars, first the bride and groom, and then a dozen other cars, many of them with their hoods down and all bewildered, but unable to stop since they were in a procession. But we hadn't reckoned on the last car. The driver had time to realise, from the ducking and weaving of the vehicles in front, what was going on. He stopped his car, jumped out, gave David a good hiding and jammed his bottom into the water bucket. I escaped.

Worse was our secret stall, which we would set up on the grass verge outside our house. We sold anything we could safely filch from house or kitchen. Our customers were the servants from surrounding houses. Most popular of course were my mother's cigarettes, followed by beer or cokes nicked from the drinks cupboard.

We didn't dare steal bottles of whisky, so we set about making our own. This consisted of weak black tea with a tiny dose of real whisky added to make it smell right. Our other offer was methylated spirits, which was, sadly, a tipple of many an unhappy African. We faked this by swishing indelible pencil-lead in water. Our stall was short-lived, however, because the hoodwinked customers told our servants, who confiscated our ill-gotten lucre to return it to our victims, and threatened to tell on us unless we desisted forthwith.

I enjoyed the stall so much I tried to run an honest trade with flowers picked from the garden, donated bric-a-brac, and fudge made with the cook's help, but soon discovered that the demand for odd saucers and second-hand slippers did not match that for booze and fags.

Emma, our nanny, was round and fat and smelt deliciously of warm black African and starched white apron. I liked her hugs but tried to land my face in the middle of her squashy bosom because the wide guipure lace frills, starched to rigid stiffness, scratched my face.

Donald, the gardener, was a painfully shy Tsonga who would giggle when spoken to and squirm like a child. Nonetheless, when I wanted to take his photograph with my Brownie, he insisted on changing into his Sunday best, borrowing some spectacles and holding a sheet of important-looking paper in one hand and the cook's new bicycle in the other. I still have the picture, and I bet so does he.

We had a laundry maid, called Joyce I think, who was so bad-tempered, old and ugly that her stream of male visitors was a source of surprise – or perhaps admiration – to my mother. We children could have told her about the *skokiaan* (illicit, home-brewed liquor made from any number and kind of ingredients) seething in the copper tub under Joyce's bed and brought out on her afternoon off to fill her customers' Cola bottles. She made it with pumpkins, which grew conveniently behind the servants' quarters, brown sugar and packets of yeast filched from the kitchen.

While prepared to be indulgent on the moral front, Mum drew the line at illegal brewing, and eventually Joyce got her marching orders. 'Good thing too,' said Charlie, the cook. 'That woman, she no good.'

But Charlie was in the *skokiaan* business too. One day the police turned up, one white corporal, one black constable and a cringing informer, to say they wanted to search Charlie's room. My mama said that there was no way our dignified old Zulu cook would be up to anything, and told them to go ahead and search. Next thing, a huge vat of moonshine was hauled out and Charlie was arrested. As the forty-four gallon drum was taken away, popping with exploding yeast sachets that had gone in whole, the white copper said, 'Hell man, they'll put anything in this stuff. Dead kittens and what-all.'

The remark has stayed with me down the years, mainly because my mother and I, then eleven, had just drowned some kittens, a traumatic experience, and for weeks I imagined those poor dead creatures might have been in the illicit brew.

Too many kittens was a frequent occurrence and there had come a day when my mother, unable to find homes for yet another litter, decided to drown the latest batch. My protests were met with a firm 'Darling, it has to be done. They are only a few hours old. They will hardly know it's happening.'

My curiosity overcame my horror, and I trailed after her as she a filled a bucket with water and gathered a thin cotton flour bag. Into this she gently put the sleepy, blind kittens one by one. They didn't yet look like cats, more like large grey rodents of some kind, with soft short fur and lumpy closed eyes. They barely stirred.

'Poor little things,' she said, as she lowered the bag into the water. 'We just have to hold them under and they will go to sleep.'

She was wrong. Dreadfully wrong. Those kittens may have been only hours old, but they fought like the devil for life. We could hear them mewing under the water, thin, long cries for help, and the bag writhed and squirmed as the kittens inside climbed over each other in desperation.

We looked at each other in horror, both, I think, willing the kittens to die. Suddenly I saw my mother's eyes fill with panic and then with tears. 'I can't do it,' she said, 'I'm going to . . .' And she started to lift the bag.

I don't know what made me suddenly take charge. 'No,' I said, as I reached in and gripped the bag. 'We can't stop now.' And somehow, while my mother left the scene in tears, I held the bag underwater until the last kitten had stopped mewing. It took a very long time. Charlie found me sobbing by the bucket, lacking the courage to haul up my cargo of murdered kittens. I wept into his apron and blurted out our story. 'Go and look after your mother,' he said, 'I will take care of the kittens. You did right, Miss Prue.'

Charlie was a Zulu. I could have learned to cook at his apron strings, but it never occurred to anyone that a white girl would become a cook, much less be taught by a black man. And anyway, I never noticed what a crack chef he was. My only forays into the kitchen were to make jam tarts while Charlie cleaned up after me. When years later I returned to South Africa from studenthood in France, I decided to teach Charlie how to make stuffed seafood pancakes. It was only as I saw him deftly un-curdle my split hollandaise, swirl the pancake batter to paper-thinness in the pan, and chop mushrooms without looking down, that I realised he needed no lessons from me.

It wasn't all gastronomy in our house. We had the colonial obsession with things from 'home'. On my father's birthday Charlie would get all dressed up in his white uniform and stick small ceremonial bones into his hair and set the silver soup tureen reverently down in front of Dad. Next to it he would place a can opener and a starched napkin.

We would all fall silent at the solemn moment when Dad lifted the lid to reveal a large tin of Campbell's tomato soup, hot, but still sealed. His hand protected by the napkin, he would open it, pour it into the tureen and then ladle it out, the smell making all our mouths water.

I never asked why the soup had to come to the table in the can. I suppose it was my mother's joke, proving that neither she nor Charlie had adulterated Dad's favourite treat.

To this day, if I'm too bone-weary to eat, a bowl of concentrated comfort in the form of tinned tomato soup will do the trick.

When I was twelve, we went camping for a few days in the Magaliesburg mountains. We'd climbed up a gorge and settled in an idyllic spot, me in a tent with my brothers, our parents in another.

There was a rock pool higher up, deep enough to dive into from a ledge. We spent every waking hour playing in that pool, David and I diving, six-year old Jamie jumping.

On the Sunday morning, long before breakfast, when we'd already been in the pool an hour or so, I went for a wee behind a bush, and discovered I was bleeding. I knew what it meant. I'd been told to expect it by Mum, and some of my school friends were there already.

But still, shame and embarrassment enveloped me. Why, I wonder? No one had told me it was shameful. But I knew it was. A girl at school had gone up to receive communion with a blood stain on the back of her dress and we had all cringed in horror and sympathy, but no one could tell her.

I crept down the mountain to wake my mother. My father, thinking I'd come to report on the baboons which were everywhere in the trees, tried to shoo me away.

'Mum's asleep. It's much too early.'

'But she's got to come, it's important.'

'Well, what? Tell me.'

'I can't.' And I burst into tears. Why couldn't I tell him?

Of course he woke Mum and suddenly it was all alright. She made me feel important and grown up. Dad had to provide his stack of perfectly ironed white hankies to stem the flow. And then he was dispatched, with David I think, to climb down to the car, drive to the nearest village, wake up the pharmacist to open his store on a Sunday, and buy thick Kotex and the clumsy pink 'sanitary belt' which held the pads in place.

*   *   *

My childhood gastronomic memories are comparatively few, but vivid: anxiously watching lest my brothers get more than I of the buttered Marie biscuits sprinkled with hundreds and thousands that Kate doled out on the beach; lying in a hammock eating nuts and raisins after a hefty Christmas lunch (the English tradition of turkey, plum pud and warm sherry was religiously adhered to despite the heat of summer); my mother's only gastronomic triumph – baked custard, smooth as silk with not a bubble in it; my parents' predilection for raw onion sandwiches made with white bread and thick butter – I would sometimes wake to find them eating these when Mum got back from the theatre at midnight.

And then there were the traditions of the South African obsession, the *braaivleis* – literally, burnt meat! – though we never *braai'd* at home. My father described barbecues, especially on the beach, as combining the triple evils of meat raw in the middle, burnt on the outside and liberally dusted with sand. But for my outdoorsy Inglis cousins *braai*-ing was the norm and they did it effortlessly: freshly caught yellowtail or kingklip baked in foil on the fire, toasted cheese and apricot-jam sandwiches, whole fresh *mielies* (corn on the cob) cooked in their leafy wrappings, then opened up and slathered in butter; sweet-smelling mealie-bread baked in a clay pot in the ashes.

Dad preferred indoor civilisation. From the time I was about twelve, he would occasionally take me, by myself, out to dinner. The Station Hotel was the most fashionable restaurant in Johannesburg in the Fifties. The waiters wore white gloves and red sashes across their jackets, and called me Miss. I ate my first snails in garlic butter there, and loved the whole performance: the hinged holders, the little pick-thing to extract the rubbery snail, the clear lake of garlicky butter, the crusty bread to mop it up, the snail shells they gave me to take home.

I also had my first chicken in the basket with my Dad. As with the snails, the 'business' of the dish added to the enjoyment: pulling the chicken apart with the fingers, a second basket for the stripped bones, a finger bowl with a floating lemon slice, the huge white napkins to cover my chest and dry my hands. It was a ritual of pleasure I will never forget.

A South African pleasure I loved, and still love, is toast spread with anchovy paste. Once, sitting on bar stools in a coffee shop with my mother, a stranger on the other side of me was eating anchovy toast, cut into long fingers. I absently helped myself to one of these and was about to bite into it when I realised what I'd done. Hastily putting it back on his plate, I said, 'Oh, I am so sorry!' to which he replied, 'Since it's been half way down your throat, I think you'd better let it finish its journey. Help yourself.' I did.

When I was thirteen, my mother took it into her head to make me a winter coat. I had to stand on the dining room table – the same one where I'd had my ear operation – on a blazing summer day for what seemed like hours on end while she pinned the hem. Mum grew more and more irritable as I shifted from leg to leg and the hemline shifted with me until she eventually abandoned the whole thing and gave the half-made coat to Emma for her daughter.

Never one to be daunted by past failure, Mum's next noteworthy sewing project was to be the dress for my first school dance. Though now fifteen, I lacked the courage to tell her that I longed for a strapless svelte affair in shocking pink or pitch black. Or that I categorically did *not* want puff sleeves or a swirling skirt in pink-bordering-on-mauve.

My hopes rose when I found her beating the hell out of the sewing machine (an old treadle Singer with a wooden frame) with the pinking shears. These she wielded in both hands as she yelled, 'You bloody well *will* work, you *will* work, you *will* work'. Sure enough, she abandoned the dress. But only to call in a dressmaker to finish it.

So when I was too ill with flu to go to the dance, I was only half sorry, especially when allowed to spend the days in my parents' bed. The crisp cotton sheets, the cool of the eau de cologne Mum dabbed on my hot forehead and wrists, and, when I started to feel better, the exquisite crustless sandwiches Charlie brought on a grown-up tea tray, turned being ill into a treat.

Mostly, my parents' room was out of bounds,

and therefore irresistible. As a little girl I would sneak in, heart banging, and poke around in my mother's jewellery box, walk about in her high heels, and experiment with her lipstick. I loved the smell of the clothes in her cupboards, especially the evening dress one: musty, but perfumed.

In my Dad's drawer I found strange white balloons, very difficult to blow up because of their wide mouth. My big brother David, then a grown-up eleven to my mere nine, enlightened me but I didn't believe him: our parents could not possibly do anything so disgusting. When I was thirteen I found a Kinsey's *Sexual Behaviour in the Human Female* and a letter from my mother to my father when he was away. The phrase *this celibate life is so withering* has stayed with me, though I was a widow before I realised the truth of it.

David and I had discovered Dad's pistol hanging behind the bed-head, but we dared not touch it. Then one day, when I was eleven, I sneaked into the forbidden bedroom to find Jamie already there, sitting on the bed with the gun in his chubby hands. He looked up, his five-year-old face stricken at the prospect of a grown-up, but relaxing slightly at the sight of me.

'Look, Prue. I found a gun,' Jamie said, his voice nervous and high as he held it up in both hands. It was shaking. My heart somersaulted. 'Look' he said, 'it's got a safety catch. When it's on I can't shoot you.' He jerked the barrel upwards with each click. 'Bang, bang, nothing happens. The bullets can't come out.' He turned the pistol and squinted down the barrel, still clicking the trigger. 'See – nothing.'

I became icily calm. I knew I mustn't frighten him. I'd no idea if the gun was loaded or not, but the thought flashed through my head that it would be stupid to have to load it in the dark if a murderer came through the window.

I walked towards my little brother and said, as casually as I could, 'Hey, Jamie, that's fantastic. Can I see? Where did you find it? I've wanted to know where Dad kept that for ages and ages . . .'

I was babbling on, but it was working. Jamie relaxed and smiled, pleased with himself. I sat down next to him on the bed and reached for the gun, 'Let me see'.

But he moved it away. He clicked off the safety catch and swung the gun towards me, 'Look! Now if I pull the trigger you'll be dead.' His face was still scared. Scared of the gun or scared of me?

'Let me have a turn, Jamie.'

He handed over the gun and I looked carefully at it, thinking oh, God, don't let it go off. The words ON and OFF were etched into the metal, and the catch was pushed to the off side and for a moment I felt panic rising. Did OFF mean the gun was off? Or the safety catch? Then my mind cleared and I knew that ON was what I wanted.

I stood up and turned on poor duped Jamie, my voice out of control. 'Are you MAD? This is a real gun, you idiot. You could have killed me. You could have shot yourself looking down the barrel . . .'

Jamie jumped off the bed, 'But you said . . .' Then he understood. 'You were just pretending, weren't you? So you could get the gun. You're mean. You cheated. You're horrible.'

I stood with the gun held over my head, out of Jamie's reach, my legs trembling and telling myself it would be all right. In my most grown-up voice, I said, 'I'm going to put the gun back, and you are going to never, never touch it again. If you don't promise, I'll tell.'

I used this incident in my novel *Sisters* and learned that the problem with plagiarising real memories for fiction is that I end up not knowing what is real and what I've made up. I *think* this little drama ended with me making Jamie swear on a Bible never to go near the gun again, and never to say a word to anyone about it in his whole life and never to come near it as long as he lived. Cross your heart and hope to die.

We all adored my father. He died when I was not yet twenty-one. He could recite more Shakespeare than my actress mother, and he was easily moved by heroic, beautiful or even sentimental words. Once my mother found him reading Paul Gallico's *The Snow Goose* to David and me, the three of us huddled together in the big arm chair. We were all weeping our eyes out.

But I realise only now, writing this, how much better I knew my mother than my father. She was more present and involved in our daily lives. I remember her climbing up a syringa tree with us and trying to swing on a high branch as we did, but her fingers were not strong enough to hold her. She swung through the air, lost her grip and landed on her stomach twelve feet below. She was badly winded and couldn't speak, and we thought she was dead. David ran for Dad, who was so relieved to find her alive that he berated her. 'You bloody idiot!' he yelled. 'How could you imagine you could swing like a ten-year-old? How dare you risk your neck? How could you, you absolute fool?' It was the only time I ever heard him shout at her.

And then he carried her back to the house, tears running down his face.

I think we always knew that the great love of both their lives was each other.

He hated to upset her. Once, when I was about fifteen and she was in a play, she decided it would be good for me to be the housekeeper for the holidays, doing the shopping and planning the menus. I loved it, and we ate well: grills and roasts and no cheap mince or stews. One day, over lunch of roast duck, the conversation went something like this:

Dad: 'Delicious, Prue. Nice change from stuffed green peppers.'

Me: 'Thanks, Dad. Mum, why *do* we have stuffed peppers and stuffed marrows and mince on toast all the time? They're horrible.'

Mum: 'We don't have them all the time. And I don't notice either of you turning them down. And duck costs rather more than mince, young lady.'

Dad (trying to pour oil): 'Of course we *like* the peppers. It's just that they do seem to appear rather a lot.'

Mum swept out of the room, into her car and drove off, hours early, to the theatre.

Dad, mortified and realising he'd touched her rawest spot – her guilt at not being the perfect domestic goddess – bundled me into his car and we drove six miles to the theatre. We knocked on her dressing-room door. Mum, her face still pink from anger and crying, fell into Dad's arms. He stroked her hair and repeated over and over again, 'I'm so sorry, sweetheart.' I stood there muttering, 'Sorry, Mum.'

How harmonious their relationship must have been if such a tiny thing, after twenty years of marriage, warranted a cross-country dash and tearful reconciliation.

They'd married in the Lake District, and I loved to be told the story again and again. The romance of it enchanted me. They had no witnesses other than the niece of the vicar. They had to walk across the fields to the little church of St John in the Vale, which they did with the dachshund puppy Dad had given Mum as a wedding present. During the service the puppy whimpered and had to be picked up and passed from Mum to Dad to the vicar's niece to keep him quiet. And then they walked back to their hotel for tea.

My mother, before she'd left Cape Town to go to drama school in London, had been engaged to be married to Dad's brother, a handsome chap with his hair parted in the middle and slicked back with brilliantine, and Granny Leith's favourite boy. But Mum jilted him for Dad, confirming her mother-in-law's judgement of her as a flibberti-gibbet. Gran once told me that it was bad enough that her daughter-in-law was an actress, but that she was prepared to be photographed ('and for the newspapers!') in a bathing suit was beyond the pale.

At one point in my childhood I rather agreed with Granny Leith. I longed for a less famous and less glamorous sort of mother. One who was fat and homely and made cakes for the school fete. My mother never came to school fetes, and she couldn't bake a cake. She wore bright red lipstick. And hats.

One day, to my horror, she came to school assembly to talk about Shakespeare. I skulked at the back of the hall, wanting to die. But within seconds she was not my famous actress mother, she became the fourteen-year-old Juliet and then the ancient nurse; she *was* Hamlet, then Horatio. I walked out of that hall puffed up like a balloon. 'My mother's an actress. She hasn't time to bother with cakes.'

I was often proud of Mum, but she could embar-rass the hell out of us. She loved to dance, and when we played records there was a real danger that she'd dance around the room on her own. Worst of all, she would put on Danny Kaye's 'Ugly

Duckling' and *be* the duckling, twitching her bottom and jerking her head, 'with a waddle, with a quack, with a very unhappy frown'; then she'd slowly become the swan and preen and sail through the lake of the living room carpet, while I shrank into the sofa, wanting to kill her.

When I was a touchy teenager, she had a way of standing in the doorway, eyebrow gently lifted, and waiting for the teenage boys, our loutish friends, to stand up. If they did not, she would say, ice in her voice, 'Good afternoon, boys,' and continue to stand there while I hated her with a passion and the boys scrambled awkwardly to their feet. We called it her 'Duchess' stare.

But she was often the go-between for us children. She persuaded Dad that we did not, as he would claim, regard front door keys as disposable and use postage stamps as sticky paper – we were just thoughtless. When he sighed over my preferring horses to reading, she'd tell him I'd come to books in my own good time.

I wasn't much good at school, but until the last few years I loved it. Except for those years in England, I'd always been at St Mary's. At first I was a day girl in the junior school and used to walk the few miles to school. I had to cross an undeveloped plot of veld, raising clouds of insects as I walked through the crackly brown grass, the sun hot through my thin cotton school dress, the cicadas making their summer racket. Sometimes I would stop and talk to an old man who camped out there. I suppose he was a tramp, a 'vagrant', but to me he was an interesting old man who brewed tea in a billycan and talked about his children in the Cape, proudly telling me two of them were so pale-skinned they could pass for white.

Johannesburg in those days was extraordinarily safe for us children. We went pretty well everywhere unsupervised. Only once, when I was about eleven, did I encounter anything threatening. I was crossing another piece of empty rough ground that ran down to a stream, taking a short-cut home after visiting a friend in another suburb. A young black chap suddenly stopped me mid-stream, gripping my handlebars as I hauled my bike across the stepping stones,.

'Come with me into the bushes,' he invited. I shook my head.

'If you don't come I will roll you up in blankets and throw you in the river.'

I dropped my bike and fled on foot back the way I'd come, leaving him with the bike. Which was probably all he'd really wanted.

When I got home, I explained the loss of my bike. My mother, alarmed, decided this was the moment to tell me about the birds and the bees, information I'd had from my elder brother years before. And perhaps this incident was what led to the ban on my playing soccer in a skirt.

Compared to today, there was little crime in Johannesburg, though people feared it and talked about it. I remember my mother's indignation at finding that a burglar had fished the eiderdown off her and Dad's big bed while they slept. Because all homes had burglar bars on the windows, thieves became adept at fishing for items with poles with hooks on the end. The poles were said to be embedded with razor blades to discourage victims from grabbing at their disappearing possessions.

Most white households owned a gun. There was great excitement when a distant relative, known as Aunt Kitty, woke up to see, through the French windows of their bedroom, a figure creeping along the path. She reached for the gun, and Uncle Alan was blasted awake by the triple sounds of a pistol going off over his head, shattering glass and the screams of the milkman, a bullet in his leg.

She was a truly dilly woman, Aunt Kitty. Not only had she shot the milkman (who lived to tell the tale and reap hush-money that made it, he said, more than worthwhile) but had done so through the French windows. When her husband asked, 'Why didn't you shake me?' she replied, 'I didn't want to wake you up.'

My school life got choppier as I neared puberty. I became a boarder and was unexpectedly homesick, missing my parents and brothers. I used to climb the trees at the bottom of the hockey pitch and gaze towards home, convinced I could tell which jacaranda trees belonged to our garden.

The nuns thought I must be up to no good – probably meeting boys or lighting fires or playing

Elvis records (all banned). I felt unjustly accused, though climbing trees was equally forbidden.

There was one member of the household I did not miss – our Great Dane, Olaf. But he missed me. Poor chap, he was old now, with drooping red eyes, bad breath, mangy patches that would not heal, and he slobbered for Africa. As the school was so near home, and Olaf had made the trip countless times, he would come to find me, usually when I was in the middle of a hockey game and could not intercept him. I dreaded his delighted, lolloping form making a bee-line for me across the pitch, trailing long ribbons of flying saliva.

I got chucked out of Afrikaans lessons for reading illicit pop magazines under the desk. This turned into a blessing because the only magazines allowed in the whole school were the Afrikaans ones in the library and I was banished there to teach myself the language. Which I did, on a dose of love stories about lusty farmers and beautiful kindergarten teachers.

I don't have a musical note in my body, but one day I heard the school choir sing Handel's *Messiah*, and it thrilled me. I went to the music master, 'Sir, can I join your music appreciation class?'

'Well, yes, but you know the others have already started and they are much younger than you?'

I said that was fine, and turned up at the next class to sit on a form with girls half my size.

'This is Saint-Saëns,' the teacher said, dishing

out sheet music. 'We will play the piece on the gramophone and you will all follow different instruments. Listen carefully.' He handed me a copy. 'You follow the piccolo, Prue.'

Since I couldn't read music and had never heard of Saint-Saëns, let alone a piccolo, that was my one and only music lesson.

I was a stroppy teenager, but ambitious. I wanted to be head girl, but was not even made a prefect. Upset by this, I mouthed off at the head nun, who sent for my mother.

Summoned to the head's study, I found my loyal mama there, protesting, 'But she's such a polite child, we have no trouble at home, etc etc'. Sister X then explained that I was to be taken home and no longer allowed to be a boarder. At this I lost my temper, stormed out and slammed the door, dislodging a framed picture of the Virgin Mary from the back of it. The glass shattered on the floor, rather spoiling my mother's case, and causing her to change sides in an instant.

After a couple of terms I was forgiven, and resumed my place in the dorm, in which a dozen girls each had a curtained cubicle. Between the dorms were the bathrooms, each separated from the next by a wall that did not reach the ceiling. After lights-out the nuns took turns in the bathrooms. We would creep into the adjoining bathroom, carrying our end-of-bed stools, climb up, and peer over the wall to observe the weekly ritual of the chaste maids of Christ at their ablutions.

It was quite a performance: first a nun would run her bath, then remove habit and headdress, then haul a heavy wooden lid over the bath, and fold one hinged end back to leave a space just large enough to stand in at one end. Then, stripped down to a cotton shift, she would climb in and wriggle down under the wooden lid, while at the same time removing the shift. Once lying down, she would close the hinged end, leaving only enough space for her head to protrude. And thus her body was hidden from prying eyes, her own as well as ours, presumably in case the sight of her own nakedness should arouse narcissistic lust.

The most exciting part was when they removed their headdresses and revealed blond, dark or grey cropped hair – an astonishing sight. It was as though we had not known they had hair. We wanted desperately to see them naked and we speculated on whether 'down below' matched that on their heads. But we never caught one skipping the wooden-board-and-shift routine. They never looked up either.

Cooping girls and women up together makes, I think, for a super-charged atmosphere. The nuns were as obsessed with sex as we were. Of course we lusted after any male under forty who gained entrance; we dreamed of marrying princes and pop stars, and fell madly in love with horses, or poetry, or religion. We also had passionate 'crushes' on older girls as they had crushes on us. Most of these were, I'm sure, innocent, but the nuns, fearing carnal sin, frowned on out-of-year-group friendships. I remember being endlessly and confusingly questioned by the Sister X, about my chumminess with a younger girl whose family and mine were friends. I had no idea what she was on about, until, older and wiser, I found myself rejecting embarrassing clinches from that same nun, now risen to headship. I soon discovered that she lusted after all and any of us between the ages of about twelve and fourteen. Her favourite technique would be to make girls cry and then offer comforting hugs and rather more. Some resisted, some bore it.

Just before the senior girls were about to leave school for good, the headmistress would invite them for a confidential chat in which they could offer advice about what they felt was right and wrong with the school. As a non-prefect, with no presumed loyalty to the system, I was deputed by my peers to be the one to tell the headmistress that we thought she should give up making younger girls cry and then comforting them with caresses which quickly turned sexual.

I started off bravely enough, explaining that we found the way she stroked her huge great dane while she lay on her back, clearly very happy indeed, embarrassing. But bravado leached away as she listened gravely. I stumbled on to our complaint about making younger girls cry, about 'kissing better' and 'touching the wrong places'.

And then the Angelus sounded. I am not sure

who was most relieved, Sister X or me, as we automatically stood and bowed our heads. The tradition was that the prayer accompanying the tolling bell was always said by the most senior person present. For the first time ever, no one said the Angelus. We stood in complete silence. I sneaked a look at the head. Sister X's face was bowed, both face and neck purple with shame. I felt like a torturer.

I had a sudden vision of her on her knees before her Maker, as she must have been four times a day. Time after time she would have to confess her sin, crave forgiveness, vainly vow not to transgress again, suffer torment as she broke her promises. Poor woman. She was probably only forty, a red-cheeked, round-faced, comfortably overweight matron who should have been a farmer's wife with a brood of children and a healthy sex life.

She was an energetic and intelligent – even dedicated – headmistress. Was it her fault that her hormones did not respect her habit?

A few years after I left the school, all the nuns were suddenly recalled to their English convent without explanation. Maybe someone braver than me, and without sin, cast the stone.

CHAPTER 2

LEARNING CURVES

Going the whole way

My adolescence was dominated by what my mother called 'popping hormones'. As soon as my obsession with horses waned, I started on boys.

At first, although I badly wanted a boyfriend, I didn't care for the lovey-dovey stuff that went with it. My first 'French kiss' was horrible, like having an athletic snail in my mouth.

We had endless discussions in the dorm about what was allowable, and the general consensus was that it was okay to let a boy kiss you, but serious groping required true love, and even then the line was drawn strictly at the waist. Of course, *sleeping* with a boy was a monstrous bridge too far: he would lose all respect for you, would leave you in the morning, and then no one would ever want you again.

My father confirmed this. He told me that women who slept with men before marriage were 'strumpets'. I doubt if he knew that my mother had not been a virgin when he married her. She told me a great story about her first affair. Her lover was a Norwegian, older than her and worldly-wise, and when she'd expressed terror at the possibility of pregnancy, he had produced some enormous pills which she had great trouble getting down. When she protested, 'Those things are like horse-pills. I could barely swallow them. Why can't they make them smaller?'

'What? You swallowed them? You're meant to stick them up your fanny.'

If I had known then that even my mother had transgressed the golden rule of no sex before marriage, and that most of my po-faced girlfriends would soon be doing the same if they weren't already, I might not have suffered the torments of guilt I did when, at fifteen, I let a lad 'go the whole way'.

I never told a soul and lived in terror of being found out. I think if I'd enjoyed it, I'd have justified my behaviour to myself, but Boyfriend One caused no stirrings of lust. However, I was not an actress's daughter for nothing, and I did a lot of heavy breathing and moaning. Joe was older than me, had left school and worked in a car dealership. Most importantly, he had an open-topped Triumph, albeit with his previous girlfriend's name painted on its side. My ambition, never realised, was to get that painted out in favour of *Prue*.

His six month's seduction campaign rested on three planks: 'You love me, don't you?'; 'You're such a baby. I don't know why I bother with a schoolgirl,' and 'You're not a virgin anyway – girls who ride horses are never intact.'

Joe's victory was played out on the living room carpet of his house, his parents asleep upstairs. The need for silence was paramount, but as things got painful (he was wrong about the horse-riding) and I panicked, then screamed, he put his hand over my mouth.

Afterwards we got a bucket and carpet shampoo and got the blood out of the rug.

My next boyfriend was a big improvement. Alexander Falk's parents were not as prosperous or as posh as mine and they had made big sacrifices to send their clever boy to private school and then to university. His father walked part of the way to work to save on bus fare. I'd never seen my dad on a bus, let alone on Shanks's pony.

I adored the whole Falk family. They lived in a small neat house, Mrs Falk did the cooking herself, no-one changed for dinner and they ate supper at six rather than eight. There were no rules that I had instinctively to divine and obey, unlike poor Alex, who would incur my mother's Duchess look if he failed to light her cigarette or to open the door for me.

Alex was my first real love, and he woke in me real desire, not just the desire to be desired. We were mooching about the wilder parts of the 'bird sanctuary' (actually a stretch of deserted veld and woodland) and we decided to cross the river by means of a fallen log. It was perhaps six feet over the water and I was too nervous to walk it, so I sat astride and shunted myself along. But it was slippery and somehow I fell into the river. It wasn't deep or fast-flowing and I was a good swimmer but my gallant swain dived in to rescue me.

And then we sat on the river bank in the sun to dry out and resumed the tentative kissing we'd started a few nights before when we'd met at a party. Suddenly I was filled with an astonishing need to meld my body into his. We looked at each other in shock. We were both shaking.

It was a true love affair, secret of course, and conducted in his house, my house, his college rooms, the backs of cars at the drive-in cinema, in my mother's big Chevrolet parked on Observatory Hill with the lights of Johannesburg below us, and of course, outdoors. I thought of little else.

Thankfully, my parents liked Alex, but that didn't mean Dad trusted him, or me, to behave ourselves. Once I set up a tremendous campaign to go with him and the university sailing team to Durban. Dad was adamant. No, no, no. My mother was less concerned. She probably guessed it was too late for my virtue anyway, and was only worried about the long car journey to the coast.

Dad gave in eventually, but reluctantly. On the morning we left, in my mother's Chevy with two more of the sailing team in the back, my father leant through the driver's window to threaten Alex with vengeance and death if he hurt a hair of his daughter's head.

This gory threat was meant, or half-meant, as a joke, but poor Alex only heard the menace. He drove the car down the drive in kangaroo leaps.

As I'd approached sixteen I'd campaigned to be allowed to leave school. 'What do I need matric for if I'm going to teach riding? It will save you money, Dad, no more school fees and no university ones either.'

'I can afford it,' he'd replied drily, 'and, darling, you are going to stay at school until you get your matric if it takes you till you're thirty.'

Right, I thought. *So he thinks I'm thick. I'll show him.* Which of course was the reaction he'd hoped for.

I surprised myself and astonished my father by following my brother David in pulling off a first class matric. If I showed signs of crowing, however, Dad would remind me that he did not think much of the subjects (other than English) I'd taken. 'No maths, no science, no classics, no history! What kind of an education is that?' Biology didn't count in his book, any more than geography, history of art, French, or Afrikaans.

However, Cape Town University accepted me, rather to Dad's surprise. He'd remarked, when filling in my application with me, 'I wish I could enter "Reading" under hobbies. I think I'll just put "Boys".'

51

I was furious, but he was right. Until then I'd read almost nothing. Today I cannot go to sleep without half an hour's reading, however late it is. I get anxious if I don't have a book in my handbag and a comforting pile of as-yet-unread books by my bed. I go on holiday with my bag weighed down with more novels than I can hope to get through, 'just in case'. But in my teens I would drift off to the sound of Johnny Mathis or Eartha Kitt on my wind-up gramophone, set to repeat.

But at university, in 1958, I started on all the books I should have read at school: Austen, Dickens, Thackeray, Tolstoy, and South African writers like Alan Paton, Nadine Gordimer, Doris Lessing.

And, being eighteen, I began to write maudlin poems about unrequited love. I wrote a predictable play about a teenager who gets pregnant and her mum adopts the child. It was called *Picking up the Pieces* and it was dire.

But I didn't give up boys. Alexander didn't survive my going away to university, being soon ousted by rugby-playing Andrew, beefy, sporty, uncomplicated and kind. But he didn't last either. I'm ashamed to say I cannot remember who followed him, or why.

I was at last becoming politically literate. I joined anti-apartheid marches and protests with other students. In 1958 the universities of South Africa were reserved for 'Europeans'. If you were black and somehow aspired to university in spite of your education having stopped at the age of eleven (only whites got free education until matric) you went to Fort Hare, which was exclusively for black students.

But I cannot claim to have been truly committed to the struggle. I joined protests because people I admired did so, and because it was exciting. When I finally left South Africa for Europe, I claimed to have left in disgust at my country's politics, but the truth was more that I wanted to see the world.

The only time I was arrested, at a student rally, I was sick with fear, but also excited at behaving like a true dissident. So I was both relieved and disappointed that the policeman sorting us in the police station did not charge me. A night in the cells would have given me some street-cred, but he saw at once that I was a mere fellow traveller and no danger to the state.

At least I was waking up to how the other half lived. I volunteered to teach remedial English in the evenings in a school in District Six, the 'coloured' (mixed race) suburb of Cape Town which was later bulldozed by the government under the infamous Group Areas Act, which outlawed different races living side by side. The schoolchildren were all coloured and their parents – shopkeepers, porters at the docks, drivers, gardeners – though poor, were not starving.

From the school yard, you could see the sea,

hardly a mile away. Yet the children I taught had never swum in it: the beaches round the city of Cape Town were designated Whites Only.

I decided to take my class on holiday. I borrowed my uncle's house in Hermanus, a seaside village eighty miles to the east of Cape Town, persuaded several friends with cars to act as both drivers and chaperones, and commandeered my grandfather's big Rover and driver.

It never occurred to me to clear any of the hurdles that one would have to jump today: written parental permission, checks on the suitability of volunteers, dietary allergies, driving licences, car roadworthiness, safety of accommodation, life-saving capability, first aid, etc. We just packed up and went.

There was one terrifying moment. We had walked along the beach to where the water from the lagoon was running on an outgoing tide through a narrow channel, a few metres wide. Opposite was a smooth and inviting sandbank.

A boisterous lad with a gang-leader reputation to uphold, was one of the few children who could swim. With a shout of joy, he dived into the water and struck out for the other side, but the current was too strong for him. He was heading straight out to sea.

One of my burly rugby-playing volunteers had the wit to run at full tilt along the channel edge, overtake the now swirling panicking boy, plunge into the sea at the wider and calmer mouth of the channel and intercept the lad to pull him to safety. The boy, I guess, learned a lesson. And so did I.

But it was a wonderful few days. We combed the beach, swam in the shallows, tried unsuccessfully to fish off the rocks, climbed the hill behind the town to swim in an icy rock pool, picnicked on the sand, played deck-quoits on my uncle's *stoep*, cooked *boerewors* (farmer's sausage) and mealie-bread on an open fire.

Not one resident or tourist complained of our bringing non-white kids onto a whites-only beach, residential area, or beach cafe. The only objection, and that was expressed in silent disdain, came from my grandfather's driver, himself a 'Cape coloured'. That his polished and pampered Rover, his pride and joy, should be invaded by ice-cream-eating ragamuffins was an outrage.

I'd left school wanting to be an actress. One holiday I'd stood in for my brother David, who was cast as one of the child actors in my mother's production of *Hamlet*. He'd quickly got tired of the part, and relinquished it to me. I had to skip down the aisle through the seated audience, do a cartwheel half way down and leap onto the stage with the rest of the Players as, tambourines, drums and whistles going, they made their entrance for the 'play within the play'.

I had to deliver three lines, which I remember to this day:

For us, and for our tragedy,
Here stooping to your clemency,
We beg your hearing patiently.

I loved it. The attention, the affection of the cast, the atmosphere of excitement, the 'smell of the greasepaint'; above all, the play itself, which each night got a tighter hold on me. *Hamlet* is still, for me, the best play ever written.

Yet drama school was a mistake. My mother said she knew I'd never be an actress when, after getting a great notice ('her mother's daughter, a born actress') in the *Cape Times* for my performance in the Ionesco play, *The Chairs*, I failed to cut it out or even tell her about it.

I thought, since I still loved the theatre, I would be a set designer rather than an actress, and I swapped to the university art school. One day the head of the school, a distinguished sculptor, came and stood behind my easel.

'What are you doing in my life class?'

'I want to be a set designer.'

'But you can't draw. You've no talent for it. I suggest you give it up.'

So I did. I then had a bash at architecture but the maths defeated me. Next, I set my sights on a BA in philosophy, but it transpired that logic and metaphysics needed some knowledge of maths too. I was never going to make it.

I blithely swapped again, this time to a BA majoring in French. I'd been at the university for less than a year and I was now on my fifth course. After another year I was still doing pretty badly, more to do with the time spent on the beach than with, as I claimed, the aridity of my French course.

Also, I was constantly broke. I started modelling for a hairdressing college. I had long thick hair and each month it would be cut by a demonstrator in a different style and often dyed a different colour: pink one week, auburn the next, purpley-brown the week after.

That job ended when my hair reached crew-cut length. I then tried modelling swimwear but stopped, ashamed, when I realised I was modelling for a 'fuller figure' catalogue. At five foot-nine and weighing less than ten stone, the description hurt.

My finances now dire, I decided to persuade Dad to raise my allowance. I did a survey of my fellow students and found I had the second lowest allowance. Fired with indignation by this discovery, I opened an account in a department store and bought a deep-blue petticoat with hundreds of yards of stiff net to go rock-and-rolling in, and some Carmen rollers to get my hair, now growing again, into flick-ups. I wrote Dad a long demand for more money, full of reproach, and justifying the store account. My clinching argument was that my mother's monthly spend on cigarettes exceeded my allowance.

Before I received a reply my courage had drained away and I knew my letter had been rude, crude and unwarranted. The reply came, a dictated, typed letter, which went something like this:

Dear Prue,

I have today increased your allowance by a third and I have paid your store bill and closed the account.

I find your remarks about your mother's cigarettes distasteful in the extreme.

The letter was pp'd by my father's secretary.

I wrote a tearful apology and was rewarded with my parents' customary forgiveness.

My first year at UCT did bring some little shafts of education: Louis MacNeice came to read to us in the Jameson Hall. He read his 'Prayer Before Birth' so badly I wanted to jump up and read it myself. I gained a liking for poetry and a smattering of French.

I also learnt a lot of rugby songs and could belt out the university Alma Mater at full throttle. It was only later that I learnt I couldn't sing in tune.

Rag Week promised much but delivered a mixed bag. Standing in Jameson Hall ('the Jammie') to watch the competition for Rag Queen, I spied a tall, good-looking boy I knew slightly. Like me, he lived in Johannesburg and our parents were friends. He was an ace cricketer and in his second year. He'll do, I thought, and was thrilled when he appeared at my side, bending to whisper in my ear.

'Can you do me a huge favour?'

'Anything,' I said, feeling blessed.

'The next girl to come on stage is Pat Kavanagh.

I'm in love with her but she's living with some wretched architect. You've got to invite her home for the vac.'

I hid my disappointment, and stared open-mouthed at the apparition on stage. All the other contenders were in typical late-Fifties fashion: full short skirts, wide belts, flat pumps, tight sweaters over high pointy breasts, flick-up hair styles, Alice bands and 'natural' make-up. Pat wore a long black dress of silk jersey, no bra but plenty of cleavage, and a falling mane of auburn hair that obscured half her face. She did not pout or smile. She looked faintly bored.

She was sensational, and had there been a public poll rather than a panel of judges, at least half the room – all the men – would have voted for her.

I did make friends with her and did ask her to stay. She captivated my parents and my little brother, but spurned the poor lovesick cricketer.

This was the first of a long line of men who fell in love with Pat and cried on my shoulder. She became the most respected, some would say feared, literary agent in London, and a lifelong friend. She never lost her looks, or her train of admirers. She married the writer Julian Barnes, just about the only one who did not regard me as a shoulder to cry on.

By the end of my second year, 1959, my little brother Jamie was a burly teenager, living a boarding school life at Michaelhouse in Natal. David was at Keele University in England, recently married to a Lebanese girl, Mary, and they had a baby, Helen. But David was still daft, brave and accident prone. The year before, he'd realised he'd not done enough work to pass the end-of-year exams. As failure would have meant being sent down, he decided to injure his writing hand and so be allowed to take the exams later, by which time he'd have done more work. His first plan was to fry his hand in boiling fat, but the attempt failed when he found he couldn't hold his hand in the fat long enough or deep enough to do the required damage. So he slammed his thumb (at the second attempt) in the car door instead – and successfully tore half the nail off.

After he'd written his final exams, David took a summer job as a bus conductor in Wales. His was one of those old-fashioned buses with a platform at the back and an upright pole to hold on to. Trying to impress the girl passengers by a look-no-hands performance of reconciling cash with ticket sales while standing on the back platform, David parted company with the bus as it swung round a corner, and woke up in Rhyl Hospital. The money he'd been counting was flung all over the road, most of it picked up and handed in by the passengers. But on David's return to the bus company, seven shillings and sixpence was deducted from his pay and he was fired.

I longed to be overseas too. I wanted to be in London, Rome, Paris, New York – anywhere but old-fashioned, provincial, South Africa. I began a campaign to go to Paris and learn French from the French. Once more my long-suffering parents acquiesced.

But first, over Christmas, we went on a family holiday to Madeira to meet David, Mary and baby Helen there. Even at the end of the Fifties, most people travelled from Cape Town to Southampton in Union Castle passenger liners, taking mountains of luggage. My mother had a set of cream suitcases, elegantly bordered in green that ranged from a trunk the size of a Great Dane's kennel, via suitcases, hat-boxes, and make-up case down to a jewellery case that she carried herself. The huge liner seemed to fill the docks and hundreds of people came to wave us off as we threw streamers from the decks. There was a brass band too, but maybe that was in honour of the most distinguished passenger, Field Marshal Viscount Montgomery.

I promptly set my cap at a young officer on the ship. Nothing happened, and he didn't respond to my overtures, but I mooned about dreaming of our eventual marriage, he in his uniform and I in bridal white. I also fancied the head chef and planned to ingratiate myself by borrowing his uniform for the fancy dress competition. But Viscount Montgomery had other ideas.

Monty was the first truly famous person I got to know and he was a disappointment. First of all, he was so *small*. I'd thought war heroes were tall, dark and handsome. And I felt sorry for a man who kept a pile of signed photos in his cabin when no-one asked him for one.

I was embarrassed by his mad assertion that apartheid was an excellent thing: he knew God had not intended black and white to mix because if you shook a black man's hand there was a negative electrical force that resisted the contact.

And then he insisted I go as him in the fancy dress contest with my thirteen-year-old brother as Churchill. My father, who revered Monty, told me I should be grateful for the honour.

I gave in, but then, I'm sorry to say, pranced around the deck wearing Monty's famous beret with my bathing costume and his long pin of miniature medals across my bosom. Dad was furious.

Monty rehearsed us, teaching us how to salute and what to say (me: 'That's impossible, Sir, it cannot be done.') On the day he was one of the judges and bullied his co-judges, 'They must win of course. No question.' We did.

Once on Madeira, I couldn't bear the cooing of the newly-weds, David and Mary, or my mother's doting on the baby. I thought it was all so *soppy*, but in truth I guess I was jealous and secretly longing for some lovey-dovey of my own. I avoided the stifling family group and mooned round the shops in Funchal. In a jeweller's I set my sights on the youngish, overweight son of the owner, and spent all my holiday money on a ring, a thick wedding band with different semi-precious stones set into it.

On Christmas Eve I insisted on going out with the jeweller's son rather than dining with my family. I spent a dull and embarrassing evening in a community hall where I knew no-one, couldn't speak the language and where the jeweller danced with his friends while I stood on the sidelines.

Then, on the ship home I fell, more seriously, for a thirty-ish Canadian who was emigrating to Australia (via Cape Town) with his wife and two babies. I think I was in love with his whole family: he was tanned and handsome, she was a beautiful, rather hippy, woman in long skirts with a thick plait down her back. She sat on deck breast-feeding the baby while supervising the toddler. Occasionally the latter would come back to his mum for a reassuring gulp from her free breast. In an age when breastfeeding in public was considered indecent, this double-feeding seemed brave and beautiful.

My admiration did not stop me longing for her husband, however. He had the dark magnetism of the hero of a romantic novel and he made my heart beat faster. I did not dare put out a hand to touch him but I suppose my adoration was obvious, and one day, hanging over the ship's rail, he kissed me. Soon we were declaring undying love.

The relationship stayed chaste only because I shared a cabin with my thirteen-year-old brother and my suitor's wife was in his. One night we agreed to meet on deck when everyone had gone to bed. Two a.m. seemed a safe trysting time. It

63

was thrilling. Both in pyjamas, we wandered round the deck, cuddling in corners.

Suddenly I heard the unmistakable voices of my father and brother, looking for me. Jamie had woken, found me gone, decided I'd fallen overboard, and gone to wake Dad.

I remember thinking, *Right. There's nothing for it, just face the music.* We stepped out of the shadows and my would-be lover rose to the occasion. He declared that he loved me, and that he intended to leave his wife and marry me.

The aftermath was grim. My poor father was ashen-faced with anxiety and refused to speak to me. My mother, angry with me, was full of sympathy and concern for the man's wife. Between them they persuaded him not to see me or write to me for a year, after which, if we were still determined, they would drop their opposition.

How wise my parents were. He continued his voyage to Australia, and I think I forgot him in a fortnight. Mercifully, he forgot me. I never heard from him again.

Three men in three weeks, but only a few supercharged kisses from one of them. That was more a matter of their good sense, or lack of opportunity, than of any principles of mine, and what really shames me still is that I barely gave a thought to that poor Canadian wife and her babies.

CHAPTER 3

FOREIGN AFFAIRS

Prue in Paris

In the late spring of 1960 I went to England with Mum and Dad because Dad had to see specialist doctors. He had a blockage of the bowel and they were worried sick by the spectre of cancer. But he was operated on in St Mark's Hospital with great success. The relief I felt when Mum told me that the tumour had been benign and Dad would be right as rain in a couple of months made me realise just how much I did love him. I stayed with them both in the little village of Penshurst in Kent while Dad recuperated. Then they went home and I went off to France, to do something about my appalling French before starting a course on French culture and civilisation at the Sorbonne in September.

I had a room in a genteel boarding house in the sixteenth arrondissement and was horribly lonely. Everyone in the house and the streets seemed middle-aged and grumpy, French classes at the Alliance Française were dull beyond belief, and I

65

made no friends. Paris was not proving the stuff of my dreams.

That changed when Louise, my friend since we were six, arrived to spend July with me. We had persuaded our parents to let us do a cooking course at the Paris Cordon Bleu school. I had booked in advance when I had no real grasp of the language, but I knew the word '*Combien?*' well enough. After much waving of arms, the bursar had written a figure. It seemed an enormous amount, but our respective parents agreed, and I paid it.

By the time we turned up, with our regulation white aprons and mob-cabs, the deadly Alliance had taught me a bit more French.

The bursar demanded about ten times as much as I'd already paid.

'But, Monsieur,' I spluttered, 'we've already paid.'

'That was the deposit, Mesdemoiselles.'

Sure our fathers would not pay such a sum, we abandoned our deposits and trailed down the rue du Faubourg Saint-Honoré, disconsolate.

We were not disconsolate for long. With the instincts of the young, we had divined that two young men were behind us. One was tall and good looking, the other smaller, but certainly acceptable. With one accord we slowed down a bit, giggled a bit, and, passing a handy outdoor café, slid into a table for four. The boys glided seamlessly into the empty seats.

The only tension was who was to have which boy. We both wanted the tall, good looking one who called himself Jackson because it sounded cool and American. He planned to be a pop star and was going to busk on St Tropez beach with his guitar. Louise won his favour and I had to make do with Guy, who worked – when he worked – as a circus conjuror. *Prestidigitateur* was one of the first words he taught me.

A great month followed. We felt adventurous and risqué, bluffing to our parents that we were at cookery school while drifting around the city, eating in tiny restaurants in back streets and listening to music in cellars and dives. In the end, Louise went off with Jackson to St Tropez and I stayed with Guy in Paris, sharing his real-life garret at the top of Montmartre. The building had not changed in a hundred years: worn stone stairs, single cold-water tap on every floor, and a stand-up WC. In Guy's room there was a single naked bulb next to a skylight. If I stood on the bed I could see the domes of Sacré Cœur.

Of course I lived with the constant fear of pregnancy. The only birth control available was the condom, and that meant relying on Guy. When, a few weeks into our affair, I was 'late' by a few days, I panicked. Guy took me to a friend of a friend of the café owner on the corner, a small silent woman at the top of a silent dark house. I was terrified that she would stick knitting needles up me and give me peritonitis, but I was even more frightened of my parents. My father's dictum that women who 'did it' before marriage were sluts tortured me. Oddly, it never occurred to me to weigh the moral question of abortion.

Mercifully, knitting needles did not feature. The woman gave me an injection, God knows of what, and relieved me of a fortnight's allowance. And absolutely nothing happened except that, as the days passed, I felt increasingly ill with anxiety. And then, a fortnight later, presto: not for the first time, the 'curse' came as a blessing.

Guy was intelligent and fun, and I tried to pretend I was in love with him, but the affair fizzled out. What had attracted me were his Frenchness and his knowledge of the nooks and crannies of Paris. I don't think Louise really fell for Jackson either, though she did find herself paying for his teeth to be fixed to help his chances as a pop star.

Louise went home and I spent August working as an au pair in the Basque country, which is where my interest in food became serious.

Madame von Bochstael, the mistress of the house, gave me two seminal lessons in my first twenty-four hours. Before breakfast we went to buy the bread: baguettes in one bakery, croissants in another and gâteau Basque in a third.

'But why do we go to all those shops? They all sell everything,' I said. She rolled her eyes at my stupidity.

That evening I watched Madame make the children's supper. They got exactly the same dinner as we would have later: tiny rare steaks, salad with French dressing, boiled potatoes, followed by a sliver of apple pie. The toddler had hers in a high chair and her baby sister had hers whizzed up or mashed. No special 'kids' food'. It was fresh food, made from scratch by a woman who could cook. And we sat round a table. And we talked to the children.

Those three principles: good ingredients; careful preparation; time to enjoy, became my mantra. I hate hurried, hand-held junk. It seems to me such a wasted opportunity. The novelist Julian Barnes, a great wine buff, once told me he didn't have enough evenings left in his life to waste one on a bad bottle of wine. I feel the same about food.

Everyone at the von Bochstaels' table talked about which shops, which restaurants, which market stall-holder, which chef, was the best. Both Monsieur and Madame cooked, and meals were delicious. At first I was not allowed to do any cooking: my English tongue guaranteed, for them, that I'd ruin the food.

I proved them right one day after a discussion with friends at dinner. What was the national dish of South Africa, they asked.

'*Mealies.*'

'What is this, *mealies*?'

'Corn on the cob. Maize.'

'*Maize?* Maize? In France, this we give to the cows.'

'But it's delicious. You eat it in your fingers. With butter.'

They were all laughing, slapping each other on the back and saying, 'Maize! That is worse than the American hamburger.'

Suddenly I was close to tears and stirred to defend my native land.

'How can you mock something you've never tasted? Have you tasted corn on the cob?'

'Of course not. We do not eat the food of cattle.'

Then Madame von Bochstael said, 'She's right. We must try it. Maize grows here.'

I picked half a dozen cobs from a field. They were yellow rather than white, the kernels harder than I remembered. Perhaps they softened with boiling, I thought.

They did not. They'd been drying all summer in preparation for grinding into cattle feed. They were inedible. I quietly binned them and Madame was good enough not to say a word.

I was learning French fast and growing up slowly. I adored my two charges but I was an irresponsible nursemaid. Walking in the woods, the baby in the pram and Frederique toddling beside me, we were startled by a large snake in the middle of the path, head raised, flicking its tongue at us. Brought up on the lethal danger of cobras and black mambas, I turned tail and fled, abandoning the babes in the wood. I suppose I only went a few paces before conscience kicked in. I turned back to find the snake gone and Frederique saying, 'Don't worry, baby, don't worry.'

I'd enjoyed au pair-ing and I knew family life was the fastest way to learn French. So, back in Paris, I agreed to work for another family. The Meniers were rich and smart and lived in the Bois de Boulogne. I was to do only a few hours a day there, leaving me time for the Sorbonne.

I hated it at the Meniers'. I was in trouble from the moment I arrived, mainly because of my inability to control their horrible ten-year-old. They couldn't control him either, and he ruled the roost.

My only friend was the Portuguese cook, Maria, who made delicious meals, but, in the French manner of very modest portions. Monsieur would dish out a few green beans dressed in butter with a sprinkling of fried almonds as a first course, and then a tiny chicken wing with a tablespoon of rice. The cook would then come round with a small Boursault and offer it first to Madame, who would cut herself the tiniest slice, making it impossible for me to have the great big chunk I desired.

I was constantly hungry, and would sneak down to the larder and cut a piece of the left-over baguette (destined to be toasted for breakfast so I had to calculate carefully) and shave another (I hoped undetectable) slice off the cheese, then another, then another, and cram my mouth as fast as I could. Of course Maria knew, but she was a kind woman. And we had a strong bond in our shared dislike of my spoilt charge.

71

At twenty I had hardly ever cooked anything. Cooking at school meant making well-named rock buns or cakes. Once I made a Christmas cake with concrete icing (I'd forgotten the glycerine) on which Dad broke the bone-handled carving knife by using it like a chisel and hitting it with a hammer.

Now Maria showed me how to make Normandy apple tart with a short buttery crust, almond filling and fine apricot glaze, and how to cook vegetables *al dente*. The only part of my job I liked was helping Maria in the kitchen.

But not all my time was spent in the Menier house. I spoke good French by now and Paris, at last, got a proper grip on me. Johannesburg is a modern city, Cape Town only slightly less so, and I was unprepared for the layered complexity, history and beauty of a European city. I revelled in the Frenchness of everything, and in the feeling of being part of the student-dominated Left Bank.

I didn't realise that my impressions and reactions were exactly the same as those of thousands before me: I was led into French poetry by Verlaine and Rimbaud, into art by the Unicorn Tapestries or the Impressionist paintings in the Jeu de Paume; heard the smoky-voiced Juliette Greco singing in a left-bank dive, saw Edith Piaf on stage (a spotlit dot miles below our cheapest seats); read *The Little Prince* in French while sitting in the Tuileries gardens; stood on the Pont Neuf and watched the Bateaux Mouches steam by; browsed at the second-hand book stalls on the banks of the Seine; drank coffee with fellow students on the pavement on the Left Bank. All these are picture-postcard clichés. But to me, a whole extraordinary new world.

And then there was the food, even the street food: melting croque monsieur, lemon-and-sugar crepes, still-hot pralines. You would need to have dead taste buds to live in Paris and not develop a love of good food. I was at last blindingly sure what my career would be. I wanted to be a cook.

Of course life wasn't all discovery and delight. Paris in the rain is grim, and the contrast of the hard and unfriendly proxy family for whom I worked with my own loving parents and brothers, or the warm Kruger clan in London, made me homesick. Once or twice I grabbed a weekend in London for a dose of Kruger warmth. Nan and Rayne had by then made their home in a modern airy flat on top of a Victorian terraced house on Campden Hill.

Rayne was always interested in the young, and I quickly fell under his thrall. He was a terrific listener. He had that trick of making anyone he spoke to feel they were intensely interesting, maybe even fascinating. I found I could tell him anything. I would fantasise that a younger brother of Rayne's, but an exact replica, would miraculously appear and fall in love with me.

In that first year I had a brief liaison which, like my affair with Guy, could only have happened in

Paris – this time with a stony-broke German student, a would-be poet who lived in a narrow room, high above Montparnasse. For not much more than a weekend I was again living the bohemian life of my imaginings. I agonised about it afterwards. I remember thinking I would go to hell if the toll of my lovers reached ten before I met 'the one'.

About this time, I landed my first writing job, a monthly column, *Prue in Paris*, for the Johannesburg *Tatler*. I am sure my mama must have engineered it – she would have known the editor and I expect she showed her one of my letters. But I still felt very grown up and pleased with myself, being paid (not a lot, but enough to give me a buzz and imagine I was a Foreign Correspondent). I have a couple of copies still, and they are a bit breathless and gushing, full of the most obvious (the Seine, the Mona Lisa, *choucroute garnie*, Les Halles, the pavement artists of Montmartre), but the excitement comes through. And I had, for the first time, that wash of pride and pleasure I still get to see my name as a by-line to a newspaper article or on the cover of a book.

One day, when I'd been in Paris perhaps six months, I had a telegram at the Meniers' house.

COME HOME SOONEST DARLING
STOP DAD IS NOT WELL AND
HE WANTS TO SEE YOU

Maria looked at the telegram and burst into tears and wails. She clutched me to her bosom. 'Oh, you poor little girl. Your Daddy, he is dying'.

I did not believe it for a second. 'No, he's been sick, but he's better. It's just that they want me home for Christmas. It's fine, Maria. Stop crying. It's okay.'

But of course she was right. My mother had lied to us, and indeed lied to Dad. She thought if he knew that the tumour was cancerous he would give up and die. And she didn't want to cloud my Paris life.

Dad was grey and thin, his chest bones, by now cancerous too, were uneven and lumpy under his pyjamas, his voice was rasping, and he was in a lot of pain. I could hear his laboured breathing from my room, two doors away.

My desperate mother was clutching at straws. She put her trust in a local faith healer, one of a long series of miracle interventions that did not work. Various nutters and medics visited: Mormons, herbalists, spiritualists. Mum first hoped, then despaired, then fell out with them.

It was torture for her. For twenty-five years she and Dad had slept in the same bed, been the closest of confidants and friends as well as lovers, and now suddenly Dad did not have the energy to talk to her, insisted she sleep in the dressing room, barely spoke to her. I think he just couldn't handle her grief as well as his own, could not manage to stifle his groans and didn't want her to hear them, needed all his energy for the business of dying. Whatever his motives, she could not understand the rejection, his turning into himself, cutting her out.

One day I felt a card in his top pyjama pocket and pulled it out. It was a picture of Christ on the Cross. I stared at it in disbelief, trying to understand why it upset me. If it helped him to suddenly believe in God, why did I mind? But I did mind. It was as though at the last he was denying the father I'd known all my life – the irreverent, merrily blasphemous, supremely rational atheist.

He gave me the ghost of a sheepish smile. 'It's your mother,' he said. 'She's trying everything.'

I found Mum too bravely bright for me to seek my own comfort from her. Until one night when I had a nightmare that has stayed with me ever since. Like most dreams, it is meaningless in the light of day. I dreamt of a young man with a green turban, close up in my vision, but from the back. I knew if he turned his head to look me in the face, that would be the end of me, the end of everything. He had begun to turn, slowly, unstoppably, when I woke up, my mother's arms round me. I had been screaming. For the first time I started to cry as she held me. I think she was crying too, the brittle bravery was gone and she did not tell me Dad would get better.

A few nights later on 20th January 1961, my brother David woke me. 'Dad's died,' he said.

I walked along the short passage, heart banging, nervous apprehension overriding any other emotions. I'd never seen a dead body before. Dad looked asleep, no longer strained or in pain, but also not like my father. I kissed his still-warm forehead. I'd longed for that terrible wheezing to stop, but now it had, the silence was horrible. He was fifty-four, my mother forty-five.

A few days after the funeral, of which I remember nothing except David's face, red and ravaged from crying, we scattered Dad's ashes in the cemetery at Modderfontein. It was horrible. The ashes came out of the sifter thing, not as free-drifting ash, but in heavy little clumps, like oily sand. They fell heavily and unevenly on the raked grave-plot. I watched in disbelief and horror. That's my father, I thought.

Soon after the funeral, David returned to his family and his studies in England and Jamie once again went back to boarding school. I stayed on for six months to be with Peggy (somehow, about this time, I'd started to call Mum Peggy or Pegs).

I did a speedwriting course, which took six weeks as opposed to the months needed to master Pitman's shorthand, and got a job as a judge's clerk. It was a job that usually went to legally trained young men but Judge Dowling hired me because, forty years before, he had done a speed-writing course in America and mistakenly thought a clerk who had done the same course would be able to read his judgements.

The judge was in his seventies, greatly respected and eccentric. Having belatedly discovered that I could not decipher his shorthand, he dictated his judgements as he drove us to some circuit court in the bush. When I protested that I got car sick and could not write while bumping over country roads, he retorted, 'Nonsense, girl. Get a grip,' and went on dictating.

His instincts were liberal, but even so, being a judge's clerk in the early Sixties was a sharp lesson in the horrors of apartheid. One day he was trying two cases of rape. The first concerned a black man who had raped a white woman, terrifying her but not physically harming her. The second accused was another black man who had raped his nine-year-old niece. The girl had been left irreparably damaged physically, and so traumatised she'd not spoken since the event ten months before.

The rapist of the white woman was sentenced to death, the rapist of the black child to one year in prison, suspended.

I was outraged. I struggled to stay seated at my desk in front of the judge's bench. It was all I could do not to jump up, turn round and cry, 'That's monstrous. How could you do that?'

The court adjourned and I followed my boss down the corridor and into the judge's chambers, then burst into a flood of recrimination ending in furious tears. Judge Dowling took little notice until I had run out of steam and was snivelling, then said mildly, 'It's generally a good idea to hear the evidence before you make a judgement.'

He explained that in the first case the law required a sentence of death if the rape victim was white and the perpetrator black. He did not like the law, but he had to act according to the law. He'd had no option other than putting a plea for mercy to the attorney general, which he would send off that afternoon.

But black-on-black rape was, in the eyes of the law, different. So here he had been able to exercise his discretion.

'But a suspended sentence! That child's life is ruined.'

'It would be further ruined if he went to jail or was hanged. That man supports her, plus eight other children and two women. Without him they would lose the corrugated iron slum they live in and would starve. There is no welfare in this country.'

'But it is so unfair. How can . . .'

'Life's unfair. All we can do is our best.'

Going round the country on circuit was another education. Every day we'd hear stories of duplicity, passion, quiet desperation. Mostly they were not the sort of stories to make the national newspapers, but they were life-shattering to the players. There was an Afrikaans farmer's wife whose damage to her arm had deprived her of her chief pride and pleasure – polishing her stinkwood furniture and buffing her red cement steps and *stoep*. And an indignant farmer whose prize cow, in calf, had been stolen. 'And,' his lawyer said, his voice heavy with meaning, 'that cow was in an interesting condition.'

Judge Dowling: 'Interesting to whom, pray?'

The judge liked a tipple. Indeed he drank like a fish. We had a system; a tap on the bench behind my head meant, 'I will adjourn in a few minutes. You leave now and make the tea. Put whisky in my cup instead of tea.'

Once he ended up in hospital, in the little town of Springs. Alcohol was firmly banned by the doctor, but as soon as the doc had left, Judge Dowling hissed at me, 'If you value your job, you will bring me a half-bottle of whisky, suitably disguised in a ginger ale bottle.'

I did value my job. Indeed I loved it. I was paid £500 a year and I felt I was in a play, acting a part, walking down wide corridors wearing my black gown with little white tabs at my neck, meeting highly intelligent lawyers and judges, seeing other people's lives in the raw.

On my twenty-first birthday, which was a few weeks after Dad's death, I came out of the house to see a Morris Minor parked in the drive with a huge pink ribbon right round it. A car! I could not believe it. I had not expected to own a car for years. Although we were a well-off family, such spoiling was unheard of. I think it was a gesture of solace in a time of grief. A week before I'd spent my first month's salary on a bone-china tea set and expensive cosmetics for Mum.

I grieved for my father and I felt for my mother. But I cannot pretend that those months were all bad. The period was a respite from the occasional stress and loneliness of Paris. Home was seldom either stressful or lonely. And I was twenty-one, in my first job, owning my first car, with lots of friends. I danced at country clubs, played tennis, went to parties, sat around swimming pools, had, I think, a good time.

I fear that I neglected Mum. I don't remember doing what I hope against hope I *did* do: hold her for ages while she wept, listen to her talking on and on about Sam, worry about her being lonely.

Of course I could find out by reading her diaries for the period, but I shy away from that. I don't want to discover that I was still the selfish, sex-obsessed girl my Dad had so disapproved of. At that time, when he was dying, I had not yet read Peg's diaries of the year before, so knew nothing of his anguish at my behaviour on that Madeira holiday, nor of her unhappiness at the effect on him. I stopped reading them after that. Even now, fifty years on, I don't want to read that he died still disappointed in me. I want to hold on to what I remember of those last weeks, which was that, in spite of his illness, he held my hand with not just love, but approval.

In a sense, Dad's death ended my mother's life. She was too feisty to mope, but there is no doubt that he was the irreplaceable centre of her being. And she of his. Years later I found this letter written from him to her as he lay in hospital the night before his operation:

Sunday, 10 pm
My darling heart,
I expect to make it tomorrow so there won't be any need to write this letter at all. And if there was any need, I can't put down in one letter, or in one lifetime what the last 25 years mean. I can't even try but the comfort to me is to know that you know without my trying. First there was you and still there is you and steady throughout the whole 25 years I have always known that my blessing and my gift and my pride and my love and my life and my heart was you. Thank you my dearest heart. First for you, then for dear, selfless, gallant Davie, for lovable, sweet, extrovert Prue and for that character Jamie who will one day set off a great rocket. Dear James, darling Prue and dearest Davie but above and beyond everything in my life is you.
Goodnight my darling one.
S

CHAPTER 4

LOVINGLY BOUND

Rayne

In May, my mother thought it was time I returned to Europe, so she suggested I drive her elderly parents and my ancient aunt round Scotland – they wanted to see the haunts of their youth – and then stay with Nan and Rayne in London for the summer until I had to return to Paris.

Like babies, the three septuagenarians would fall asleep as soon as I started the engine, so I mostly admired the Highlands by myself. Once I threw an apple core into the long grass and Great Aunt Peg made me stop the car and pick it up: I was littering the countryside. I shared a room with her and her frail old body emitted snores worthy of a gargantua. I would clap my hands gently, then louder and louder until she harrumphed and turned over, whereupon I would race her back to sleep.

After the Scottish trip, I headed for Nan and Rayne and Airlie House in Kensington like a homing pigeon.

Donald was a now a trainee doctor and married. John was with the BBC and set on a career in film and TV, and Angela was at the Royal Academy of Dramatic Art. That summer of 1961, I was gently civilised by the Kruger family and gradually lost some of my South African rawness or, some would say, brashness. I learnt to have grown-up conversation at Sunday lunch (for which you were expected to take an interest in current affairs, the arts, politics) and occasionally met Nan's theatre friends, some of whom – Alec Guinness, John Gielgud for example – were awesomely famous and very polite and socially polished. Nan taught me not to nick fruit from the fruit bowl every time I passed it, to bring home the occasional bunch of flowers or mini-present. Rayne taught me, not very successfully, to talk less and listen more. Ange let me into her circle of drama-student friends. They were a fascinating, intelligent, generous and loving family.

Only Angela was still living at home, but she was at RADA during the day and often out with friends at night, and Nan was at the theatre. So I saw more of Rayne than of the others. Being a writer, he worked at home, and I would make lunch or supper for him and we'd talk. He was by far the most interesting person I'd ever met.

Rayne was born, illegitimate, in 1922 in South Africa. Pat Kennedy, his adored mother, married Victor Kruger when Rayne was three and Rayne took his name. He hated Victor, who beat him mercilessly, though in time he came to have some sympathy for a man unable to control his temper and dealing with a clever lad who had the devil in him. The family's fortunes veered from riches to bankruptcy and back again but Rayne viewed his childhood as generally happy.

By the time he was twenty-two, Rayne had worked down a gold mine; prospected for tungsten in Rhodesia; been thrown out of Witwatersrand University for organising a donkey derby and failing to return the donkeys to their owners (the lads in charge had got drunk and let the animals go); become an articled clerk while pursuing his law degree by correspondence; acted in several plays with my mother and Nan; joined the merchant navy and gone to war; come home to Johannesburg, where he resumed his law studies, as well as working as a radio announcer and actor. And he was writing his first novel.

That novel, *Tanker*, is a ruthless coming of age tale based on Rayne's own experience in the merchant navy, working as a steward on a tanker ferrying oil from the Gulf.

In June 1944, while Rayne was on his tanker, Nan had received the telegram dreaded by every woman with a husband away at war. Bill had been killed in a plane crash in Algeria. Donald was eight at the time, John four, and Angela just three.

In 1946 Nan and Peggy decided to stage *Pygmalion* and Rayne auditioned for the part of Henry Higgins. My mother, who directed the play, had her doubts about the pairing of a greenhorn in his twenties as the forty-something Higgins playing opposite forty-year-old Nan as the twenty-something Eliza. But Rayne got the job and during the round-South Africa tour of the play, Rayne and Nan fell in love. Rayne wanted marriage but Nan anguished over the seventeen-year age gap and the danger of Rayne, so young and infatuated then, falling out of love as the years passed. My mother's diaries also record Nan's concern for Rayne, fearing that taking on a family of four would hamper his career as a writer.

But by the end of 1947 Nan and Rayne had indeed married, and were in London living in Nan's house with Nan's three small children.

As an impoverished writer newly arrived in England, Rayne took what jobs he could get. He went to the Congo to write a newspaper profile of Albert Schweitzer, the legendary leper doctor. His account was not entirely glowing. He could not reconcile the image of a saint with a man whose principles about not destroying life meant a refusal to use antibiotics or to kill the rats that ate his patients' nerveless feet.

Rayne took a job writing horoscopes for the *Daily Sketch*. Knowing nothing about astrology but needing the money, he bought a book and mugged up enough to mention what star was where that week, and then proceeded to pontificate with harmless stuff like 'Do not pat unfriendly dogs today' or generalised nonsense like 'You will make a major decision soon' or 'Today is the day to sort out what has been troubling you'.

He gave it up when women started writing to him: 'I took your advice and I've left my husband'; 'You know you said I would cross the water? I did. I've emigrated to Australia.'

Tanker was followed by six other novels and by *Goodbye Dolly Gray*, his Boer War Book. This was followed, in 1960, by *The Devil's Discus*, about the mysterious death of King Ananda of Thailand (then Siam). At twenty, Ananda had been found dead in bed, a bullet through his head. Few educated Thais believed the official story that two faithful royal pages and an ex-secretary, who had served the Royal Family for many years, were the killers. But neither of the two alternatives was acceptable: that a demi-god king would take his own life, or that a divine prince would murder his brother-god. Such concepts were too dangerous to both the monarchy and the regime, so the three men charged, after ten years of trial, appeals and more trials, were executed.

Rayne decided to investigate and took ship for Bangkok.

On arrival he tried to get a rickshaw to take him to his hotel, but his inability to speak a word of Thai meant he had to go back to his ship and get an English-speaking Thai to write the name and address of his hotel in Thai characters. The incident revealed to him the utter madness of his mission. Imagine, he thought, if a Thai

87

writer, without a word of English, arrived in London set on discovering the truth about the killing of the Queen.

Without any real hope of a result, he asked the receptionist at the hotel to put the word out that he needed a female assistant who would have royal blood, good English, charm and personality. She must also have no belief in the divinity of kings, no close acquaintance with the ruling elite and no political ties or allegiance to the current regime. She should be able to travel, willing to work night and day, and be completely free for the next month!

Rayne then went for a massage and thought he might as well spend a few days seeing the sights and then go home, but two days later a young woman came to see him. She was an aristocrat, but more socialist than royalist. She had been to university in the West, she was charming and beautiful, could type, and was free to work, etc. Above all, she was brave.

Between them they discovered that Ananda had fallen in love with a Swiss girl when at college in Switzerland. Knowing the impossibility of marrying her, dreading his future as a god-king and with no one to turn to, the young prince had shot himself through the head.

The Devil's Discus was banned in Thailand and still is, but it remains in print in successive underground versions today.

★   ★   ★

Since writing is a precarious occupation, Rayne worked part-time on property development. While I was staying with him and Nan at Airlie House, he would occasionally have to visit some property or go to a meeting and I'd go too. Sometimes we went by bus, but more often on foot. He knew London inside out – its history, art and architecture – and, ignoramus that I was, I soaked it up. He was a good storyteller, and I fell back into my old hero worship of him. Soon there was nothing I would rather do than be with Rayne.

I told myself I was not falling in love with him, that he was out of bounds. And anyway, he loved Nan.

And then one evening, when we were in the kitchen, he kissed me.

I wish I could say I objected, but I didn't. Guilt about Nan would creep in later but what I felt at that moment – apart from a leaping desire – was surprise and delight that he considered me kissable, a woman, not a child.

So began a thirteen-year affair. I was utterly infatuated. Far cleverer and better educated than me, Rayne nonetheless found me interesting. He made me feel talented, beautiful, admired. There are few things more seductive than someone who delights in you, believes in you, wants you to be happy. And few things more attractive than that someone knowing much more than you do. To this day I am an intellectual groupie. Not clever, artistic or particularly talented myself, I remain in awe of writers, artists and musicians, am 'turned on' by interesting, achieving people.

Of course I realise my affair with Rayne was unforgivable. I still believe adultery is wrong and feel genuinely angry with men who betray their wives, and prefer to forget that I encouraged Rayne to do just that: I fell completely, thunderously and irredeemably for the husband of my mother's best friend and partner. Rayne had been a kind of godfather to me. Poor Nan had no idea what a serpent she had allowed into her nest.

I had never met anyone like Rayne before. Ironic though it might sound in view of his secret life, he held almost Victorian values of honesty, probity and kindness. He was also, in those early days, beautiful.

But what captivated me most was his off-beatness. He became more conservative in later years, but in the Sixties he was something of an anarchist. He thought the police were no different from the villains they chased, he knew where to get hold of illegal joints, and numbered some dodgy (but interesting) Soho low-lifes as his friends – alongside, but quite separate from, the Kruger coterie of actors, writers, artists and business people.

Betraying the hospitality and love of Nan should have been impossible for me, but I pushed all feelings of anxiety and guilt away. I refused to think about it, at least at first. I told myself I was no threat to her, that I loved her and would never hurt her. And neither would Rayne. Somehow, I cannot now imagine how, I managed to persuade myself that what we were doing was nothing to do with anyone else. In the age-old excuse of all adulterers, I couldn't help it.

After that first kiss, we spent more time exploring London, a good bit of it looking for a flat or a room for me and both of us falling in love. It is not much of a boast, but I'm glad we never slept together at Airlie House. I can't claim any credit for this because, if he'd wanted me to, of course I would have. I would have stripped off in Piccadilly Circus if he'd asked me to. Rayne would never talk about Nan or his loyalties, but we agreed I should move out.

So, love unconsummated, we tramped the streets, galleries or museums. We would sometimes end up in the Studio Club, a raffish haunt for artists and writers in Swallow Street, near Piccadilly Circus. Rayne was relaxed there – it was a club where none of his or Nan's acquaintances was likely to come. We were not yet sleeping together, but I imagined the rather louche members assumed we were, and I liked that. I felt flattered, grown up and bohemian.

We found a room in Leinster Terrace, Bayswater, and one evening after a Studio Club supper and a bus ride home to my new flatlet we finally made love. It had been about a month since that first kiss.

The Leinster Terrace room was tiny, with almost no space to stand between cupboard, single bed, kitchenette and tiny shower room. It became our island. I would spend all morning preparing first me and then the supper. I had long hair which had to go into rollers, and I would struggle with Sixties false eyelashes. (When one fluttered into my glass of wine at a party I gave them up.) There were only a fridge and a kettle, so fixing supper was easier – it came cold from the deli. There was no table, but a flap on the wall opposite the bed was wide enough for a tray. We ate sitting on the bed, and then squashed into it.

I did not want to go back to France. 'I'll never be a linguist, the Sorbonne is wasted on me. I want to be a cook,' I told Rayne.

'Even if you become a cook, another year in Paris can only do you good. You could get an evening job in a restaurant or café.'

'I'd be better off going to the Cordon Bleu in London.'

'You can do that later. Besides, darling girl, isn't it time you finished something you started?'

Maybe he hoped we would forget each other. Perhaps it was a last-ditch effort not to fall completely in love with me. I don't know. Rayne had an extraordinary power to prevent conversations he did not want to have.

So, at the end of August, I went back to Paris, taking a room with a middle-aged Frenchwoman to further improve my French. But she hardly spoke to me, and I ached for Rayne all the time.

Not being able to speak to him was agony. I

couldn't ring the flat for fear of getting Nan. Once, I telephoned when I thought she would be at the theatre for a matinee, but I mistook the day. In those days you had to make long distance calls through an operator and when she said, 'Mr Kruger is not in, but would you like to speak to Mrs Kruger?' I heard Nan's voice, concerned and kind, 'Prue darling, it's me. Is something wrong? Can I help?' I panicked and put the phone down, and curled myself into a ball of anguish, eyes shut tight, teeth clenched.

Long-distance, Rayne continued my education, fanning my dawning interest in art and architecture, getting me reading writers he loved: Montaigne, Dickens, Bernard Shaw, all sorts. I was twenty-one and at last beginning to see the point of learning. I was certainly a better student for him than I was at the university. I wanted to please him, and to have opinions as he and the rest of his family did. The few lines of love in every letter were the manna that kept me going.

He extracted a promise from me that I would destroy his letters, which I dutifully, painfully, did. The only thing I have that dates from our clandestine years is a hand-made booklet of Rimbaud's *Le Bateau Ivre*, 'lovingly bound for the recipient at the Armitage Press'. (Guy Armitage was our secret alias for him.)

After a month back in Paris I decided to try for a part-time job in Maxim's, then the most fashionable restaurant in Paris. The head chef was dismissive:

'You cannot work in the kitchen. You're a girl.' He said I could help pluck and gut the poultry and peel the potatoes with the women who did this first thing, but I must be gone by the time the chefs arrived.

'But I want to learn from the chefs. Watch them at work.'

Gallic shrug and shake of his head. End of interview.

On the first day of my second attempt at the Sorbonne course I spotted Jane Cluver, a girl I'd known since school in Johannesburg. We fell upon each other. Both of us were miserable and lonely in our respective digs, so we promptly hired a furnished flat on the fourth floor in the fourteenth arrondissement, with the classic grumpy concierge lurking on the ground floor. The flat was small, just a bedroom (we shared the double bed), a tiny sitting room and a kitchen which also housed a shower behind a curtain.

Jane became my closest friend and, forty years later, still is. Of course I told her all about Rayne. She is extraordinarily discreet and, apart from my friend and agent Pat Kavanagh, in whom I confided a year later, I never told anyone. I introduced Jane and Rayne and they liked each other at once. It was wonderful having one friend in common who knew of our relationship. I don't know why this should have mattered but it did, and it was wonderful.

I tried not to think about the future. I was too

happy to concern myself about what might happen to the relationship, whether I would marry and have children, or what discovery of our affair would mean to my family and Rayne's. Mostly I managed not to dwell on any of that at all. But sometimes I lay awake, asking myself how I could have got into a love affair with my mother's best friend's husband, a man who had always been half uncle, half godfather to me; whose stepdaughter was one of my closest friends; whose whole family was like an extension of my own family, people I loved. It was practically incest.

There weren't any answers. I just loved him, I told myself, and I could not make myself un-love him.

Because of Rayne, I was not, as before in Paris, on the hunt for a boyfriend. But I was grateful for any social life, and we would go out with fellow students to eat couscous in the Moroccan quarter or drink coffee on the Boul' Mich'. One day, Pierre, a French-Canadian who worked at the Banque de Paribas, told me about a risqué club which he thought would be fun. I put on my best new dress and we went.

We knocked, and finally banged, on a nondescript door in a nondescript street. Eventually the letterbox opened a slit and Pierre had a whispered conversation. I felt we were in a movie, with him muttering a name and password and the door reluctantly opening. We walked down a corridor and then into a warren of rooms, every one of them crammed with naked people. One room was carpeted with wall-to-wall copulation, young bottoms going up and down like bouncy castles.

It was an organised orgy, and we were the only people with any clothes on. I would have given a lot to have escaped, but I tried to look cool. Pierre, only slightly less taken aback than I, said, 'When in Rome . . .', took his clothes off and disappeared into the throng. I kept mine on for a while, but soon realised that this just encouraged treaties from men to join in. So I undressed too and at once became less conspicuous.

I spent the next two hours walking purposefully from room to room, trying to look as if I had a sexual tryst arranged in the next room or was on my way to the bar or the loo, and avoiding the men patrolling the party, cocks aloft. They brought to mind cars prowling about in search of a slot to park in. I was amazed at the variety of models on offer: penises that were stubby, fat, bent, grey, pink, brown, crimson. I was torn between wanting to look and not wanting to be seen looking. One guy was so proud of his – and it *was* impressive – that he never put it to use, but merely paraded about like an athlete with an Olympic banner.

Rayne came to visit me when he could contrive a few days away and it was heaven. Paris *is* for lovers: the tree-lined Champs-Elysées, the river and the bridges, the intimate little bistros; the city reeks of romance. On one visit, Rayne stayed for four days in the flat (Jane kindly disappeared for the duration). I carefully planned what we would eat and drink every day, and did much advance cooking, most of which we never got round to. We strolled the streets, ate in cafés, and one night went to the Folies Bergère, which was a great, if dated, spectacle.

Once, holed up cosily in the Hotel Cimarosa, Rayne came down with flu. I brought him aspirins, orange juice, and the occasional cup of consommé or boiled eggs from the café next door. I read the whole of Victor Hugo's *Le Ventre de Paris*, in French, lying beside him, his body too hot to cuddle up to. When he left, I went back to the flat – with flu.

It was still less than a year since Dad's death, and my mother could not face Christmas without him and with only Jamie at home. So she brought Jamie, then fifteen, to Austria – where I met up with them – to visit a Doctor Hoenig, an old man who had known my father. It was an odd thing to do, since we didn't know him well, but I imagine she couldn't face Christmas at the Krugers' either, which was the other obvious alternative to home.

We stayed in a small mountain hotel, and went to Midnight Mass on Christmas Eve, walking through the snow. We could hear *Stille Nacht* – 'Silent Night' – being sung, unaccompanied, at Oberndorf, in the tower of the little church of St Nicholas for which it was written. The clear voices coming through the crisp air, in the snow, were magical. And afterwards, in Doctor Hoenig's house, curtains were ceremoniously drawn apart in the living room to reveal the Christmas tree, lit by hundreds of real candles and hung with gingerbread biscuits. It was so pretty I burst into tears, to the gratification of my hosts and the embarrassment of my brother. My mother tried to explain that our Christmas tree at home was a summer apple tree stuck with cotton wool balls in the blazing sunlight.

Doctor Hoenig impressed me deeply by keeping a large live carp in the bath. This meant no one could have a bath until after New Year, when I'm afraid we ate the carp with a great deal of pleasure. He was delicious.

After New Year we went skiing, something none of us had done before. My mother, then forty-six, managed to fall down even as she was standing on dead flat snow. At twenty-one I was enthusiastic but clumsy, and almost at once sat down on a lump of ice and cracked my coccyx. Very painful. For the rest of the fortnight I lay on my tummy on a hotel lounger, dreaming about Rayne, and sitting up on a rubber ring to eat my meals. Fifteen-year-old Jamie, needless to say, was slaloming happily down the slopes almost at once.

One of those hotel meals was memorable, if farcical, and was my first insight into the dodgy practices of the catering trade. There were large tanks of live trout in the dining room and the guests could choose their victims. Ever greedy, I chose the biggest trout I could see and the waiter duly fished it out with a net and carried it in a bucket to the kitchen.

When, twenty minutes later, the trout came back, sizzling in brown butter and fried almonds and smelling delicious, it was frozen solid and raw inside. I wondered how many trips that magnificent trout had made to and from the kitchen. The waiter put his finger to his lips and gave us dinner on the house.

One evening my mother announced she was going to marry Robert Langford, a theatrical producer and motor-racing aficionado. It was less than a year since Dad had died and I couldn't believe she could love anyone else. But Jamie liked Robert and I knew she was lonely in spite of her glamour and fame. Having always preferred her husband's company to anyone else's, she had few real friends, and we children were all away, Jamie at boarding school, David in England and me in Paris. They married a few months later. Fifteen-year-old Jamie gave her away, but neither David nor I was there.

When I hobbled off the plane at Orly airport, Rayne was at the gate. Jane had told him what flight I was on and he'd booked us a room in a small hotel on the left bank.

Jane and I took it in turn to manage the household kitty, shopping in the tiny food shops and local markets and occasionally eating in underground bistros with gingham tablecloths and a *menu du jour*. We drank Nicolas red wine every evening because it was cheaper than Coca-Cola, which we regarded as a treat for Saturdays. We developed an enthusiasm for steak tartare, which I had eaten with Rayne and thought enormously smart. (He liked it with chips, which inevitably made the waiter think he didn't know it was made of raw chopped steak. But the hot fried chips are perfect with the cold, rich and spicy meat.)

One day I asked Jane, 'Can we really afford steak tartare again? It must cost an arm and a leg.'

'Oh, it's fine,' she replied. 'I got it from that cheap butcher on the corner with the horse's head over the door.'

And that's how I know that horse fillet makes a better tartare than beef does.

The *Cours de Civilisation Française* was to end in June. And though I was longing to get back to Rayne, Jane and I decided that we might never again have a completely free summer to travel round Europe. We planned to buy a combi-camper to sleep in so we could save on youth hostel costs. Jane took our combined savings to buy the car, and we arranged to meet up in Amsterdam.

Arrived in Amsterdam, I walked down the canal outside the youth hostel where she was staying, and saw her suitcase in the back of the smallest car in the world: a little two-seater Isetta bubble car with the engine at the back and only a huge plastic door-cum-window in the front. It was all that the money had stretched to.

I swear, but Jane denies, that when driving up

a Swiss mountain we went so slowly that a farmer leading his cow outstripped us. But that car was a valiant little thing and crossed the Alps once and the Pyrenees twice.

In six weeks we rattled through Holland, Belgium and France, and had a week on Corsica. By then I was desperate to get back to Rayne, and I expect Jane was sick to death of me talking about him. She went back to Amsterdam, and I took the Isetta to London. We would share it, swapping every six months.

CHAPTER 5

KILLING LOBSTERS

From cook to caterer

Rayne helped me find my first long-term flat, a bedsit in Baron's Court. It cost four pounds a week, a pound more than I could afford. Rayne chipped in the extra pound, and teased me about being a kept woman.

That first flat – I called it a flat but it was just a room with a groaning geyser and a bath in one corner and a tiny circular kitchenette under a pointed turret in another. The room was on the top floor and you had to negotiate old mattresses and upturned tables on the landings. My landlady was of the keep-yourself-to-yourself school and had no interest in the goings-on of her tenants. Her basement flat had a separate entrance and she rarely left it.

She also had no sense of smell, which was just as well since I cooked all the time and if she had realised I would soon be running a business from that room I'm certain she'd have upped the rent. Apart from a permanently out-of-work middle-aged actor living in the flat below, who would sometimes come in for a cup of tea (and then cheerfully and without embarrassment take the dead teabags home with him to use again), I knew no-one, and Rayne and I felt safe from detection.

I was inordinately happy. For the first three months I was at the Cordon Bleu cookery school in the day and I would bring home little boxes of Coq au Vin or pots of chocolate mousse, a quiche Lorraine or a soup, and Rayne and I would toast bread on a barbecue fork in front of the two-bar electric fire and talk about my business-to-be.

I was taught by a Mrs Proctor. She was a brilliant teacher. 'Looks like hedge clippings', she'd say of my inadequately chopped parsley. She made us wash the spinach in seven changes of cold water to ensure there was no grit in it (no bags of pre-prepped spinach in those days). The water was freezing and when her back was turned we would turn the hot tap on.

We made delicious, and adventurous, dishes, food that today seems old fashioned, but deserves reviving: kidneys turbigo (lambs' kidneys casseroled with sausages and mushrooms); butter-laden puff pastry made into vol-au-vents filled with sweetbreads in a cream sauce; veal escalopes with marsala and spinach; eggs Florentine.

I got my first freelance catering job while still at the Cordon Bleu school. Two of us students were sent to cook a dinner party: egg mousse, roast pheasant, hazelnut meringue cake with a raspberry coulis. We had to lay the table, decant the wine, do the cooking, carve the pheasant, wait at table, make the coffee and wash up. We were terrified: neither of us had ever seen a pheasant, never mind plucked, drawn and roasted one. The first course and the pudding were classic Cordon Bleu recipes and we had done them at school. But they were not simple: we had to make mayonnaise by hand for the mousse, and the meringue stuck like a limpet to the foil. But we managed.

Euphoria changed to exhaustion at about midnight and we spent our entire earnings on a taxi home.

That first job taught me to charge extra for washing-up and waitressing. That way the customer might hire a proper waitress who would also make the coffee and wash up, and I could go home when the pudding was served. And years later, when my business was employing just-fledged cooks, I'd try to make our chefs sympathetic to the terror and tears of newcomers.

The job led to more evening chef-ing, and when I left cookery school I took a three-day-a-week job cooking for the embryonic law firm, McKenna and Partners. The three partners had a dining room which doubled as a boardroom in Whitehall. The kitchen was so small you couldn't open the fridge and the oven at the same time.

I worked there for two years. I'd been taught the principles at the Cordon Bleu, but now I set about cooking my way through the twelve hundred-plus pages of the *Constance Spry Cookery Book*. The partners were extraordinarily good about it. When I got to the chicken chapter they ate chicken, in different guises, for weeks. I never gave a thought to nutrition or variety. I was intent on learning classic French cooking, and if it came with large quantities of butter and cream, well, hadn't Fernand Point, the great French chef, said, '*Beurre beurre, donnez-moi du beurre, toujours du beurre.*'

Once, experimenting with making cream cheese and yogurt, I forgot a bowl of fermenting milk behind the radiator, hidden by the curtains in Reception. I arrived on Tuesday to find men in white coats, wearing surgical masks and looking for the source of the smell.

I started to cater from my bedsit, carrying pies and casseroles round on the tube, or using the bubble-car when it was my turn to have it. I sometimes took jobs cooking for private weekend parties, or shooting parties in Scotland where I rapidly learned to make porridge, cook game and bottle raspberries.

Most customers would recommend me to their friends. But some would not. I remember cooking for a woman in Holland Park and hearing one of the guests complimenting her on the food.

'This is delicious, darling. Any chance of getting the cook's phone number?'

'Oh, no, I do all my own cooking. I just have a little girl to help with the serving.'

A little girl! I'm a great clumsy five foot-nine

and I'd cooked everything. So I put business cards into the guests' coat pockets, with a note on the top: *Your dinner at Mrs X's was cooked by . . .*

Another time I heard a hostess protesting that there was no point in giving her friend my details because 'she is just *so* busy. You have no idea. You have to book her weeks in advance and, honestly, it would be a waste of time.' The temptation to fling open the kitchen hatch and yell, 'Lies! I'm desperate for work,' was strong.

My mother brought my new stepfather on a visit. She told me later of her horror at my room – worn lino, junk on the stairs, the groaning geyser, the candlewick bedspread and thin curtains, the ancient free-standing gas stove. She wanted to sub me to stay somewhere better, but Robert dissuaded her. 'She's so excited and proud of the place. Don't ruin it for her. She wants to manage her own life, and she's doing fine. Leave her be.' It was good advice. To me that first flatlet was my pride and joy.

From the start, Rayne was my advisor in all things, from cutting my hair (he disliked long hair) to running a business. He wasn't a Svengali – did not control or dominate me – he just knew a lot more about absolutely everything than I did. Except food to which, ironically, he was pretty indifferent.

He visited me whenever he could, egging me on and making me extraordinarily happy. He encouraged my first harebrained idea, *Matinée Collations,* a catering delivery service to actors in their dressing rooms between shows on matinee days. It was a resounding flop. I hadn't reckoned on the stage doormen demanding a cut in return for access; I'd not realised how many actors want to go for a walk between shows or sit in a pub; I'd wrongly imagined matinees all took place on Wednesdays and Saturdays, and, worst of all, I hadn't figured that shows would close without warning – I'd arrive with a load of picnic trays to find the theatre dark.

In spite of this dead end, I began to make a living, though I was still flying by the seat of my pants and still remarkably ignorant.

Lady Elizabeth Anson, whose company Party Planners organised fashionable events, asked me to cook a lunch at which Princess Margaret was to be the guest of honour. The menu, she said, was to be caviar, followed by lobster.

I'd never cooked, indeed I'd never seen, either delicacy. But I had a book, and plenty of time to mug them up. The caviar was easy. All I'd have to do was open the tin and serve the caviar with toast, finely chopped egg, shallots and parsley.

The lobster, however, put the wind up me. The instructions were perfectly clear: I had to kill it by splitting its head in two. I bolstered my resolve. Cooks had to learn to kill things.

What the book failed to mention was that when lobsters are alive they are black and when cooked, bright red. Which is why Declan the butler found me, knife in hand, solemnly despatching boiled lobsters. He teased me about it for years.

A few customers were a nightmare. One, incredibly, refused to pay her bill on the grounds that I'd forgotten to wash the egg white off the whisk in the Kenwood machine. She admitted the dinner had been perfect but, she said, 'You promised to leave the kitchen spotless, and you didn't.' We settled for a twenty-five per cent discount, slightly more than my profit.

On one occasion I went to cook dinner in a kitchen so filthy that I had to spend a couple of hours cleaning it. Every surface was covered with greasy bottles and jars, the floor was dark and sticky, the fridge full of evil-smelling leftovers, manky vegetables and unidentifiable substances growing mould. I'd have liked to add an item to the bill, 'to de-toxifying kitchen: £10', but of course I didn't.

I was keen to get into food writing and Rayne encouraged me. My first jobs included a food column for a small newsletter published by Berry Brothers, the wine merchants, and edited by Quentin Crewe, and the food articles for *Nova*. Everyone in the publishing world thought this new and decidedly irreverent fashion magazine, launched in 1965, was cutting-edge and revolutionary, a view not shared by enough subscribers: *Nova* died ten years later.

My landlady finally realised I was running a business upstairs and wanted me out. And I needed a proper kitchen. So Rayne masterminded my first small property development, funded by loans amounting to £9,000 from Mum and the bank. We found a near-derelict row of four garages with rooms above in Upbrook Mews near Paddington Station. They'd been built as stables and grooms' sleeping quarters for the big houses in Gloucester Terrace that backed onto the mews. I couldn't afford to turn the whole property into a house for myself, but Rayne helped me build two tiny cottages, numbers 25 and 25a, with kitchen and garage downstairs, sitting room above, and bedroom and bathroom on top. Number 25 had a narrow second bedroom and loo on the living room floor. I let this house and lived in the smaller one.

Every inch was designed by Rayne to be both practical and good looking. I discovered the excitement of building – something only rivalled by the satisfaction of nesting – choosing furniture, colours, putting up pictures. I loved both and still do.

Rayne took me to a wholesale warehouse in the docks where we bought flat-pack Scandinavian furniture, including a mini-office which folded up to look like a cupboard so that I could banish my day's work when everyone went home.

My first tenants for number 25 were the pop group the Hollies, of which Graham Nash was the lead singer. I was twenty-six by then, they were a few years younger and we became friends. I still have a beautiful Victorian tippet (a kind of short cloak) that Graham bought in the Paris flea market and gave me. I used to have his cast-off jeans too, but soon got too fat to wear them.

Crowds of screaming girl groupies would sometimes gather outside the house, hoping for a glimpse or a touch. The group would rehearse loudly all afternoon and often all night, but the neighbours – I guess we were all young – never complained. Years later, when Graham had formed Crosby, Stills and Nash, he invited me to a concert at the Festival Hall. Afterwards I walked forward to the stage and he came out to chat. He looked at the front row seats and nodded with satisfaction. 'Good concert,' he said. 'If they don't wet their knickers you've failed.'

I used to hide the group's hash for them among my dried herbs, but no one ever came asking. Once or twice when I was still cooking in the small hours they would come in, high as kites, and marvel at the sparkle of sugar on a pie crust, or the wondrous design of a lettuce leaf, or want to tell me the secrets of the universe. They would occasionally offer me a spliff, but I'd refuse. I've always been frightened of making a fool of myself. I must have seemed very staid and respectable to them.

But with Rayne it was different. In all those years of secrecy, if Nan was not in a play, he would only see me perhaps one evening a week, sometimes not even that. He would have to invent business reasons to be out without her. But, as mistresses go, I was lucky. Nan was a successful actress and often in work, and then Rayne would see me every night while she was at the theatre, and, best of all, on matinee days we could hole up all afternoon and evening with food, wine, and bed. And sometimes a joint or two.

Once or twice things went badly wrong. Rayne believed drugs should be legalised, and I believed whatever Rayne believed. But then one night he appeared with two small white pills. They were LSD.

We both had a horrible time. Blissful at first, as promised: floating, aware of the beauty of anything and everything, music sounding like never before, food ambrosia, love transporting. And then suddenly we were into a nightmare of terror and hallucination. The walls seem to breathe in and out and the air became visible and moving, like a 3D fabric. My arms melted, the flesh dripping off the bones; I could not look at Rayne for fear he would turn into a devouring monster. Even his back swelled like an orang-utan's and I knew if he turned round that would be the end of me. Somehow he managed to comfort me without my looking at him. But he told me afterwards that he'd had a similarly terrifying trip.

That night my cavalier attitude to drugs was changed forever. I realised how incredibly dangerous they can be, and how LSD, at least, can affect your brain. Nearly fifty years later if I wake from a deep sleep, especially from a nightmare, and stagger to the bathroom, I can see the air moving, patterned and pulsating in the same way, though much more mildly, as it did that night. I have to put on the light and blink away the vision.

Many chefs took the occasional Drinamyl tablet, known as 'purple heart', to keep them working all night. I would be horrified today if a Leith's kitchen boss offered them around as casually as I did. But I was never offered cocaine and I knew no one who became addicted. And eventually we stopped smoking joints too. Age does, maybe, bring some sense.

Not all my tenants were as amiable as the Hollies. Once I let the house to an Australian doctor who turned out to be an abortionist – this before abortion was legalised. He drove a Ferrari and failed to pay his rent. At first I believed his 'It's in the post' line but having discovered his secret trade from one of the young women who visited him, I decided he had to go.

He owed me six months' rent and I realised that a court order, and the subsequent appeals, could take months more. And I really needed the money. As usual Rayne came to the rescue, this time with the help of an amusing Maltese friend, Micallef, a bit of a villain. Rayne had met him when buying a dodgy strip club from him to complete an office block in Soho Square.

Micallef turned up in a van with three heavies. They picked the lock of number 25 in no time and had the tenant's gear out on the pavement within minutes. Rayne and I were in the sitting room, directing operations, when the Aussie tenant pounded up the stairs. He stuck his head out of the window and yelled, 'Call the police,' at the top of his voice. Micallef grabbed him by his hair and yanked him back inside, but not before someone heard him and did call the police.

The force of the law turned out to be a mild-mannered copper who was more impressed by Rayne's respectability than by the Australian's rightful claim of illegal eviction. Possession (mine) proved to be nine-tenths of the law. The policeman told my now ex-tenant to be on his way and go to the civil courts if he wanted redress. Micallef offered to take his possessions in his van anywhere he wanted for an advance payment, but, unsurprisingly, the doctor called a taxi for his stuff and followed in his Ferrari. I never heard from him again.

I was luckier than most secret lovers in that Rayne and I had a genuine reason to be together – he was the finance director and chairman of my company. We almost never risked it, but we could have explained away a lunchtime date if we'd had to. Theatres and exhibitions were absolutely out of bounds, and only once did we go to the movies together, to a little flea-pit, and we had to leave before the end so Rayne would get home before Nan. We could walk in the parks, providing we kept to little trodden paths and kept a wary eye out for acquaintances, and sometimes we would openly play tennis together at the Campden Hill Club, where he was a member and I would be there as a family friend.

Occasionally we did take risks, going together to supper with Pat Kavanagh, my only confidante apart from Jane, in her flat in Camden Town and later in Bayswater. And when Jane, now living with a new boyfriend in Paris, came to London, we once went to a nightclub and another time to the revolving restaurant at the top of the Telecom Tower – which at the time was new and the talk of the town. The excitement went to my head and, for the first and last time, I got so drunk that I was sick and threw up in the gutter.

Best of all were our rare holidays together, which took a lot of contriving. I would pretend to be staying with friends but would set off to some remote holiday spot or little-known town. Rayne, having told Nan he was away researching a book or on property business, would arrive a few days later and we'd have a brief week, or less, of unbelievable happiness with next to no chance of being discovered.

It wasn't all champagne and sunshine, of course. A vengeful God would sometimes punish us. I got lobster poisoning in La Palma. I thought my puffy face was due to too much sun, so I lay in the shade and ate more lobster. On arrival back at Gatwick my eyes were tiny dots in a moon face.

The doctor said, 'That's the clearest example of shellfish poisoning I've ever seen.'

In Germany I had gastro-enteritis and couldn't swallow my birthday dinner at Bonn's best restaurant, which upset Rayne since it cost a fortune and was supposed to be a treat. We ended up quarrelling in the street.

The necessity for discretion often meant I spent time alone in foreign places, staying on so that we wouldn't provoke suspicion by arriving back in London at the same time. Usually I would just stay in our hotel room and write (from 1970 on I was producing cookbooks) or work on some catering project or other. But one morning, after Rayne had left me in Sardinia, I went out on a boat on my own and managed to stall the engine miles out in the bay. Not wanting to drift, I threw the anchor overboard – only to discover it wasn't attached to the boat. I watched it sink to the sandy bottom. I thought it was shallow enough for me to dive for so I leapt in after it. But it was too deep and I couldn't retrieve it. Then, exhausted, I couldn't climb back into the boat.

Mercifully, I somehow stayed calm. I hung on to the shaft of the outboard motor, took deep breaths and rested until I had regained enough strength to haul myself back into the boat.

But my troubles were not over. I still wasn't able to start the engine, and after an hour or so the gentle breeze turned into a brisk wind and I was being blown out to sea. Occasionally other boats would pass in the distance, but their occupants would merely wave merrily in response to my frantic hand signals.

I told myself that sooner or later the boatyard would send out a search party, but since I had hired the boat for the day I knew that might not be until evening. Scared of sunburn, I sat under my towel feeling sick, whether from fear or from the increased rocking of the boat I knew not. My helplessness was the most distressing thing: the boat was blowing along steadily now, heading for nowhere.

At last a speedboat came close enough to recognise my desperation. The relief was overwhelming, but short-lived. My hero was a Sardinian with little English, but enough to bellow at me that I was a complete idiot; that I could have been blown all the way to Corsica; that a storm could blow up in minutes in these waters; that I had no business hiring a boat if I could not start an engine; that I should not be alone anyway; that I gave tourists a bad name and he should leave me to my fate. He was right of course, but his rage when I expected sympathy was too much for me and I burst into tears. He stopped shouting and towed me home in silence.

That week in Sardinia, staying in the Cala de Volpe (a fake village of real charm and great luxury) is chiefly memorable, not for my marine adventure, but for our drives into the hills for lunch or supper at tiny remote village inns. The simple pleasure of holding your lover's hand, of feeling his arm round your back, of a quick kiss, with absolutely no chance of being recognised is extraordinarily potent.

Declan, the butler who had caught me killing dead lobsters, became a helpful business ally. He got me a job delivering lunches to Grieveson Grant, stockbrokers in the City, for whom he worked three days a week. This meant I could afford to leave McKenna (where I had to arrive in time to serve the morning coffee and stay until I'd served the afternoon tea). Now I could just deliver to the City and scarper, which meant I could cook for several clients at once and do one round of deliveries in the morning and another in the late afternoon.

It's true that word of mouth is the most effective marketing tool for a caterer, but in those early days the good opinion of other freelance cooks, waitresses and butlers was more important than the approval of posh hostesses. Declan, whom I recommended as often as he recommended me, introduced me to the butler mafia. Word spread that I was reliable and would go anywhere. And that I would work weekends, which a lot of the middle-class Cordon Bleu graduates with mummy and daddy in the country and hunt balls to go to, would not do. I was more likely to be cooking at the hunt ball than dancing at it. Most importantly, in Declan's eyes, I didn't pocket the tips meant for the serving staff.

And then Mrs Henderson, a freelance waitress, introduced me to more clients. She became my head waitress and worked, first for me and then for my company, for twenty odd years. She was a motherly soul who, nonetheless, was a stickler for how things ought to be done. She'd started out in Lyon's Corner House as a teenager and one of her jobs was to save the end-slices of tomatoes and make tomato paste out of them. She also taught me how to wash a lettuce, and I still think of her every time I do it. It only works with big open lettuces like oakleaf or escarole but it's brilliant. You fill the sink with cold water, grip the lettuce by its root end and sink it head first in the water. You gently plunge it up and down in the water and twirl it gently clockwise and anti-clockwise, then put it on the drip rack to dry. Running the cold tap brutally through the leaves bruises them, Mrs Henderson told me, and washing it leaf by leaf takes too long.

Most of the time my customers were delightful and delighted. If things went wrong, which happily was not often, it was usually my fault.

Once, at Grieveson Grant, Declan was coping with an unusually large sit-down lunch and I had stayed to help him dish up the first course, a seafood salad. I went round the table with the (unwashed) watercress garnish. I broke off the stems of each bunch of cress and planted the leaves into the side of the heaped-up seafood. By the time I got round all sixteen places and back to the first plates, there were shoals of little fresh-water creatures, like tiny prawns, frantically swimming through the French dressing.

Even worse was when I was doing an eighteenth birthday party for the twin children of Kate and Ronald Searle, the cartoonist. Delicate icing not being my forte, I'd ordered a cake from a confectioner and assured Kate that it would be delicious. But when we opened the box the confectioner had taken no notice of my instructions for simple fondant roses on the top, and instead had festooned the cake with plastic bits and bobs, silver trinkets, ribbons and every bit of tat you could think of. Kate was horrified. I shoo'd her out of the kitchen with 'Don't worry. Really. I will fix it long before we need to do the cake-cutting.'

What to do? If I pulled off all the tat, I would need to re-ice the whole thing and there was no time for that. And then I saw the neighbours' rose-garden out of the kitchen window. I was over that fence in a flash, kitchen scissors in hand.

Ten minutes later Kate came in to find the most perfect yellow roses and a few trailing ivy leaves, hiding the damage. They looked lovely and she was as delighted as she was relieved.

But when we came to cut the cake, it was alive with hundreds of little black creepy crawlies who had forsaken the nectar of roses to overdose on the icing. Not good.

Both that and the watercress disaster came from not washing things, but I've also got into trouble *because* I wash things. I was delighted when the partners of a firm of shipping brokers said it was high time I sat down to enjoy my own cooking, and would I join them for lunch?

All went well until the senior partner looked intently at the salad in front of him, then reached into it with his fingers. Ah, I thought smugly, he's never seen a designer salad before, he's curious about the radicchio, arugula, lambs' lettuce, pea tendrils . . . And then he had a piece of string between his fingers and was gently pulling it out of the salad. The string turned into a length of chain, and then – out popped a bath plug.

Fast as anything, I said, 'Well, at least it proves I washed the salad.'

I had an Abyssian cat, Benedicat, known as Benny, who liked to roam the nooks and crannies of Paddington. He was forever getting stuck on scaffolding or locked in someone's garage. Once he climbed into a caravan and ended up in Cornwall.

Today it seems incredible that I let Benny sit on my kitchen window-sill and watch me cook, but I did. He never so much as put a paw out, and if he wanted to get down he would jump cleanly over the worktop.

One day a voice on the telephone said, 'Do you have an animal called Benedicat?'

'Oh Lord,' I said, 'yes, I do. He's always going walkabout. Is he stuck on your roof?'

'No,' came the reply, 'but his collar tag is stuck in my trifle.'

I must have had plenty of triumphs or the business would never have grown, but it is the horrors that I remember.

One of the worst was when I went to cook over a weekend at Lord Verulam's mighty house in Hertfordshire. It was a ball for, I think, his son's twenty-first. He had hired caterers to do the main event – the marquee, the bars, the enormous buffet breakfast – but I was to do the dinner party for the twenty odd guests actually staying in the house. The menu was poached salmon followed by roast beef fillet and strawberries. Not difficult.

But when I arrived I found the six-oven Aga barely warm. I'd been sabotaged by the Verulams' own chef, an old boy who deeply resented not being trusted to produce the goods. He'd been given the weekend off, but before he left he did his best to ensure my downfall by not refuelling the Aga. It was already five p.m. and an anthracite-burning Aga takes many hours to get up to temperature. And anyway he'd locked the coal store.

Thankfully, the tap water was near boiling and I made the court bouillon for poaching the two ten-pound salmons, and then set them on the Aga top. More in hope than belief, I put the beef in to roast, fearing the oven was so cool that the juices of the beef would run out, making it dry and tasteless.

Salvation suddenly seemed possible when the maid told me that there was a modern electric kitchen which the family used in the summer when the Aga was turned off. But hope died when we found the chef had locked that too.

Desperate, I searched the warren of kitchens and stores, and found a butler's pantry with an electric tea-urn which I commandeered for boiling the potatoes.

And then there was nothing I could do but wait and fret. I remember crouching between the fridge and the freezer, curled up, foetus style, racked with anxiety.

But once again Declan, whom I'd employed as head butler, saved me. He was brilliant: first of all he did not announce dinner. Drinks overran by half an hour until Lady Verulam questioned the delay. 'Oh, no delay, my lady. I was waiting for a nod from you. So sorry. I will do it at once.'

When the guests were seated, he had his waiters spin out every action to funeral tempo. Very slowly they placed napkins ceremoniously on each guest's lap. Very slowly they removed the decorative service plates. Very slowly they filled the water glasses. Very slowly they put fish plates in front of everyone. By the time they had milked every possible delaying tactic, I was ready.

That was the best salmon I have ever produced! It was barely cooked in the middle, as perfectly moist as only a slow-cooked fish that has just come out of the court bouillon can be.

But I still had the raw fillet to deal with. I ended up slicing it into steaks and cooking them directly on the iron top of the aga, without a frying pan or griddle. I'd just got them to a dull grey, still very rare inside, when Declan came in to chivvy me and I had to fling them onto the serving dishes. Fortunately I had made the mushroom sauce at home and managed to get it hot by suspending the saucepan in the tea urn with the potatoes. I poured it all over the steaks, tossed a handful of chopped herbs on top and sent it up. I flung the frozen peas in with the just-cooked potatoes to heat through. They were delicious with a heap of mint and plenty of butter.

Lady Verulam never knew what a snake her chef could be. I was tempted to tell her and make the old bastard's life a misery, but then I thought, Hell, what would I feel if *my* boss didn't consider my cooking good enough for the most important family dinner ever?

CHAPTER 6

OUT OF THE FRYING PAN

The birth of a business

In 1966, I hired my first full-time assistant and learnt Employer's Lesson Number One: Insist on Flexible Hours, the hard way. I went out cheffing most nights to earn the money to pay Jean on Fridays. During the day we seldom had enough work to keep us busy, so we played a lot of tennis. Once we'd built up enough business to occupy her full time, she left.

The next girl, Amelia, was on flexi-hours, but she was hopeless. I had not yet learned Employer's Lesson Number Two: Check References. Amelia was a pretty, charming friend of a friend, a few years younger than me, but stupid and lazy. She would tip a bag of fresh oranges onto the remaining layer of mouldy oranges at the bottom of a box; she would leave gallons of warm soup out in a hot kitchen all night and be astonished when it fermented; she would bring the van (by then we had a tiny mini-van, proudly painted with Leith's on the side) back with no petrol in it.

What finally did for Amelia, though, was her

cavalier attitude to hygiene. One evening, coming in late after a job, I found the kitchen grubby and smelling nasty. Bad-temperedly I set about washing the floor and wiping down the work surfaces. Behind the Kenwood mixer I found a filthy cloth with which she had wiped up smoked salmon and other debris and, too lazy to use the bin and wash out the cloth, she'd simply pushed it, fish and all, into a corner. Seething, I cleaned up. Upstairs I found Amelia's chef's clothes flung in a corner and all the drawers and cupboards open. I picked up her things, intending to stuff them into the drawer I'd allocated to her, but the drawer stuck. And then I lost it. I yanked the drawer right out and slammed it as hard as I could down on the next drawer. The chest was a cheap affair and all the drawers, the one I was using as a weapon and all those underneath, fell to pieces. It was hugely satisfying.

That was the first time I'd lost my temper at work and at least I was alone. The drawer-battering incident was on a Friday and I had the weekend to get up my courage to sack Amelia. On the Saturday night I went out with a friend. He said the secret of sacking someone is to use the magic words 'I have to let you go', which allows the victim some dignity in feeling that you are doing them, or at least pretending to do them, a favour.

On Monday morning, I buzzed down to the kitchen from the living room which doubled as my office, asking Amelia to pop up to see me. As

I heard her shoes clunking up the stairs I rehearsed to myself. 'Amelia, I'm afraid I must let you go . . . must let you go . . . must let you go . . .'

She stepped into the room. I jumped up and said, 'Amelia, you're sacked,' and she said, 'I know I know, I'm completely useless.' And we both hugged each other and blubbed.

Within two years, I had four people working for me, all young women. We all shopped, cleaned and drove the van as well as cooked. I did all the organising, pricing, billing and event management, making it up as I went.

Rayne had been astonished to discover that I added up on my fingers and didn't know my times tables. He bought me a little calculator (this was before the age of electronics) on which you used a thin stylus to push numbers up and down the columns. He taught me the simplest of basic bookkeeping: money in on the left, money out on the right. For several years all my accounts were kept in blue cash-books with a carbon copy.

A lot of my work still involved small dinner parties, which were not wonderfully profitable, but every now and then I'd be asked to cook a really grand dinner for really grand people, usually by Lady Elizabeth Anson of Party Planners. If the jobs were for business grandees or movie stars I would generally be very well paid. If they were Royals, the money would be lousy, but of course I would accept, both because I'd be flattered and pleased to be asked and because I figured it would be good for my reputation.

There is something about the Royals that ensures drama and disaster. I don't understand why even I, a republican from South Africa, should get into such a tizzy at the prospect of cooking for any of them. But I don't think I have ever done a 'royal do' without drama. One such was for Princess Alexandra and her husband. Thirty years later I was to translate my adventures that evening into fiction, in my second novel, *Sisters*.

The Princess was entertaining the Shah of Persia at her home, Thatched House Lodge, in the middle of Richmond Park, for a late supper after the Opera, and I had time to kill. The pheasants had just gone into the oven, the breadcrumbs, bread sauce, bacon, gravy were made, starter and pud ready and waiting. But I thought the cheese looked colourless and could do with some black grapes. I jumped into my van and went off to get some.

When I got back, the great iron gates to the park were closed. I was locked out. No problem, I thought, plenty of time, and set off round the park perimeter. Ham Gate was closed too. Keep calm, I told myself, Kingston Gate has a lodge. Presumably with a lodge keeper, who'll let me in.

Huge relief, the lights were on and my ringing the bell brought a speedy response – from a small offended woman.

'All right, all right,' she said, eyeing me with hostility and suspicion.

'Please, I've got to get into the park. It's urgent. Can you let me in?'

'No, I'm just babysitting. I don't live here.' She nodded with satisfaction.

'But this is the lodge-keeper's house. Surely there are keys to the gates.'

'Well, if there are, I don't know anything about them. And if I did,' she said, smug and smiling, 'I couldn't just let you in, could I?'

I ran back to the car and slewed back on to the road. I drove fast, swallowing panic. Dinner was now due to start in ten minutes. Would anyone think to take my pheasants out of the oven? The resident housekeeper had not been friendly.

At Robin Hood Gate there was the sound of television from the front room. I banged the brass knocker. Nothing. I did it again, more loudly, trying to penetrate the canned TV laughter. Nothing. I stepped into the flowerbed and banged on the sitting room window.

Thank God, I thought, as the TV died. The curtain flipped open and a man, bearded and angry, mouthed silently at me through the glass. The curtain dropped back and the next minute the front door opened and he was shouting, 'Them's my petunias you're standing on. What the hell do you think . . .'

'I'm so sorry, but there was no answer . . .'

'Too bloody right there's no answer. I'm off duty.'

He made to close the door. I stuck my foot into it. He banged the door on it.

'Ow, that hurt,' I yelped, hopping up and down and trying to keep my leg in the door. 'Look, I'm really sorry about the petunias, but you've got to help me. I have to get into the park. I'm cooking Princess Alexandra's dinner, and she's got the Shah of Persia with her.'

'Princess Alexandra! The Shah of Persia!' His mouth curled. 'Fucking toffs.' He opened the door wider and for a second I thought he was going to come out and clock me one, until I realised he was opening it wide the better to slam it shut. I jumped back as he did so.

I'd been close to tears when I'd arrived at his door. Now I was just furious. My foot hurt, and I'd had enough of uncooperative lodge keepers. I hammered again on the door, shouting through the letterbox.

'If you've got a problem with royalty why the hell are you a gatekeeper in a royal park? And why take it out on me? I'm only the cook, comrade. And I'll lose my job if you are too bloody-minded to help. How about some solidarity for the bleeding worker, hey?'

No reply. I turned away, muttering, 'What is it with you anyway? Or are you always such a bastard?'

I heard the door open, and thought, Oh God, he's going to clobber me. I started to run down the path.

He called after me, 'I don't have a key, lady. The police have them. Ring the cops.'

I swung round, 'Oh thank you. Could I use your telephone?'

The sneer returned, 'Don't push your luck, lady. There's a box over there.'

The phone box was yellow, and announced itself as an emergency telephone connected to the park police. Thank God, I thought, as I picked up the handset. Dead. Nothing. No dial tone. No friendly park copper.

Fighting the tears that were threatening to return, I drove on, found a BT box and dialled 999. But the police, reasonably, did not regard my situation as an emergency and told me to ring the local station.

I rang Directory Enquiries. They gave me the number. I had no pen and had to memorise it. I dialled.

'Richmond Police.'

Relief flooded through me. But then, beep-beep-beep. It wasn't a free call. And I had no money with me. I dashed back to the van. Got some money. Dialled again. As soon as the female voice answered I launched into my tale of woe.

She listened in silence, then said, 'Well I'm terribly sorry my dear, but I don't know how I can help you. I'm a housewife in Slough.'

She did help though. She looked up the Richmond police number and this time I memorised it successfully and got through.

'Calm down, Miss. We'll send someone round to Richmond Gate with the keys. Meet you there, right?'

I hurtled round the perimeter road – I'd now driven right round the park and I was back where I'd started. And then I waited. And waited.

It was agony. The dinner should be on the table by now. Finally I could stand it no longer and I knocked on the door of a big double-fronted house, its garden overlooking the park.

The woman who answered was wearing a silk shirt tucked into well-tailored trousers, pearls at the neck, and buck teeth. She did not open the door very far.

'Could I possibly use your telephone?'

At that moment I heard a car behind me and turned to look.

'Why?' she said, suspicious and peremptory. 'Who are you looking for?'

'The police,' I said and immediately regretted it. I would have to explain the whole saga all over again.

I did, but my troubles were not over. I wanted her to let me use the phone while she stood by the door in case the police came. But she wasn't going to let a tear-streaked young woman with blood down her apron (pheasant blood, but she was not to know that), so she came with me.

The officer was apologetic. The panda car was on its way; should be with me any minute.

I ran back to the front door. It was now almost dark and as we emerged into the street I saw the tail lights of a convoy of cars, the middle one containing the Princess and the Shah, disappearing into the park, beyond the once-more locked gates.

'Oh God, no,' I cried, all control finally deserting me as I ran to the gates and shook them. I felt tiny, like Alice in Wonderland, and utterly despairing.

And then the police arrived and let me in.

The housekeeper had rescued the pheasants. They were in the warming oven, succulent, pink and perfect. And the guests were still having drinks, so I had time to do the veg.

And the Princess came into the kitchen to tell us how delicious it all was.

If Royals paid badly, at least they did pay, and raised my reputation. But sometimes (not often I hasten to say) I would make a hash of a job and damage my bank balance and standing at the same time.

I was asked by Mr and Mrs Ryder (he was the boss of Reed Publishing) to cook a dinner. She would buy the ingredients.

The pudding ingredients turned out to be a pineapple, eggs, cream and gelatine. The instructions were to make a cold pineapple soufflé. I didn't have a pineapple soufflé recipe but I knew how to make a lemon one, so I juiced half the pineapple and substituted that for lemon juice. I put a jam jar in the centre of a big soufflé dish and poured the mixture round it. When it was firmly set, I intended to fill the jam jar with hot water to loosen it, lift it out and fill the resulting hole with chunks of fresh pineapple mixed with chopped mint. It would look pretty and unusual and use up the rest of the pineapple.

What I did not know was that pineapple contains an enzyme which prevents gelatine doing its setting job. When the main course was in the dining room, I set about the last-minute decorating. The mousse looked wobbly, but set, I thought. But when I removed the jam jar the whole thing collapsed into a gloopy soup. I served it in soup plates with apologies. And had to tear up my bill.

Mrs Ryder, gratified by my not charging her, offered me a second chance the following week. Disaster! Waiting in the kitchen was, I could not believe it, another pineapple! It hadn't occurred to me that she'd want to risk the same dessert, and I hadn't yet discovered the cause of last time's failure. So I made exactly the same mistake. Again I could not charge her. Reasonably enough, she gave up on me.

Another venture was cooking for pubs and retail food shops. Wholesaling food means you have to share the profit with the retailer, and I never managed to do much more than cover my costs, but I learnt a lot. My first attempt was to make pork terrines for Balls Brothers pubs in the city. I would deliver the terrine whole and they would sell it by the slice with toast and chutney. The terrine was a classic French recipe, cooked in a loaf tin lined with streaky bacon and filled with a mixture of minced pork and pork liver, garlic, spice and herbs.

We made six terrines twice a week and the worst part of it was the mixing. My butcher up the road minced the pork and liver for us, and we would tip them into the biggest container we had, a huge fish kettle. The mix was too thick to stir with a wooden spoon, and we didn't have a machine strong enough for the job, so there was nothing for it but to stick your hands into the freezing gloop and stir away for a good thirty minutes. We all hated doing it.

At one point I hired an undersized twelve-year-old lad, the son of my hairdresser who was anxious for him to get an after-school job. It might, she said, keep him from nicking stuff from Woolworth's and smoking on street corners with his mates. We paid him three shillings an hour and he was a terrific worker. Today I'd be had up under child labour laws, I think. Poor little guy, too small to reach into the kettle on the work surface, he would kneel on the floor in a sleeveless tee-shirt, up to his armpits in freezing liquid liver. He must have been happy enough though. He worked for me until his family moved away, and when he left he gave me a heavy glass ashtray which I still have. I suspect he'd lifted it from an antique stall, but he was so proud of it I hadn't the heart to question him.

I only had one oven, a double Belling, so I baked the terrines at night when it was free. They had to cook slowly and they needed to be rotated from shelf to shelf every two hours. This meant I had to wake up, stumble down to the kitchen, move the hot terrines about and go back to sleep quick before doing it all again.

It's extraordinary what you get used to: when, later, in 1969, I added a restaurant to my activities, I would get my sleep in varying chunks: on Mondays, Wednesdays and Fridays I'd be up at four a.m. to go to the markets, sometimes ending with a breakfast fry-up in the old Billingsgate fish market, before getting back to work in the catering business all morning. I'd deliver to the City at noon, sleep in the afternoon, work in the restaurant in the evening, and go to bed after midnight. On the other days there would be no four a.m. rise, but on Tuesdays and Thursdays, I'd have to tend those wretched terrines. I grew to hate the smell of their cooking permeating the whole house. I don't think I've eaten a pork terrine since.

Whether my allotted sleep-time was two hours, four hours or eight hours, somehow my sleeping brain would wake me exactly five minutes before the alarm went off. I'm sure being a good sleeper is an essential ingredient for success, just as enthusiasm and energy are. And those things are nothing to do with talent, just luck, of which I've always had more than my rightful share.

By 1968 I had a serious management problem. Rayne was brilliant on the finances but he knew nothing about food. We needed new premises for the catering company and, since I couldn't be in two places at the same time, I needed a partner or a managing director.

Annie Langford was the closest thing I had to either and I'd wanted us to work together ever since we'd met in the early Sixties. At the time I was still in my bedsit and up for anything that would earn me some money, so I'd agreed to teach a Tuesday evening 'dinner party' cooking course in Kentish Town. I quickly realised Annie knew a lot more about food and wine than I did, and was a better cook than I. I was much impressed that she knew that claret was the same stuff as Bordeaux and the bottles had high shoulders while Burgundy bottles had sloping ones.

But Annie cooked for Jim Slater, of Slater Walker, then the most famous name in the City and hugely rich. Despite his wealth, all he ever seemed to eat was melon, roast lamb, peas and fruit salad, so it was a boring job for a keen cook. Every time I managed to persuade Annie to chuck it in and work with me, he would increase her salary and she'd stay.

In the end I persuaded her. We agreed on a partnership to be called Langford Leith, which would run the outside catering business, and it was a huge relief to hand the whole shebang over to her.

We had to find new premises, and Rayne came up with an old dairy depot in Sebastian Street near the Barbican, just north of the City. It was perfect. We inherited a huge loading bay, big enough to park our vans, with a raised platform which meant we could stack trays and crates directly into the vans. The enormous walk-in milk fridges became our kitchens and storerooms. And it was a stone's throw from our City customers.

For a while Annie's boss-ship of Langford Leith worked well. The business expanded, we had a dozen or so people working in Sebastian Street and the quality of our food steadily improved.

Then sadly, Annie became ill. One day she rang me to say that she just could not cope. I went and sat with her in the office, trying to list the things that needed to be done and get them into some sort of order. Annie, highly agitated, alternately tearful and excited, kept jumping up and dashing off to do urgent things, which were not in fact urgent at all. It was the start of a breakdown and the first serious indication of chronic depression.

Poor Annie. She ended up in a clinic in Australia, from where, oblivious of the time change, she would ring me in the middle of the night to berate me for ruining her life. And it is possible, I guess, that had she stayed as a private cook, working for one person or small company, and avoiding the stress-soaked event-catering business, she might not have cracked. Eventually she recovered, came back to England, and forty-plus years later is still a dear friend, but one I feel faintly guilty about. She was to have been my partner, and I have had the most successful and happy life, while she has had an unfairly tough one, plagued by depression, money worries and family tragedy, none of which she complains about.

Langford-Leith reverted to its previous name of Leith's Good Food. My beloved elder brother David, who had joined the RAF and risen to the rank of squadron leader, left the air force to become the catering division's managing director. After sending him on a brief course at the Cordon Bleu school to learn something about food and cooking, we installed him in a new office we had built to cope with the expanding business.

Our reputation grew. Caroline Burrows (later Caroline Waldegrave) became our head chef, rising rapidly from a junior cook just out of the Cordon Bleu to run the kitchen with enormous efficiency. Her success was as much a surprise to her as it was to me. When I rang the Cordon Bleu school for a reference for her, the reaction was: 'Caroline Burrows? Surely not? She is the naughtiest girl in the class.' I think it was this schoolmarmish response that made me think Caroline must have a bit of initiative.

She certainly did, but she was hardly the knowledgeable foodie, in love with cooking, that she became. She had gone to cookery school because she'd had glandular fever and the doctor decreed that studying for a degree would be too much for her and she should do something less taxing – like cooking. He obviously knew nothing about the catering trade! She obeyed reluctantly, angry at not going to university and generally prepared to bunk off at any opportunity.

Caroline started as a junior cook but rose rapidly to boss-ship. She developed a management style which made her both popular and successful. She disliked confrontation and seldom raised her voice, though her language was – for those days – singularly X-rated.

Probably due to her classy connections, a lot of our cooks and drivers, washers-up and barmen were ex-public school. It was the end of the hippy era and both boys and girls had long hair; some wore bangles and beads. One sported long hair and make-up on one side of his head and very short hair and stubble on the other. I spent a lot of time explaining that they had to look as the customer expected them to, not as they preferred. Think what your mum and dad would like to see, and aim for that, I'd say, but often to no avail.

Not all our staff came out of the top drawer. The catering trade is generally a melting pot of the posh and the working class, and a perfect illustration of how class does not matter. All that matters in a busy kitchen is that you pull your weight.

My wanting to be a cook had stemmed partly from a horror of working in an office, yet I found as much satisfaction from a profit and loss account with the right number at the bottom as in cooking a perfect dish. And I enjoyed running a company and I grew to love almost every aspect of business.

But my brother David, in agreeing to take on Leith's Good Food, drew a short straw I think. He had to cope with the worst thing that has happened in my long career, one that no one will ever forget.

Literary agents Peters, Fraser and Dunlop had booked us to cater for their fiftieth anniversary party in the middle of Vincent Square in Westminster. All went well except that it poured with rain all day and all night. But our marquee-tent suppliers had done us proud with a big service tent and covered passages, as well as the grand tented ballroom. The party was a great success in spite of the downpour.

When the staff were clearing up, two of our student casual workers, young men of perhaps twenty, were walking through a covered passage. One of them, Sebastian, half running and swaying as exuberant young people do, reached up and grasped a guy rope as he swung past it. He was electrocuted. The chandeliers had not been earthed and the water running down the guy ropes was a lethal conductor.

He was taken to Westminster Hospital in a coma, and not expected to live. All anyone knew of his family was that they were in Spain. David contacted the Foreign Office for help in tracing them and within two hours, the British Consul had found them and arranged a flight. They got back in time to be at their son's bedside when he died. His co-worker, who'd been holding on to him, received burns down his side.

David had to deal with the police, the contractors, and our shocked staff, and meet Sebastian's parents. They were extraordinary: they regarded their son's death as a tragic accident, not a criminal failure on anyone's part, and their courage and dignity in grief were heartbreaking.

It was a tragedy for all involved. The electrician who had failed to earth the cables was a highly qualified master electrician, had worked for the marquee contractors for years and was a few weeks off retirement. He knew how lethal electricity could be and had trained hundreds of young electricians. He could not believe what he had done but had to accept the truth that his moment of inattention had caused the death of a young man.

Later that year, David had to cope with the classic caterer's nightmare, food poisoning. One day I was in the Mosel in Germany, buying wine for the restaurant, when he rang me.

'The Council has closed us down. Everyone at Grieveson Grant has food poisoning. They're doing tests to establish the cause.'

Every caterer worries about food poisoning and we took a lot of trouble to avoid it. We kept very clean kitchens, trained all our staff in how bugs multiply and spread, ensured our fridges and refrigerated vans were at the correct temperature, rotated our food stocks.

But here we were, poisoning our customers. The cause of the outbreak was soon established: coronation chicken. *Our* coronation chicken.

What had happened was this: we were due to deliver lunch for twenty-five people and the cold chicken, poached the day before was mixed with the curried mayonnaise sauce. It was in the fridge.

Next morning there was a message asking us to cater for five more people, so the cooks hurriedly poached another chicken and added it, still warm, to the cold chicken mix, dished it up and delivered it.

And then, since Grieveson Grant had little refrigeration and the customers were about to have lunch, the food was left in a nice warm room with the sun streaming through the windows. And lunch was very late.

A classic recipe for salmonella poisoning. Although the poaching of the chicken would have killed any bacteria on it, there must have been small colonies of salmonella somewhere else, maybe on the container the chicken was mixed in, the wooden spoon it was mixed with, the jug used for the mayonnaise, the egg yolks used in the sauce. None of this would have mattered if everything had been kept well chilled, because bugs only breed to dangerous levels in the warm. But adding that warm chicken to the mix, which would have raised the temperature of both chicken and sauce, and then letting it sit unrefrigerated for hours before serving it, meant we poisoned everyone who

142

ate it. Two people, one an elderly high court judge, ended up in hospital.

David did everything right. He immediately called in the Council food inspectors – the first time, they said, that a possible culprit had initiated an inquiry. He went to see the bosses at Grieveson Grant who, instead of sacking us forthwith, accepted the inspector's verdict that both we and they were to blame and promptly installed more refrigeration.

Stress, interrupted sleep and long hours are the lot of almost all caterers, yet most of us love the job. Weddings are the bread and butter of the event-catering world, and are generally a formula for maximum stress. There are no rehearsals, no second chances. And there is the mother of the bride, a stress machine all on her own.

I remember once, when I had failed to give the wedding cake icing time to harden, the top two tiers were in danger of sinking lopsidedly into the ones below, like the leaning tower of Pisa, only a lot less stable. We had to stand the pillars on plates, which distributed the weight more evenly, and disguise the plates with hastily piped fresh icing and ribbons. This worked fine until it came to the cutting of the cake, when the bride and groom found they could not get the knife through the obstruction of the plate.

One summer we had a wedding job in Surrey on the same day as one of our clients was entertaining the Queen Mother in Kensington, and Elton John was having a party in north London. Needless to say all our staff wanted to gawp either at the Queen Mother, or at the mother of all Queens, so I got the short straw and went to supervise the wedding.

There were no tablecloths for the buffet. They'd been sent to Elton John's house. Since he was having a cave-man party with our waiters in loin-cloths and our waitresses in leopard-print bikinis, he really didn't need tablecloths, but they were too far away to fetch. One of my staff had a horrid time driving round Esher trying to borrow linen from hotels and pubs, or buy anything white – tablecloths, curtains, sheets. No luck.

The bride's mother appeared in pink silk from head to toe. She looked in dismay at the flowers and candelabra, napkins and plates, sitting about in boxes on the floor. I comforted her.

'Madam, please don't worry. Really. We never, *ever* do the buffet until the wedding party has left for church. We need to keep all the food in the refrigerated vans you see. Health and safety. And anyway, we hate to spoil the surprise by letting you see it half-finished.'

She bought this tosh I'm glad to say, and went off to see her daughter married. Meanwhile, I was up to her linen cupboard in a flash, whipping out her sheets and tablecloths. I think if she'd not had enough I'd have stripped the beds.

We were ready and smiling when the wedding

guests arrived. Our client, perhaps in relief at seeing the buffet, or having got her daughter safely married, got stuck into the champagne.

'You were quite right,' she said, 'I should never have worried. It all looks beautiful. And how *clever* of you to have our monogram on the tablecloths. No wonder you wanted to keep it a surprise.'

I thought discretion might be kinder than the truth. At least on her daughter's wedding day. I rang her next morning though, and she was good enough to laugh and forgive us.

Event catering has always been, for me, the most exciting side of the trade. My brother Jamie once said of me that I would rather do a dinner for four hundred well than a dinner for four exquisitely, and he's right. I love the logistics – it suits my organising nature.

I love big events that come together like magic – when hundreds of people, all doing their little bit, produce something remarkable. Once we had to cater for a conference lunch in Yorkshire for four thousand delegates – *in a tent* – and get it over and done within twenty minutes. The challenge was irresistible. I couldn't bear the thought of bought-in aeroplane trays of plastic food, so we devised a plan. It was not gastronomy, but it was delicious, and fun. The delegates were seated for the plenary sessions at long trestle tables, facing the stage, and we had to feed them in the same tent.

We got the organiser to ask them to clear their

tables, putting their papers and briefcases underneath them, then go out of the doors at the back, collect their food and come back. In the outer tent were twenty service points, all dispensing identical plates of food with everything on it. No choice. I don't like the idea of salmon, pork pie, rare roast beef and several salads all on the same plate but I figured that at buffet parties people mostly pile their plates with everything on offer, so we just did it for them. While their colleagues were handing out the plates, teams of waiters were preparing the tables back in the main tent. Serving staff dashed down the rows of tables, rolling out different coloured wallpaper rolls as a runner down the middle. Then waiters hurried down, dumping baskets of knives and forks and trays of ten glasses (each one containing a folded coloured paper napkin) at intervals along the tables. Finally we ran down liberally sprinkling all the tables with fresh flower petals of every possible hue. It wasn't a sophisticated or expensive transformation, but it was colourful and bright and it worked.

And for pudding the waiters served ice cream cornets from cinema-style usherette trays slung round their necks.

The whole thing worked like clockwork and I was as proud of that event as almost anything, I think.

It goes without saying that I care about the quality of food – indeed, poor food makes me cross, especially if I am responsible for it. It seems to me that to waste the opportunity to eat well or

146

cook nice food is a crime, but I'm not obsessed by gastronomy. I seldom want to spend all day clearing consommé to crystal brightness or painting perfect pictures on the plate with fancy ingredients, or drive half way across the county to get the best ostrich fillets or morning-picked microleaves. Very occasionally I want to show off and will do a grand dinner party, but my idea of heaven is to be at the end of a huge table of family and friends, ladling out slow-cooked, wholesome, great-tasting cassoulet.

CHAPTER 7

INTO THE FIRE

The economics of watercress soup

My television debut was hilarious. In the late Sixties, a friend, Fiona, worked as a presenter for the BBC's pilots for colour television. In those days official programming only started in the afternoon. These unadvertised pilots were broadcast in the mornings so that the boffins could check that everything was functioning properly.

Fiona asked me if I would do a bit of cooking for one of the programmes. As I would only have a few minutes I decided on a sort of instant risotto. There was almost no budget for these programmes and my 'cooking rings' were four black rounds painted on a white tabletop. So when I put the butter into the frying pan to melt nothing happened. 'Just pretend,' the producer had said to me.

'When the butter is sizzling,' I said, desperately squashing the lump of solid butter with the fish slice, 'put in the cooked rice and . . .'

The combination of my nervousness and the lack of action in the pan made me dash through the recipe in record time. In less than a minute I had added the peas, the chopped hard-boiled egg, diced tomato, flaked fish, the lot, stirred them together into a horrible lump – everything seemed to get glued to the un-melted butter – and said, 'and there you have a delicious supper dish', probably with little conviction.

Fiona looked at me in dismay and said, 'Prue, we still have a few minutes left, and I know that you can chop an onion like a professional chef. Perhaps you could show us how?'

I looked wildly round. 'Of course, only we don't have an onion,' I said.

'Never mind, show us on a tomato.'

So there I was, trying to dice an overripe tomato with a blunt BBC knife on a painted tabletop.

I was more successful on radio. I got my first regular radio job a few years later – bizarrely, on the current affairs *Today* programme. I had a two-minute slot every Friday in which I would make weekend cooking suggestions to the nation. The presenter was Jack de Manio. He was famous not only because anyone who presents the *Today* programme becomes famous, but also because his catchphrase, uttered in a memorably gin-soaked voice, was 'And the time now is *precisely* 8.20' (or whatever), only it was very often really 7.20. He had a great deal of trouble telling the time. And he drank a lot.

After Jack resigned from the *Today* programme – I suspect it wasn't entirely voluntary – he took a job for Tyne Tees television in Newcastle, presenting an afternoon show consisting of interviews, domestic advice and celebrities. In 1973 he asked me to replace the Italian chef they currently had doing the cooking spot. How hard could it be to make a simple dish while Jack asked questions, I thought . . .

Just before filming was due to begin the producer rang me. 'How would you like to present the series?' he said. 'Jack is indisposed.'

Actually, poor Jack was sacked. Of course I said yes in a flash, without giving a thought to the fact that, apart from the humiliation with the squashy tomato, I had never been on television.

David Coleman, the well-known sports commentator, had a training studio. Mostly they schooled top policemen and football managers in handling the press. They said they'd need a week to teach me the rudiments of presenting a magazine programme: how to talk to camera, interview live guests, listen to the floor manager talking to me through an earpiece, manage the timing, look relaxed . . .

I could only afford to train for half a day. I learnt that a finger drawn across the throat meant 'Kill it', that two forefingers held like a crucifix meant 'Half a minute left' and that 'Camera right' meant your left.

So, armed with even less confidence than before, I set off for Tyne Tees, where my director, who had been a schoolmaster, did not believe in spontaneity and liked everything scripted. I'd have my questions on an autocue under one camera and the poor guest would have his or her answers under another camera. And if, in rehearsals, I'd put the wooden spoon down on the right, he'd get very upset if I now put it down on my left.

I hated the whole business. I would lie awake in the Swallow Hotel the night before filming, muttering to myself, 'Hello and welcome to another afternoon with me, Prue Leith, and blah blah blah.' I was terrified, and as the weeks went by it got worse.

I suppose I couldn't have been wholly dreadful because, to my amazement, we did a second thirteen-programme series. I hated that too, although there were some good moments, such as my interview with my wine-buff friend Joseph Berkmann, then the wine writer for the *Daily Mail*.

When he had given his tips about how to store wine, open a bottle, read a label and so on, I asked him, 'Joseph, you live and breathe wine. You are passionate about it. What is it about wine that has so captivated you?'

I thought he would say what was on his autocue, something about wine being a living thing and wine-making an ancient and fascinating art. But, eyes shining with merriment, he looked straight to camera and answered, 'It makes you drunk.'

One day my guest was Lotte Berk, the then-famous fitness coach I went to for weekly torture sessions. Her language was as strong as her German-Jewish accent and she was obsessed with the 'inner core', which included not just abdominal, but also vaginal, muscles.

My warnings to Lotte that this was a pre-watershed show proved quite useless. She had me lying on my back on the floor while she, seventy if she was a day, tiny, thin as a stick insect, in black leotard and tights, pranced around like a demented teenager, exhorting us, 'Squeeze, squeeze, make like fucky-fucky. More, more, fucky-fuck, squeeze, squeeze, tighter, tighter. Think of your lover as a string bean: he is getting away, quick, hold on to him, squeeze . . .'

I doubt if anyone on the programme will ever forget it. Most of the footage ended on the cutting room floor – I'm just glad YouTube didn't exist then: someone would have posted the clip.

Less amusingly, Jason of Jingles, a then fashionable London hairdresser, came to demonstrate his cutting skills on my thick mop. To save time next morning he wanted to wash my hair the night before at the hotel, but he hadn't brought shampoo and the hotel didn't provide any. So we begged some washing-up liquid from the kitchens. I had in mind some mild Squeezy-like stuff, but what they gave us was industrial sterilizing detergent. Although we rinsed my hair a dozen times, that night I was kept awake by the smell of bleach and next morning my hair was dull and felt like string.

But worse was to come. Jason was so nervous

that he accidentally snipped my ear and blood poured down my cheek. In the end we had to keep my non-bandaged side to camera.

I was perfectly happy with the format of the programmes, which mostly consisted of items in which I would be taught something (how to tap dance, how to buy wine, how to get fit, how to put up a tent, what to keep in my freezer – Mary Berry produced a pig's trotter which had been in hers, she said, for ten years). We provided a good mix of amusement at my uselessness and helpful information for the viewer.

Unhappily, I never got on with the director, who stifled all spontaneity and terrified the socks off me. Then, towards the very end of the second series, the floor manager, a sympathetic guy who knew how terrified I was, offered me a small yellow pill.

'It's Valium,' he said, 'it will calm the terrors.'

I took it gratefully, and spent a wonderfully happy day floating on air, unruffled by anything, confident that I was doing a marvellous job. My brother Jamie said afterwards, 'God, Prue, what happened? You were awful. Half asleep and looking like a zombie.'

Ever since my Paris sojourn in 1960 I'd wanted a restaurant. I started with the dream of a tiny basement bistro with checked tablecloths, affordable food, a bohemian atmosphere and unknown painters' works on the wall – a perfect recipe for losing money.

Happily, by 1969, when I could afford to open a restaurant, I'd grown up a bit. Now I wanted a biggish restaurant, very classy, with great food and wine, stylish design and an informal atmosphere. I found most smart restaurants stuffy: men had to wear ties and jackets; women were not allowed to wear trousers. (A great trick was to arrive in a trouser suit with a long top, and when refused entry, to slip off the trousers and claim to be wearing a mini-dress. I only pulled this off once, at the Ritz.) Sommeliers looked down their noses if you ordered the house wine and a kind of holy hush dominated. Worst of all, there were some fancy chefs so precious about their food that they wouldn't allow customers to add salt and pepper, or to have their steaks well done.

On the other hand, restaurants with a relaxed atmosphere, though cheap and cheerful, offered bog-standard food, horrible wine, amateur service and were deafeningly noisy.

Of course, there were some great establishments. The two I admired most belonged to people who, interestingly, had not grown up in the restaurant trade. Albert Roux, who had just opened Le Gavroche and was later to be awarded three Michelin stars, had been a cook in private service, and Robert Carrier, whose eponymous restaurant in Islington was the talk of the town, was a food writer. They both thought more like customers than caterers. I aspired to join them at the top of the trade.

I had, by 1968, enough money saved to persuade the bank to lend me some more. I also borrowed £11,000 from my mother, and sold ten per cent of the equity in the restaurant company for £3,000 to Richard Eldridge, a City high flyer whom, a year later, I was able to buy out for three times that sum.

Rayne's property ventures were doing well. He and his partner bought a row of crumbling Victorian terrace houses in Notting Hill, most of which they sold off to another developer, but they kept three and restored them. In 1969, with great trepidation and excitement, I took the lease of the ground floor of two of them for my first restaurant.

Leith's Restaurant, which opened in October 1969, cost £30,000 all in all, which seems like nothing today, but was a real stretch for me then. We had enough reserves, we thought, to run at a slight loss for six months. But then it would be sink or swim.

I never considered the prospect of failure, which is just as well: more restaurateurs go bust than anyone except builders. I shudder now to think how ignorant I was. I'd never had a proper job in a restaurant, never mind run one. I knew next to nothing about wine, I had no idea that the best place to open a restaurant is between two other restaurants in a street of shops. I thought that the best place would be in a residential area where there were no other restaurants.

I just sat down and thought about what I would like as a customer. I decided on a four-course dinner menu with a fixed price. My thinking was that what customers were *really* paying for was being there – for occupying a seat as in the theatre, not for the food they ate. We'd not be tempted to harry people who were only having one course out of their seats. The all-in price would be just that – no surprises at the bottom of the bill: no tax (at the time there was a new Selective Employment Tax), service charge, cover charge, or supplements.

There would be no dress code. And we would not be precious about the food. It would be excellent, but if the customer wanted to ruin it with a ton of salt, or have his beautiful Aberdeen Angus steak cremated, or put ice cream into his Chateau Lafite, it was none of our business – he was paying for it, after all.

I thought it would be nice to have a selection of starters and puds on big trolleys so customers could have a little bit of lots of different things.

I liked big wine glasses and even bigger water glasses and I adopted the American habit of automatically giving customers tap water as they sat down, rather than expecting them to buy bottled water.

I hated the way waiters repeatedly interrupted the conversation to top up your wine, so I bought a lot of ornate silver soda siphon holders which served as both table decoration and to hold wine bottles.

156

To avoid that feeling that the staff are willing you to go home, lingering customers would be given a hand-bell to call a waiter from the bar if they needed anything.

To me the most comfortable chairs in the world were office chairs on casters. They swivelled to make getting out easy and they were designed to be sat on all day.

I liked the 'theatre' of smart restaurants: steak tartare mixed at the table, ducks carved, fish filleted, and crèpes suzette flambéed by the waiters. I had been knocked out by a visit to the Tour d'Argent in Paris, famous for its pressed duck, so I bought a duck press for special occasions. Pressed duck, rarely done now, is still the best duck dish in the world: you roast a small duck very briefly in a blazing oven, then serve the still rare breasts with the juices pressed out of the mostly raw bones and legs. Not for vegetarians, but truly delicious.

We hired an architect, Nathan Silver, who had never designed a restaurant and was as ignorant as I about how they worked. We managed to build a restaurant without a chef's office, without a wine cellar, without changing rooms or loos for the staff, without a walk-in fridge, without a freezer at all. But Nathan was full of ideas, and we ended up with very original décor that got us into all the fashion and design magazines and put us on the map. Nathan decreed a hard grey brick floor, false windows of glittery amber mirror all round the walls, deep turquoise carpet on the ceiling and an expensive printed velvet for the rolling office chairs.

Of course we were wildly over budget. Nathan wanted to design every door handle and window latch. Once I took him to lunch at the Ritz with the intention of sacking him, but by the end of lunch I had not only failed to do so, I'd agreed to an increased budget and to his designing the hors d'oeuvre and dessert trolleys. I still have one of them, a thing of beauty: huge, heavy, made of oak and stainless steel.

Restaurant openings, I now know, are always attended by panic and drama, but this, my first, was worse than anything to come. For a start we were unable to resolve a ridiculous planning issue. The Fire Department decreed that the door between kitchen and dining rooms should be solid and fireproof. The Health and Safety Department said it must be louvred to allow a flow of air from dining area to kitchen. I had discovered that the officials of these two departments had offices on the same corridor in the Council building. I suggested they sort it out. They refused to speak to each other. In the end we put in two doors, a louvred one for everyday use, and a fire door on a fusable link which would close if there was a fire.

Naturally, Nathan didn't want the casters that came with the chairs and had ordered specials, large and expensive and in polished steel. They didn't arrive until the day before we opened and my stepfather (who had come over with my mother for the opening) had to spend all night putting them in.

The first manager we hired changed his mind the week before opening.

The London black-taxi drivers decided to boycott us because we had done a deal with a mini-cab company. (We quickly came to heel: you cannot have London cabbies advising their customers against dining with you.)

I lost my voice completely, something which, in times of stress, tends to happen. I rang a Harley Street specialist. An actress friend had told me he could prescribe some spray to get my vocal cords functioning. But he gave me very short shrift.

'Prescribe over the telephone? Certainly not. You must make an appointment.'

'I can't,' I croaked, 'I've got an interview with the *Daily Mail* and we need the publicity.'

'Are you telling me that getting into the papers is more important than your health?'

'Yes, it is.'

'Well, I can't help you.' Click.

At about lunchtime on the opening night I walked into the bar to find Nathan's plain white walls and pale oak bar festooned with Chianti bottles in straw baskets and plastic vines dripping with fake grapes. And a head barman absolutely delighted with himself for jollying up Nathan's minimalism.

Poor man. I don't think he ever forgave me for insisting he take it all down again.

I had some idea that having a restaurant would mean drifting about in long earrings and false eyelashes, receiving compliments on the food and dishing out brandies to favoured customers. In fact (complete with earrings and false lashes) I spent most of that first evening in the ladies lavatory, unblocking the loo with a plunger.

The kitchen porter didn't turn up and my mother manned the wash-up.

But we were a huge success. Undeservedly. At the start our food was not marvellous, but at the time few restaurants cooked well, and most used frozen vegetables and canned celery, mushrooms and asparagus. The mere fact that we served only fresh food was newsworthy.

But most of the press homed in on the originality of the design, the trolleys of pick-your-own hors d'oeuvres and puds, the fixed inclusive price, the chairs on castors, and on the fact that I was a woman in a man's world and only twenty-nine.

Humphrey Lyttelton, writing in the *Tatler*, said, 'If you can rob a bank, or beg or borrow a fortune, and then risk being mugged, go to the seamy end of Notting Hill . . .'

Thanks very much, Humph, I thought, that will pack them in.

But in fact it did. Those posh folks from the south side of the park made the journey into the jungle and discovered Notting Hill Gate.

Within a month we were packed. Our timing had been spot on, though we'd not known it. The area, peeling and cheap in 1970, became first gentrified and then fashionable. Tina Turner bought a huge house across the road for a million pounds, probably worth sixteen today.

But for all our success, we were losing money.

Belatedly I decided I should meet some restaurateurs and ask for help. The only restaurateur I knew was my hero Albert Roux, who had agreed to let me pick his brains before we opened, but I did not then know what questions to ask. I did remember (and still do) several things he said then. One was to write the laundry's name and number in letters of fire over my desk because I would be ringing them up weekly demanding to know where the hell our linen was. He was right. And he held up one hand and counted off his fingers: 'If you are open five days you have one day to make the money to pay the wages, one for the cost of wine, one for the cost of food, one for the overheads and one for you. If you are open six days you may have to pay the tax man too.'

Now I needed Albert again, and he agreed to come and have a look.

I also went to a cocktail party given by the embryonic Restaurateurs Association of Great Britain on the terrace of the House of Lords. At that reception I joined the Association (I was later to become its chairman), but more importantly,

Joseph Berkmann was there. Joseph was, and is, a successful entrepreneur. He had a clutch of excellent restaurants and a wine business.

'Congratulations,' he said, 'You're doing wonderfully well.'

'But I'm losing money!'

'You can't be. You charge a fortune and you're booked up weeks in advance.'

'Well, I am. If we don't turn it round, we'll be out of business in four months.'

He too agreed to come and see what I was doing wrong and turned up the following Monday. He looked at our account books, and within minutes said, 'Your chef is robbing you blind. Your food bills are astronomical.'

I'm ashamed to say that I answered, 'He can't be. He's English.'

Joseph, who is Austrian, raised an eyebrow. I hastily amended this to, 'I mean, he was the Lord Chancellor's chef. And he cooked at the British Embassy in Paris. He's a terrific cook.'

'Terrific cooks can be terrific crooks too.'

He was right of course. The chef was due to go on holiday, something I'd had to agree to when he applied for the job. When he was away the costs dropped dramatically, and we found he was being paid kickbacks from our suppliers, who were also selling us a lot of fantasy food.

When Albert arrived one evening on the same rescue mission, I thought he would do as Joseph had and look at the books, but he positioned himself at the bin into which the waiters scraped the leftovers. After half an hour Albert summoned me.

'Either your food is deesgusteeng, or you are giving the customers too much. A third of it is going in the bin. Rich customers who 'ave 'ad a business breakfast and a business *déjeuner* do not want 'alf a duck falling off the side of the plate. Not if they are paying for four courses.'

He fished an apple out of the chefs' bin.

'*Regardez.* This is criminal. Why throw this away?'

I took the apple and turned it over. 'It's *bad*, Albert,' I said.

'No, no, no. It is only 'alf bad.'

And then he fished out a bunch of watercress stalks and explained that there was more flavour in the stalks than the leaves and they would make good soup. And that we should not buy the cream in half-gallon jugs, because if the chef has a big container of it he will tip it in with abandon, using far too much. If it comes in half-pint domestic containers he will be use it frugally, scraping the last drop out with a rubber spatula.

We took both Joseph and Albert's advice. We sacked the chef (and his wife, who was our cashier and in league with him) and we dropped the portion size for main courses. This should have been obvious to me from the start, because the first-course trolleys were so popular (and our Spanish waiters so generous by nature) that most diners were pretty full before they came to the main course, never mind the pudding.

After six months we were breaking even and by the end of the first year we'd made a decent profit.

On top of my existing catering business and new restaurant, I was soon coping with a secondary career as a food columnist and with writing my first cookbook. One of our customers, a publisher, got me to write *Leith's All-Party Cookbook*, published in 1972. It was probably the most original of all my dozen cookbooks. The cover had a picture of a loaded buffet party table on it, but that was on the back. The front was of the same food, but after the buffet has been trashed by the guests: empty lobster shells, ham bone stripped, bare salmon bones, Stilton dug out, bottle upended in the ice bucket, even a cigar stubbed out in a dish. And I had fun hunting down suitable paintings or etchings to illustrate the parties covered by the chapters. They included Cruikshank and Gillray cartoons, a detail from the Bayeux tapestry, Poussin's *A Bacchanalian Revel*, *Fêtes Champêtres* by Watteau and Tissot. They were not all exactly suitable – the barbecue chapter was illustrated with a 1575 engraving of a Brazilian human barbecue, complete with people being butchered and cooked.

My getting the job as cookery columnist for the *Daily Mail* was a stroke of luck. Soon after Leith's Restaurant opened, the newspaper launched a pull-out section for women, *Femail*. The editor wanted someone with a name, fame, and style and he alighted on Lady Elizabeth Anson, by now a friend. She was the Queen's cousin, sister of the wildly sexy photographer Patrick Lichfield, and her company Party Planners was growing ever larger. The editor asked her to be their cookery writer. Although she was a good cook, she told him she could never write a recipe. And then added, 'But I know a woman who can.'

And so I was offered the job of ghosting Lady Elizabeth, but I managed to do a deal with the editor: I would write her column one week if I was allowed my own the next.

I gave Lady Liz all the posh stuff, the iced soups and dinner party game, the chocolate desserts and elegant savouries. And under my name I produced family fare of endless mince, stews and homely puddings.

All went fine until I wrote a recipe for a ginger peach brulée under her name. It was basically a crème brulée, with stewed peaches and an ounce of stem ginger at the bottom of the ramekins, but I failed to specify what kind of ginger. And an ounce of ground ginger is the whole pot, enough to blow your head off.

That was not the last disaster. I was very confident of my Oxford orange marmalade. I liked the slightly bitter caramel taste that two tablespoons of black treacle gave it. I did not yet have a typewriter and I sent the recipe in handwritten.

But I'd forgotten to cross the T of two tablespoons, so it appeared, not 2 tbs, but 2 lbs. And two pounds of black treacle is rather a lot for a couple of pounds of oranges.

The *Daily Mail* switchboard went white hot with readers ringing in to complain of the sticky goo in their saucepans or, worse, of solid black rock and wrecked pan, and curtains that smelt of burnt molasses. The *Daily Mail* had to pay out seventeen shillings and fivepence (this was before Harold Wilson turned this into 87.5p) to every reader to compensate them for the ingredients.

Then one woman rang up and said, 'Look, how many oranges and how much sugar must I add to the treacle to get the proportions right again?' Sensible woman, I thought. From now on we'll pay out no more compensation – we'll just encourage people to make a few years' marmalade at once. I worked out that she would need to make 160 pots of marmalade. We paid her the seventeen shillings and fivepence.

I was sure this time I must be for the chop, but no summons came from above. But next day when I arrived at my desk I found a letter bomb on it. I knew what it was because we were in the middle of the IRA letter bomb campaign which targeted newspapers and we had all been given training: if you could feel something squashy that would be the Semtex, and something that felt like wires was not good news either.

My envelope had the squashy bit in the middle and wires on both sides of it. I remember thinking this an over-the-top reaction to a mistake in a recipe, but I did what we were trained to do and cleared our room (I sat opposite Linda Lee Potter and we scuttled out together). I phoned the post room, who phoned the police and a copper came and took away my envelope.

After a couple of hours they told me to collect it. It contained a lump of marmalade toffee with a dental brace embedded in it, two teeth attached. And a large orthodontist's bill.

It is every restaurateur's dream to have their place heaving with famous people. They are rich and spend a lot, and other people want to be where they are. And in the early Seventies, Leith's clientele included all sorts of very famous people. Nan knew everyone in the theatre, and so Alec Guinness, John Gielgud, Diana Rigg, Vanessa Redgrave, would all come. We had pop stars like Lulu, the Rolling Stones and the Beatles. (I was disappointed that all the Beatles wanted was a bacon-and-egg fry-up. 'And don't make it fancy with chopped herbs and stuff on the top,' said Ringo.)

Music people tended to stay later, and drink more, than actors. Our rather ordinary brass bell given to late-stayers to summon service, was replaced by singer Harry Nilsson's girlfriend, Kathy, who gave us an engraved silver one in thanks for the many hours they sat over a bottle, or three, into the small hours.

In the first months before we were really fashionable, we were often empty. One Monday night at about ten-thirty I'd just had dinner with Rayne, the chef had already gone home and most of the waiters had been let off early, when three more customers arrived.

Rayne said, 'Who is that dumpy little woman? She looks familiar.'

I looked up. 'Oh God, that's Princess Margaret! And the restaurant is stone empty.'

So we summoned our friends. Rayne rang his chum, Peter Parker, chairman of Mitsubishi UK, and later to be chairman of British Rail, and his doctor wife Jill. Jill had washed her hair, taken a sleeping pill and was fast asleep. But she gamely got up, wrapped her head in a bandanna and, groggy and swaying, ate another supper. Nan was about to leave the theatre; she gathered up most of the cast and brought them along too.

I dashed 'backstage' and told the waiters, busy changing out of their uniforms, to hurry into their civvies and come round to the front and try to look like a crowd of fashionable, happy customers.

Those waiters had a ball, clicking their fingers, sending food back, complaining about the wine and generally having fun at the expense of those colleagues forced to serve them.

I took over the kitchen. I wasn't, and never became, a restaurant chef. Whatever the waiters ordered they got sole doria – fillets of sole, shallow-fried in butter and served with glazed cucumber balls. It was the simplest thing on the menu.

At the time we had a know-it-all waiter, François. He was technically good at his job, but a snob and unfriendly, and though I longed for him to leave, I hadn't real grounds for sacking him.

Princess Margaret's party were seated in his section. He came into the kitchen and announced that 'Madame la Princesse and her companions will have le faisan roti.'

'Roast Pheasant? That's not on the menu. And it will take fifty minutes. Are you sure she didn't ask for the pheasant casserole?'

'I will not serve stew to la Princesse,' he pronounced, while pouring meths into a flame lamp preparatory to re-lighting it. But, busy arguing with me, he did not notice that the lamp was still alight.

Whoomph! Massive explosion and François had little spots of flaming meths down his front. Needless to say, I failed to follow proper procedure (smother with the fire blanket) and instead beat the flamelets out with my floury, fishy hands, leaving Francois with great white handprints all over his black jacket and trousers, and so unable to serve anything at all, never mind stew, to the Princess.

That wasn't all. The kitchen porter, happily with his back to the explosion, lost a good bit of hair, and the laundry basket, into which François had knocked the flame lamp, was now on fire. Someone threw water from the coffee machine at it, missed, hit the wall and fused the ice-cream machine.

But otherwise it went like a dream. Compliments to the chef on the excellence of the pheasant casserole.

Throughout the Seventies and Eighties, we would get the occasional Royal arriving unannounced and booked in someone else's name. I remember Princess Anne and a 'John Smith' sitting where everyone entering the restaurant would see them. I said to the manager, 'How could you seat her there? Doesn't she want privacy?'

'It was worth a try,' he replied, 'and she didn't object, so be grateful. She'll do us a power of good.'

I was never good at judging where to seat famous people: would they want privacy, or an audience? In 1975, when the film *Shampoo* was on everywhere, I got it wrong with Julie Christie and Warren Beatty. The newspapers were full of their affair, so I showed them at once to a discreet corner table, but they shook their heads. I offered them various other tucked-away tables but they chose a table right in the middle of the room, under a spotlight.

'How was I to know they wanted to be seen?' I moaned to a restaurateur friend.

'What were they wearing?'

'What has that go to do with it?'

'Just tell me. What were they wearing?'

'Well, oddly, they were both wearing white. She was in a trouser suit, he in cream linen. They looked stunning.'

'That's your answer. No one puts on a white trouser suit if they don't want to be seen.'

In my experience, few celebrities want to hide

away. Michael Winner, the film director, food critic and maddening telly person, put it very well. The picture of grumpy distaste, he gazed round our bar, 'But Prue, where are all the glitterati?'

'Michael,' I said, creeping like only restaurateurs can, '*you* are the glitterati.'

'But don't you realise, rich and famous people only want to be with other rich and famous people.'

How to cope with that much ego? By lying, I decided. 'Well, we have Michael Parkinson and Mary dining with Ian Botham round the corner, and the Mamas and the Papas are in the private room.'

He at once relaxed into good humour.

Relations with Kensington and Chelsea Council were never great. They had been unhelpful about planning and ridiculous about health and hygiene (one inspector would tell us to have lids on the rubbish bins to keep the flies out, the next that we must not have lids because the chefs would contaminate their fingers by touching them), but we came to war over the dustmen. They were meant to collect from commercial premises every day and we had three huge 'paladins' in our yard: one under a chute from the flats upstairs, one for the kitchen rubbish, and one for the bottles.

In the Seventies they seldom came more than twice a week but it didn't matter much because the pig man collected all the organic waste to feed his pigs. But when, in the Eighties, the Council outlawed the pigswill collections, we really needed them to take away the rubbish before it rotted, stank and attracted rats. I rang the Council frequently to no avail, and then rumbled what the problem was: the dustmen wanted private payola to do their job. I refused. They got their revenge by scattering rubbish all over the yard and down the basement steps.

Beside myself, I reported them to the Council. More rubbish down the steps. I then rang Esther Rantzen's TV show *That's Life* and they sent a cameraman to secretly film the men asking for bribes. Sadly a new gang appeared that day and wheeled away the paladins with no demands or menaces.

But the following week we got no collections at all. At which I loaded up all the black bags into one of our vans and deposited them on Kensington Town Hall steps, with a note saying that next time I'd call the press to photograph me doing the dumping. It worked.

Over my twenty-five-year ownership of Leith's Restaurant, we had some just-okay chefs, some lazy ones and some brilliant ones. And our reputation went up and down with them. One of the things that stood in the way of excellence, I thought, was the poor relationship between kitchen and front of house, a common problem in restaurants. The chefs think the waiters have an easy job of it, just putting food in front of customers, absorbing the praise (and the tips) and deflecting complaints to the kitchen. The waiters think the chefs are a temperamental and arrogant lot who never have to face a customer and who go home two hours before they do.

One day in 1973 I was eating lunch in the Berkeley Hotel with several other food writers and restaurateurs, all of us there to judge the food for a chef's competition. After an excellent meal, the chef came out to talk to us. He was called Jean-Baptiste Reynaud, and he was utterly charming: passionate, funny, and with the sexiest of French accents. As he left, my neighbour and fellow judge, the fashionable restaurateur Mario (of Mario and Franco fame) said to me, 'Do you steal him, or do I?'

I stole him – but not for the kitchen. I offered him the job of restaurant manager. I figured that you cannot be a head chef in a top London hotel without knowing how to manage people, budgets and suppliers. And I thought the kitchen could hardly run rings round a former head chef. And he would be the perfect man to unite the kitchen and front of house in harmony.

I was mostly right, although success in the kitchen/dining room peace stakes was always patchy.

Jean Reynaud (known as JBR) did greatly improve the quality of the food, but my great ambition, to get a Michelin star, remained unfulfilled. He stayed with us fifteen years and then one day announced he was leaving. He explained, 'I want to run a tiny place of my own. Not a great big place belonging to someone else.'

'But JBR, you run this place. I hardly interfere.'

'Yes, you do. You never stop. I'm tired. After five years I'm fed up with the staff, always complaining; after ten years I'm fed up with the customers, always complaining. And now I'm getting fed up with you! Always complaining: "JBR, there's a light out in the passage; JBR, the water for the flowers needs changing; JBR, there's a crack in this glass."'

He opened his own place in Islington, and we stayed good friends.

In 1988 JBR was followed by Nick Tarayan, a lovely guy. In those days you could ask prospective employees questions that today you cannot, like: how old are you? Are you married? Are you pregnant? But even then, you did not ask people about their sex lives. But I said, 'I know you're gay. That's fine by me, but are you committed to anyone, or are you still hunting?'

He looked at me for a moment, then burst out laughing. 'Wow, you don't beat about the bush, do you? Why do you need to know?'

'I don't if you don't want to tell me, but I'd like to know as much about you as possible. I suppose I want to be able to judge whether you are going to be flirting with the young waiters or going sedately home to slippers and pipe.'

He said he was still single. And I decided I was

being an idiot. Why would a single gay guy do more flirting on company time than a single hetero guy?

I asked him to come and eat in the restaurant incognito and write me a report. It was devastating, especially about the wine. Nick was a real wine buff, and he correctly concluded that no-one was putting any effort into our list. When I'd first opened Leith's, Cyril Ray, the journalist and wine writer, had helped me with introductions to wine people and he'd chosen the wines for my first list, which was small but excellent. I had hastily done the Higher Certificate course in wine and quickly became a crashing wine-bore, giving my friends tasting lessons at dinner and talking of little else. And I spent all our profits on building up a really good cellar.

But gradually other interests crowded out the wine obsession and our list, as Nick pointed out, now had too many poor vintages of great wines and little of really good value. I had let the wine explosion from the 'new world' of South Africa, Australia, California and South America, pass me by. Nick overhauled the list, and much acclaim and multiple awards, including best wine list in the UK, followed.

He also tackled the décor (we had just been described, to my humiliation, as 'stuck in a Seventies time-warp' by *Time Out*).

And we promoted our sous-chef, a young Scot who cooked like a dream, to the top job. Alex

Floyd instantly made the dishes lighter, more interesting and exciting.

By now we also had a vegetarian menu, which surprised us with its popularity. This came about because one day my vegetarian sister-in-law, Penny Junor, replied to my enquiry about her main course, with a rather lukewarm, 'It was fine. I always have the gratinéed veg with hollandaise.'

This was the off-menu 'vegetarian special' the waiters always suggested.

'Why don't you choose from the menu?'

'Because the waiters always suggest the special and I don't like looking for vegetarian dishes among your carnivore's delights like veal kidneys, calves' liver and roast suckling pig.'

It got me thinking, and I proposed a separate vegetarian menu. At first the kitchen was resistant. In those days chefs regarded vegetarians as a flaming nuisance, but they cheered up when I pointed out that by increasing the size of some of the vegetable garnishes from other dishes – little mushroom pastry parcels we served with veal, baby peppers stuffed with pea risotto that accompanied the lamb, endive confit with orange that came with the duck – the veggie main courses need not be much trouble. And they would certainly be more profitable than the meat and fish dishes since we'd still be charging the full dinner price.

To my simultaneous astonishment and dismay, we proceeded to win 'Vegetarian Restaurant of the Year'. Astonishment because we were not a vegetarian restaurant, and dismay because I figured that a lot of customers wouldn't come if they thought we were.

In fact it did us a lot of good. I once calculated that twenty-five per cent of customers would choose at least one dish off the vegetarian menu. If you are overfed or tired, you might prefer not to be faced with a great plate of meat.

CHAPTER 8

CRACKS IN THE AFFAIR

I sometimes wished I did not love him so

I must have been a very good liar to keep my love affair with Rayne secret for so long. But I did not fool everyone. One day, soon after Leith's Restaurant opened and eight or nine years into our relationship, one of Nan's friends cornered me in the ladies' loo. When I emerged from the cubicle, there she was, her back to the door, barring the only way out.

'You're sleeping with Rayne, aren't you?'

I spluttered indignant denials, I'm sure unconvincingly, and only escaped by saying that if she wanted to talk to me I would come and see her the next day, at teatime. And then, coward that I am, I didn't go.

Life went on through the Seventies. I was very busy, of course, and I was happy. But as I got older I sometimes resented what I considered Rayne's pulling rank on me, just assuming that he knew best. I was good at controlling my temper in the business, but sometimes Rayne would drive me mad and I would lose it, yelling and crying at the same time. Once we had a ludicrous argument when I was driving and he was navigating. Looking at the map and not seeing the No Entry sign, he told me to turn right. I did not, he expostulated, I retaliated, and he found himself declaring – to my fury and his later shame and amusement – that if he told me to turn into a brick wall, I should do it.

I can't remember what our quarrel was about when I threw a glass-topped coffee table at him. It was not a success: the glass fell backwards as the frame flew forwards, and splintered into shards at my feet. I ran out into Upbrook Mews and set off, sobbing, down the cobbles. At the end of the mews I became aware of a pain in my ankle and looked down to see blood all over my foot and still pumping out of my leg. I hobbled back and Rayne had to staunch the flow and tape me up.

Rayne became ever more involved with my business and his own property ventures, and stopped writing the history of China that he had begun after the publication in 1964 of *The Devil's Discus* about the Thai king. I used to feel I was responsible for his abandoning his writing career, but he claimed he would return to it – and eventually he did – but that now he must concentrate on making some money.

The first cracks in our long idyll started to appear in the early Seventies, when I was a few years into my thirties. Nan and Rayne's children were all married and having babies. My friend Jane, now living in Canada, was married with one child and planning a second. My brother David's youngest was already a teenager. And every visit to my beloved brother Jamie and his talented, beautiful, pregnant Penny, fed a longing for marriage and a family of my own.

One night in 1973, my mother, on a visit from South Africa, had a drink or two too many and suddenly banged her glass down on the table.

'I want a grandchild!'

'Mum, you already have two. Helen and James.'

She countered, 'They're David's children. I want *my daughter* to have a baby.'

I wanted to yell, *Well, so do I!*

Jamie and Penny's first son, Sam, was born in January 1974, and the embryonic family lived in a flat over a dental surgery in Westbourne Grove which Rayne, in his capacity as pseudo godfather, had helped them buy. They had very little money. Jamie was a struggling actor, trying to make a few bob on the side by cutting the top half off wine bottles and polishing the rims to make tumblers. Penny had been a journalist on the *Evening Standard* and, once Sam was born, went freelance and wrote when she could.

I longed to tell Jamie about Rayne. I wanted him to know that I, too, loved and was loved. But somehow I just couldn't. I knew he would be sympathetic but I also knew he, and particularly Penny, would ask some hard questions about where the affair would end. And didn't I want children? And what about Nan? They all loved her too, and would be rightly appalled.

These were questions I asked myself all the time and I didn't like the obvious answer: I should leave him, find a mate, have a baby, get the Jamie and Penny life, and leave Nan's husband to her. But I loved Rayne, and I understood that he couldn't leave Nan. It was an impasse that I could not unblock. I just pushed the frustrations, longings and guilt away and got on with my business, tucking up with Rayne whenever we could.

But once into my thirties, I was getting very tired of lying to everyone. Inexcusably, I would sometimes encourage men who fancied me, just to have the smokescreen of a 'boyfriend'. I used them mercilessly, refusing even a kiss, but displaying them to family and friends to disprove the ever more frequent assumption that I was lesbian.

One day I was visiting my brother Jamie's parents-in-law, Sir John Junor, the famous and controversial editor of the *Sunday Express*, and his wife Pam. John had a way of lowering his head like a charging bull and looking up at you with his somewhat droopy, but popping, eyes,

'Don't try to fool me. I know you're a dyke. It's obvious.'

I longed for a baby. Rayne's baby. I wanted to live with him openly, to do the things families do. I wanted to go out to dinner with friends as a couple, to ask people to dinner other than in Leith's

Restaurant, where I had to pretend it was just business promotion we were up to. I envied women gossiping about husbands and children. I lied to my women friends. Even the closest of them, other than Jane and Pat Kavanagh, had to be kept at a distance.

I resented my image as the hard-driving businesswoman with no time for anything but making money. I no longer wanted to spend night after night in my restaurant, chatting up customers or working in the office.

From the outside it looked like a great life, and in many ways it was. The business was doing well enough for me to swap cottages, letting the smaller and living in the larger. The errant doctor had pretty well trashed it, so I got Rose Underdown, friend and fashionable decorator, to do it over for me. It ended up very Seventies, with cork tiles on the kitchen walls, zebra print in the loo, and thick, almost padded, blue curtains and quilt. I loved that quilt. Forty-odd years later I still have it, now a faded picnic rug.

So there I was with a dinky house in Upbrook Mews, a fashionable restaurant, and a fast-growing and profitable catering business. I was a published cookery writer, who knew lots of interesting people, and yet at the very centre of me was this uncomfortable ache: a never-ceasing longing for Rayne to belong to me, and for us to have a child.

Yet I never beseeched Rayne to leave Nan. I proposed our having a child that I would bring up myself, somehow pretending it was the result of a one-night stand with someone I never wanted to see again. But Rayne would not hear of it. He had already brought up three children, he had no desire for more, and he thought my scheme a romantic dream. So we went on as before.

At times I wished I did not love him so, and that someone else would come along who would do instead. I had, in our time together, very occasionally found other men attractive and been pleased by their attentions, but doing more than a bit of flirting was unthinkable. If I was lucky I'd end up turning them into friends.

Ed Gottesman, an American lawyer whose marriage was on the rocks, was the only serious contender in all those years. I really wished I could leave Rayne and give in to Ed. He was a million times more suitable: available, good-looking, knowledgeable, clever, rich, educated, cultured, funny. But I twisted and turned and he got tired of my behaviour and fell in love with Pat Kavanagh instead.

But not before one hilarious interlude when I had invited him and another friend (a Scottish rugby-playing distant cousin called Mick Grant, whom I had only recently met and who believed himself passionately in love with me) to join me over Christmas with Jamie and Penny in Perthshire. They had taken a tiny cottage in the middle of snowy nowhere while Jamie was in a play at the Perth Theatre.

We had a very boozy Christmas Eve, not least because Ed made a bucket of American eggnog which started with bottles of bourbon and rye whiskey, two dozen egg yolks and a couple of litres of vanilla ice cream.

The house was full of family, so Mick, Ed and I were billeted in a B&B to which Mick and I staggered off around midnight. I fell asleep at once but was woken in the wee small hours by Ed climbing in my window from a low roof. He'd lost his key after John Junor had taken him on a late-night pub crawl, intending, he said, to 'teach him how to drink'; John was unaware that Ed's first employer, the Secretary of the New York Bar association, had already made a handsome fist of the task.

I had a second bed in my room and Ed lay down on it, fully dressed, and went out like a light.

Some of the men were due to play golf on the famous St Andrews Old Course in the morning and had an early start, after which Mick was to travel south. At first light, Mick came in to say goodbye. I woke to find Mick looking aghast at the sleeping Ed in the bed next to mine. Pain, grief and horror were written all over his face. He backed out of the door and disappeared without a word.

I have no idea why I thought it so important that Mick should know I was not sleeping with Ed. I had no intention of sleeping with him either. But I got caught up in the melodrama of the thing and insisted Ed and I belt along deserted country lanes in pursuit of Mick. Hours later we tramped across the windy fairways of the Old Course to catch the golfers up and explain my innocence (if it could be called that) to Mick.

There was also an unfortunate banker who pretty well rumbled that I was inventing a French lover. He questioned me remorselessly and would then tell me that there was no Guy Armitage working for Crédit Agricole, that the street I'd said he lived in did not exist. He concluded, like so many others, that I had a darker secret to hide and Guy was probably Gayle.

And then one evening in the summer of 1973 I got talking to Jake, a customer in the bar at Leith's. Jake was confident, self-made, good-looking, my age and obviously attracted to me. He made my heart beat faster. When he rang me the next day and suggested dinner, I knew, and also feared, that I would sleep with him.

In a bid to avert the inevitable, I went to see Rayne in his office that afternoon and chatted away about how I'd met this guy and we were going on a date. I thought, perhaps, that if I made it sound like the many, many times I'd been out with other men, it would ensure that the evening ended as innocently as always.

Jake arrived in a chauffeur-driven limo and took me to Tramp. I'd not been to a nightclub in years, and we had a blissful evening. Ever since then, Carly Simon's 'You're so Vain' continues to take me right back there. In contrast to the understated tastes and quiet confidence of Rayne, there was something bold and even flashy about Jake, which, oddly, I found appealing. I spent the night with him in his grand house in Notting Hill Gate. Next morning, we ran away together.

It was crazy. We hardly knew each other. He was trying to extricate himself from his marriage, and I saw him as my escape route from an impossible situation. I told myself I was acting for Rayne's good as well as mine. If he hadn't the courage to leave Nan, at least I had the courage to leave him.

I left Rayne a note, just saying it was over and I was going away with someone else. I asked my secretary to look after my cat, the senior staff of Leith's to look after the business, and Pat to look after Rayne.

Jake and I flew to Austria, where he had some business to do. I was so anxious (or excited?) that I was unable to eat hot brioche for breakfast. We went on to Israel, where Jake bought me a leather jacket and a gold necklace and we went on a trip to Eilat.

Being whisked away on a whim felt like a dream, a Mills and Boon romance. But I thought about Rayne a lot, while at the same time desperately wanting Jake to be the answer. After a week we flew to Cape Town, where we stayed at the best hotel, the Mount Nelson, and went to my Uncle Jack's house in Durbanville for a barbecue party so I could show Jake off. My uncle put our suitcases into separate rooms and I proudly told him, no, we'd bunk up together.

It was a joy being openly with a boyfriend, able to be publicly affectionate, and Jake was good company. But when we were alone, he was occasionally silent and unapproachable, presumably thinking of Elspeth, the wife he'd left. Most of the time, though, he was satisfyingly passionate.

We flew on to the seaside resort of Plettenberg Bay and stayed at the Beacon Island hotel, built on the rocks over crashing seas. It was there that I first began to come to my senses. I missed Rayne dreadfully and was increasingly worried about him.

I rang Pat in England to find out about Rayne, to be told that he had left Nan and was living in a hotel room on the Bayswater Road.

I simply could not understand it. All those years of fidelity (of a sort) to Nan, and now, when there was no need, he'd abandoned her. My emotions veered from anger – why could he not have left her before? – to anguish at the depth of unhappiness that must have led him to leave her now.

Poor Jake. I was now the pre-occupied and silent one, thinking all the time of Rayne. And Jake, affected I guess by my anxiety, became ever more moody and morose. In three weeks the zing had gone out of the relationship.

Of course I thought of abandoning Jake and flying straight back to London in the hope of rescuing my relationship with Rayne, but I didn't know if he would have me back. And if he did, could I face both families? And what about children? Presumably his stance would not have changed – he'd done plenty of parenting, and that was enough for him. Besides, he'd said many times there were too many children in the world.

So I said nothing and we continued on our trip, flying next to Johannesburg. I was keen to show Jake off to my mother, to give her the comfort of seeing that at last I had a man in my life. Things were only intermittently good with Jake but I was trying to pretend I was ecstatically happy.

Peggy was not bowled over by Jake, especially when he recognised a Lalique vase, admired it, turned it over and said, 'No maker's mark. Pity. Might be a fake. It would be worth a lot more if it was signed.'

More seriously, she was troubled that since he had only just left his wife, he was probably not ready for serious commitment and she didn't want me dragged into his divorce.

Peggy was full of the terrible news of Rayne leaving Nan. He had written a letter full of sadness, telling her of his departure and asking her to write to Nan, that she was in a bad way, in need of her friendship. She handed me the letter and as I read it I bit my lip to stop myself groaning or wailing. He said nothing of his now defunct, long relationship with me.

She questioned me as to whether I had seen any cracks in his and Nan's marriage. 'Is there another woman, do you think?' I shook my head, not trusting myself to speak. Then made an effort and said I didn't know, but no, I didn't think so.

'Poor darling Nan,' she said. 'She said before she married him that if he gave her five years it would be worth it. But it's harder to be left after twenty-five than five.'

Jake and I flew back to England via Israel. One night, in the middle of dinner in the Tel Aviv Hilton, the waiter told me there was an urgent phone call for me. I took it in the bar. It was Rayne. He was more emotional than I had ever known him, desperate, close to tears. He said all the things I'd longed for him to say for twelve years: that he could not live without me, that he wanted us get married. That I should come home and we would have a baby.

I said, no, it was too late, I was with Jake now. He should return to Nan. Soon I was in tears too.

I went to the Ladies, mopped myself up and walked round the lobby for a minute or two. Then went back to the restaurant, sat down, smiled.

'It was Rayne,' I said. 'It's okay.'

Jake said nothing, but dropped his pudding spoon and fork on top of his pudding, threw down his napkin and pushed his chair back with sudden violence. I followed him from the room. That night we made love with a new desperation.

On arrival back in London I went to see Rayne in his office. I'd thought of little but him since our phone call and I longed to see him. But I told myself that I was in love with Jake now, that I didn't want to go back to Rayne. True, he dominated my thoughts, but after such a long time together wasn't that natural? It did not mean I wanted to spend my life with him.

So why did I take such pains to look my best? I'd lost a lot of weight, collected a suntan and was better dressed than was my wont, wearing the tan leather jacket that Jake had given me, the gold necklace and a silk shirt.

My heart was banging in my chest like a schoolgirl's. Rayne was composed. He said he loved me for good, would wait in the hopes that the Jake thing would run its course. And then he would bear whatever he had to bear.

I was secretly relieved when he said he could not go back to Nan, at least not yet. I suppose I just wanted to keep my options open. I knew if he returned to Nan he would not leave her again. He had left, he said, because my going had made him realise that I had been the counterpoint that balanced his life and made it possible to stay in a marriage that had long ago lost any spark. If I married Jake then he would know it was over, and then, yes, if Nan still wanted him, going back and trying to make her happy was the least he could do.

In the event my affair with Jake lasted perhaps another six weeks. His wife was still in their country house and she wanted him back. He went to see her sometimes but mostly he stayed in

London and we went about together. We had a party at his Notting Hill house for some of his and my friends. But my heart was not really in it, and neither was his. He missed his wife, I missed Rayne, and neither of us admitted that we'd made a mistake.

In the end he dumped me and went back to Elspeth. Considering that I thought more about Rayne than about Jake, it was surprising how hurtful it was, more, I suspect, to my pride than my heart. I'd never been dumped before. But deep down, I knew he was right.

I continued to see Rayne about the business and tried to think of him now as my chairman and friend. I kept telling myself that having made the break, I should not go back, that he should return to Nan, that we would all get over it eventually. He'd said on the telephone to Tel Aviv that he wanted to have a baby, but I was sure that wasn't true. Least said, soonest mended, I kept saying to myself.

But I couldn't keep it up. How could I pretend, just because I had made a desperate and abortive attempt to get away from him, that Rayne was not the great love of my life?

One evening I went to him in his hotel room. And that was that. It felt so right, like coming home.

CHAPTER 9

IT'S A BOY

Daniel

Rayne and I resumed our clandestine relationship, but now at least we were contemplating a baby. Rayne was true to his word, he *had* changed his mind about a baby. He'd have preferred not to add to the world's population and would have chosen adoption, but he could see how desperate I was to have my own child. We agreed we'd have one home-made, and one ready-made.

We didn't want to come into the open yet. Nan was desperately unhappy and Rayne knew that a confession of his love for me would be unspeakably hurtful so soon after his desertion of her.

Six months after my abortive bid for freedom Rayne agreed to abandon birth control. I think he hoped it would take a year or two for me to get pregnant and that by then Nan would have become more reconciled to life without him. He saw her once or twice a week and spoke to her frequently, but of course she was miserable.

I think Jilly Parker, Sir Peter Parker's wife, and friend to all of us, must have realised I was in the picture because, one day early in 1974, she rang me up.

'I think you must be having a bit of a grim time. Can I help? Do you want an ear to bash?'

Bound by my promise of secrecy, I rejected the offer, protesting that I was fine, had nothing to discuss. But I knew then that one day when Rayne and I could be together openly, she would be a non-judgemental friend. And indeed she became one of my dearest friends until the day she died, in 2010, aged eighty-five.

In March 1974 I suspected I was pregnant. In those days you had to go to a clinic, pee into a bottle and wait a week for the result to come back from the lab. I picked up the plain white envelope and drove home up the Buckingham Palace Road, unable to open the envelope lying on my lap. I knew it held either ineffable joy or deep disappointment. At Hyde Park Corner the traffic slowed to a halt and suddenly I ripped the envelope open and read the paper inside.

Positive.

A rush of pure delight, a hot blush of happiness flooded my face, my heart felt as if it might just stop from too much emotion. A baby. I was going to have a baby.

I did think of Nan. Of the rest of the family; Ange; my mother. They would all be aghast. But my happiness just steam-rollered less selfish emotions. Rayne and I would have a baby. And the terrible secrecy would be at an end.

I was nervous of Rayne's reaction. He hadn't wanted a child of his own. He'd agreed because he knew that the lack of a child might be a continuing and increasing source of unhappiness to me, and it could ruin what we had.

To my surprise he was delighted. I think the realisation that he had actually *made* a baby came as a shock – an exciting shock. And his response to my worries about our respective families was typically calm and wise.

'Darling, they are all good people. Of course they'll be upset, but that's because they all love Nan. And Nan is the most generous woman on earth, and if she can come to terms with it, and she will, you'll see, they will too.'

He was right, but of course it took a while. We decided not to tell anyone about the length of our involvement. Rayne said it would be bad enough for Nan that he had so swiftly taken up with me after leaving her, but worse still to know that he'd been deceiving her for so many years.

So he told Nan that we had suddenly fallen in love, and I was pregnant. Her sons were naturally outraged, and he was particularly distressed by Ange's reaction, though he acknowledged the fairness of it. She said she had thought the world of him, had him on a pedestal, but now realised he had feet of clay.

My mother astonished me. She had, after all, been Nan's friend for thirty years. They had founded and run a theatre company and shared a house together, and she had been deeply angry with Rayne for leaving Nan. But when I told her that I loved him and that I was pregnant and that, in spite of everything, I was happier than I had ever been, she was wonderful. She told me later that she thought I had always adored Rayne because he had filled the gap my father left when he died when I'd been not quite twenty-one.

Nan asked me to come and see her. She gave me lunch on her roof terrace. Heart banging, feeling sick, I followed her up the steep circular staircase, watching her sensible shoes treading carefully on the iron steps and knowing that in a few minutes I would have to admit to loving her husband.

Naturally she wanted to know when we had started our affair and I stuck to the lie Rayne and I had invented. I said it had happened in January, five months ago, at a New Year party given by his friend, Gerry McKnight. And that the baby was a mistake (also not true) but that we both wanted to keep it.

That conversation must have been torture for Nan, but she behaved impeccably. For me, it was the most difficult conversation of my life. Maybe it would have been easier if she'd ranted and raved or cried, but she was calm and generous. Not forgiving – of course not. But if she could not forgive my treachery, she understood my falling in love with Rayne. She had done so herself twenty-five years before, and many a woman had done so since. All through their marriage there had been younger women mooning after him.

The more hurtful aspect for Nan was Rayne loving me, not me loving Rayne, but even that she tried to understand. At the beginning of her marriage, she told me, she had looked ahead and feared that when he was forty and she nearing sixty he would surely meet someone younger, fall in love, and leave their marriage. She'd thought they had successfully navigated the danger zone. He'd seemed happier and more content all through his forties, right up to his leaving her nine months ago at the age of fifty-two – just before her seventieth birthday.

Rayne was indeed wise. How could we possibly have told her that she'd been right about the danger zone, and that the age of thirty-nine was exactly when he'd fallen in love with me?

But, selfishly, I was very happy. The man I loved now lived with me, I was to have his baby, and we were to get married. We went to Florence for a long weekend to celebrate, staying at the then charmingly dilapidated Villa San Michele above Florence. It was a magical time, the first holiday where we could be openly together.

On the Ponte Vecchio, heaving with tourists, Rayne bought me an antique ring, a single large diamond in a complicated setting, the gold soft and pale with wear. The charming old rogue who sold it to us told us a fairy story about the ring being passed down the female line of a noble old family for generations until the present countess, whose husband had abandoned her and left her penniless, had been forced to sell it. Rayne paid £500 for it, and we were surprised when we later had it valued, that that was exactly what it was worth. And that the stone was indeed a diamond, albeit a badly flawed one. I wear it still.

We lay in the big bed with old, soft linen sheets at the Villa San Michele and talked about the baby. If it was a girl, we decided we'd call her Jane, but we couldn't agree on a boy's name. On Easter Day we planned to go down to the Piazza del Duomo to see the fiesta, but we couldn't get a taxi and we had no car. Finally, a waiter who had the day off and was himself going to the square, offered us a lift. We had no Italian and he no English so conversation was rather limited, but I did manage to ask him his name.

'Daniele,' he replied.

Rayne and I looked at each other and simultaneously cried, 'Daniele. Daniel. That's it.'

So Daniel is named for a Tuscan waiter.

That day was significant for another reason. It was the first time I felt my son move inside me.

The activities in the square seemed to me quite as much pagan as they were Christian. We sat on stands erected to the side and front of the Duomo and below us a troupe danced and waved multi-coloured ribbons and flags. They were followed by marching and music and a general air of fiesta. Finally, a procession of clerics led by, I think, a bishop (he had a crook and a tall hat), processed round the square and up to the great Duomo door, which was closed. Three times he banged on the door, and on the third time it opened. At which point an electrified dove hurtled out of the open door along a hawser stretched tight across the square and ending in a construction like a massive unlit bonfire. When the dove – or bundle of dynamite wrapped in feathers, who knows? – plunged into this, all hell broke loose. Fire crackers and rockets went off like gunfire and the square was filled with cheering Italians, smoke and noise.

I was terrified. As was my unborn infant. Up till then the baby had not given me so much as a nudge, never mind a kick. He made up for it now. It felt like somersaults and cartwheels in there.

For the first time I felt real love for the baby and a desperate desire to protect him. I tried to cover my belly to shield him from the noise. Daniel, Daniel, I said, it's all right.

'Maybe it's Jane,' said Rayne, amused at my distress.

After years of eating catering leftovers, pots of yogurt, cans of beans or even, shamingly, Birds Eye Roast Dinners for One, cooking domestic suppers for two was a huge new pleasure, though

I found it difficult to scale down quantities. To this day I cannot make stew for two.

Of course there was still unease in the family about our betrayal of Nan, and she must have still felt very wretched, but work, Rayne, the coming baby and looking for a larger flat filled my life.

I had written to Ange, trying to explain, and failing. She'd not replied. But when, a few months later, I was in danger of losing the baby, she came round and we had supper. And by then her brothers were speaking to Rayne.

That both families remained friends was due to the determination of Nan as well as Rayne. Nan told her children that they must try to behave well to us, because the families had been friends for ever and a feud would be unbearable. And Rayne did not show me the letters Nan wrote him, or let me even open the two letters she wrote me, or allow me to write to her. All explanations and recriminations would only add fuel to the fire, he said, and there were not so many people he loved in the world that he could afford to lose any.

I was able to accept his being so controlling, frustrating what was essentially something between Nan and me. I knew what Nan must have said in those letters, and she would have been right. But I didn't want reminding of my sins. The coward in me was happy to let Rayne manage relations with his family.

In the summer, when I was very visibly pregnant,

we went, at Nan's insistence, to her seventieth birthday celebration. I think she wanted us there to show the world that she accepted the situation and to get it over all at once: the entire Kruger family was there, plus all Nan and Rayne's friends. It must have been incredibly hard for her. But she was as strong as she was generous.

Rayne found a flat in a new-build development, which we bought off-plan. The Colonnades is a hideous yellow-brick block near the railway line but the flat, on the sixth floor at the top of the building, looked south over the rooftops of Queensway and north onto Porchester Square. There were three bedrooms, a living room, a study and a big sunny terrace. Completion was scheduled for well before the baby was born.

I loved being pregnant. Other than a few weeks of slight nausea on waking, when Rayne would bring me tea and a biscuit in bed, I was wonderfully well and continued working hard in the business. I added the task of furnishing and decorating our first real home together with gusto. The Colonnades was still a building site without a working lift, so right up till the day I went off to hospital to have Daniel, I was cheerfully puffing, panting and heaving to get smallish items – lamps, kitchen gear, bedding, pictures – up six floors to the flat. I was also lugging a very big belly with me. 'Eating for two', even then, was frowned on but somehow greed and hunger prevailed.

A few days before giving birth was probably not

a good moment to stand in for the head chef at Leith's. Although I sometimes cooked in the restaurant during the day, preparing puddings or first courses for the evening trolleys, I hadn't done an evening service since the Princess Margaret episode, and that had hardly gone smoothly.

This time I managed to stab a fellow chef. I slipped, and went over like Humpty Dumpty. As I fell, my hand jerked up and I felt the short sharp knife I was holding penetrate flesh. I looked up to see Ahmed, a junior chef, clutching his genitals while a blood stain bloomed in the front of his checked chef's pants.

I stared in horror, thinking I'd unmanned him.

It was appalling at the time but it was farce too. Ahmed refused to take his trousers down in front of a woman, and I was stranded like a hippo, unable to get up unaided. The manager decided that the victim should be given a brandy. The wine waiter, better trained, protested that would make Ahmed bleed more. While they were shouting at each other, Ahmed managed to quiet them by saying he, a good Muslim, didn't drink.

Eventually I was hauled to my feet and went to throw up in the Ladies. Stabbing someone is not nice for the stabbee, but it's not great for the stabber either. While I was out of the room Ahmed deigned to reveal his wound, which, to his and everyone else's relief, was in the upper thigh.

By the time the ambulance arrived we had a restaurant full of very cross customers who wanted to be fed. The manager had told them that 'Chef has cut her finger,' an excuse bound to enrage them further.

Unsurprisingly, Ahmed elected for compensation. He said it was the easiest money he had ever earned and came to thank me personally.

That was my last attempt to run the service as head chef.

It was Nan who pushed for a speedy divorce: 'I'm not going to be responsible for your baby being born out of wedlock,' she said.

It was a close-run thing. We were married on Monday, 21st October 1974, and Daniel was born on Wednesday, 23rd. The day between was our honeymoon, spent at the Ritz in Piccadilly.

The wedding was memorable, but not for the right reasons. I was wearing a full-length lime green dress made by Thea Porter, the only smartish dress I owned that I could get into. It was as far away as one could get from a wedding gown. Apart from the colour, it had a pinafore top and a huge tent-like skirt. It needed to be – I had put on sixty pounds of which only six pounds, four ounces was the baby. In an effort to distract attention from what could never be called a bump – it was a mountain – I had my thick hair permed into a corkscrew Afro.

The lift was out of order at the Harrow Road Registry Office and the four of us (Rayne and me, my mother and stepfather) had to walk up several floors. As I heaved my great bulk onto the top landing, we were met by the registrar.

'Don't worry,' she said, 'I'm a midwife too.'

My stepfather, Robert, was in charge of my little Kodak cine-camera. He'd gone ahead to film our arrival, so he recorded this exchange, the marriage, the precarious descent to the street, and then tea for four in a suite at the Ritz. That was it. Three minutes of film, which we sent off to Kodak for developing.

When, weeks later, we got it back, it was the wrong film. We got some old codger's day out in Skegness, with shots of the backs of pensioners getting onto a coach, of rainy streets through the bus window, of the road sign 'Welcome to Skegness', of seagulls whirling through grey skies, and then more rear views of the day-trippers climbing back into the bus. I hope the old boy thought a film of a gargantuan green bride with a ludicrous hair-do worth losing his gloomy little masterpiece for.

Daniel's birth was not without drama. Rayne had managed to duck all invitations to join me in ante-natal classes and, though he didn't say so, I knew he was not looking forward to being in at the birth. His one and only concession had been to come to a National Childbirth Trust evening where we were to be shown a movie of the birth of a baby.

The proceedings were charming and amateurish, with young couples sitting together on the floor on beanbags. Since I had puffed and panted through breathing exercises with my fellow prospective mums and shared the excitement and fear of imminent childbirth with them, I confidently strode towards a space in the middle. Rayne did not follow. I looked round to find him sitting on the only chair in the room, at the back. I was about to fight my way back to him when the lights went down and the class tutor began her talk. So I stayed where I was.

The film was pretentious and preachy with an embarrassing voice-over declaring 'Born the brow, born the nose, born the chin' as the baby's head, emerged. But it was informative and I was glued to it until I was suddenly distracted by a familiar sound from the back of the room. My future husband was asleep and snoring.

Given his lack of pre-natal training it was no surprise to find Rayne more distressed than I was at birth pangs. He was plainly in a bad way, not helped by the fact that his secretary, the wonderful Miss Joshua, chose this moment to resign. She adored Rayne; indeed, I think she'd been in love with him since she'd joined him twenty years before. Rayne, overwrought and anxious about me, gave her a roasting over the telephone for telling Nan that the baby was on the way. He was a great believer in never giving more information than strictly necessary, and I guess he wanted to tell Nan himself.

So, between contractions, there was I trying to

broker peace and reconciliation when Miss Joshua arrived at the hospital in person, resignation letter in hand, tears distorting her dear old face.

While Rayne was out in the corridor patching up his office relations, things were getting serious in the labour ward. My baby was showing signs of distress and the doctor on duty was called. He had a look.

'Nurse, how long has she been in labour?'

'Twelve hours, I think.'

'Has her consultant been in?'

'Not yet, Doctor.'

He turned to me. 'Mrs Kruger, I think we need to help your baby out. You are hardly dilated at all. Frankly, you should not have been induced. You are not ready to give birth.'

I knew it. I had not *felt* ready, I thought I still had a fortnight to go, but my consultant, a private (and expensive) gynaecologist known to his patients as *divine de Vries* was more interested in selling me pheasants from his shoot for my restaurant than in my baby, and was no more enthusiastic about natural childbirth than Rayne was. He'd never examined me in the whole nine months – he would do so at six months he said, when the baby was safe from interference, but by then he was on holiday and his locum thought he'd leave it for the great man on his return. It never happened. He'd been keen on induction from the start, and had blinded me with guff about how much safer it was for elderly first-time mothers (I was thirty-four) to have an induction followed by an epidural, and if that didn't work, then a Caesarian.

Later, a nurse in the private wing of the Westminster Hospital said, 'Oh, Mr de Vries's mums all have their inductions on Wednesdays. We think he plays golf on Thursdays.'

So here I was, husband freaking out, contractions every few minutes, baby being squeezed at one end and unable to get through the gate at the other. A Caesarean sounded like a very good idea to me.

When I came round I couldn't see Rayne. Anxious that he might have been creating all hell, I asked the nurse whether he was all right.

'He's lovely,' she said. 'Ten fingers, ten toes, he's perfect.'

He was. My first sight of Daniel was in Rayne's arms, or rather in not much more than the palm of his hand. He had the hairy back of the premature infant, pitch black hair (later to become blond curls and later still a rather ordinary brown), blue eyes, and the unsquashed face of a baby that has been lifted out by Caesarean section. We both fell instantly and permanently in love with him.

Wednesday's child was not full of woe, but he *was* full of sleep. I remember the Irish nurse holding him out of the window of the Westminster Hospital so the cold air would wake him up to feed.

'There you are, young fella,' she said, 'have a good look now. Over there is the Palace of

Westminster where all those politicos make up our stupid laws.' Maybe that's why Daniel went into politics.

Wates, the developers, had repeatedly sworn the Colonnades building would be ready by the time Daniel was due. Of course it wasn't, but at least we were able to move in. My mother fetched me and my infant son from hospital and drove us straight there. And we promptly got trapped in the lift, stuck between floors.

We could hear the builders' radio blaring, but with all the banging and drilling going on there was no attracting their attention by hitting the doors. And the emergency telephones were not yet installed.

I was unworried. The babe had his milk supply safely stored in me, and I sat on the floor and contentedly awaited rescue. But when my mother started screaming hysterically, 'Help, help, there's a new-born babe in here,' I remembered that she was claustrophobic. I lumbered to my feet and smacked her smartly on the cheek.

She turned to me, perfectly calm. 'What did you do that for? I'm just trying to get some attention round here. I do a very good line in hysterics. I'm not an actress for nothing.' Sure enough, builders appeared with crowbars and apologies.

That flat was never homely but it could not have been more convenient. I could walk to the restaurant in ten minutes, there was a car park under the building and porters at the entrance.

I awarded myself unlimited maternity leave and settled down to be a Mum. Daniel was sleepy and content for the first few weeks and then became fractious, twisting about and crying. The district nurse put it down to pain from a slow-to-heal belly button, but when I noticed what I took to be pus coming from his navel, I called the doctor. In fact it was curdled milk. It was coming directly from his intestine, via a tube through which the placenta feeds the foetus, and which should have disappeared in the last stages of pregnancy.

The next morning we were in the hospital awaiting surgery to remove the tube. Daniel was less than four weeks old and the thought of a general anaesthetic and a long operation was terrifying. His operation was scheduled for four p.m. and I was not allowed to feed him all day. It was agony. If I held him he would twist his little head, rooting for my breast. All we could give him was a dummy, on which he would give a few desperate sucks, and then resume his crying.

Rayne sat opposite me, his face drawn and grey. I think it was a relief when we realised we were due to meet a prospective nanny at our flat at two o'clock. We'd forgotten, and not brought her telephone number with us, so Rayne decided to go and meet her anyway. It meant I could stop worrying about Rayne, and he could get away from crying Daniel for a little while.

I won't ever forget the bleak feeling of loss when a nurse carried Daniel away to the operating theatre. Now exhausted from screaming and hunger he was keening rather than crying. A vision of a silent dead baby being returned to us would not leave me.

It was the surgeon, smiling broadly, who carried him back. He handed him to Rayne. I had to sit down, my legs too weak to support me.

Meanwhile, Rayne had hired the Nanny from Hell. Karen, poor girl, had recently given birth to a baby of her own, an illegitimate child by an unknown father. She'd had an emergency Caesarean, and the baby had died. Her own background was one of foster parents, care homes and institutions in Australia, and she was looking for a baby to replace hers. Rayne, not exactly rational at the time, felt sorry for her and thought she might be perfect.

That Christmas we went to Morocco, to the Gazelle d'Or, a fancy hotel among the orange groves in the Atlas mountains. We took Karen with us. Disaster. She had absolutely no sensitivity at all, and to the horror of the other guests she would festoon the bushes outside our chalet with drying nappies. The dignified Berber porters would look askance as she walked about the grounds in her bikini. She was desperate for attention, and probably for love. The hotel manager complained that she was spending her afternoons off in the bedrooms of his waiters. But far worse in my eyes, she was a terrible nanny.

One morning I watched Karen put Daniel's

bassinet on the edge of a coffee table. This was obviously precarious and I made a dash to grab it. Too late. Daniel fell head first onto the paving slabs. Happily the bassinet protected him and he was fine, but it gave me the excuse to do what I'd been longing to do since we arrived: send the girl home.

CHAPTER 10

BUT CAN YOU BOIL AN EGG?

Leith's School of Food and Wine

Once, in 1973 I think, I'd watched Caroline Burrows (later Caroline Waldegrave), head chef at Leith's Good Food, with her arm round a weeping cook. 'Don't cry,' she said, 'the first day in a new job is always horrible, but you're doing fine.'

And then she took the girl's knife out of her hand and demonstrated the Leith's way of cutting carrots (batons, not rings). Caroline was as firm about maintaining standards as she was encouraging. What a great teacher she is, I thought.

As we employed more young people, the need to train them to do things our way and give up the habits learned at college, began to grate. I complained to Rayne. 'If we had our own cookery school the cooks could pay us while they learned, and then we could hire them. At the moment we pay them while we teach them.'

My husband thought a chef school one of my better ideas, but by then Caroline had left Leith's and was travelling round the States. I telexed her, asking whether, if I opened a school, she would come home and run it. Yes, she said.

Rayne enlisted the help of his old friend Gerry McKnight, who was a whiz at finding a bargain. Gerry equipped the space we rented – the old Byam Shaw painting school in Notting Hill Gate – on a shoe string. Almost everything was acquired at trade auctions or second hand. We bought twenty second-hand cookers from Stirling Moss, the former racing driver, who was upgrading the flats he let. And we got a huge box sign which came out of a launderette and put it over our entrance alley off the main road. LEITH'S SCHOOL OF FOOD AND WINE it shouted in yellow neon.

The school opened in 1975 with only thirty students, mostly the overflow from the successful Cordon Bleu school. But we wanted to be different. The Cordon Bleu was considered more a finishing school than a chef school. Their students were all girls, mostly there to acquire a domestic skill, or aiming to be chalet girls, or perhaps set up their own little catering business as I had done. Few went into the restaurant trade.

On the other hand, Caroline and I didn't want to ape the state colleges either. We both liked the simplicity and honesty of Cordon Bleu food. We didn't want to teach students how to make sculptures out of butter or blown sugar, or how to carve vegetables into flowers and fold napkins into swans.

We wanted to encourage students to love good food, to be offended if they were served bad food and furious with themselves if they produced it. And to know something of the history of cooking and appreciate not only European cuisine, but also that of India, Mexico, Thailand, China, the Middle East. We wanted top chefs from the industry to lecture and demonstrate at the school. In brief, we wanted to light a fire in our students that would burn all their lives, giving them a passion and a profession, or at least a skill and a lifetime of pleasure.

Apart from the long professional courses we ran, we embarked on short courses for gap-year students, evening classes for amateurs, wine courses, restaurant management lectures, team-building evenings for corporate clients, and much more.

There were, of course, a few problems. Caroline, grandly titled principal, was only twenty-three and not a qualified teacher. Nor was I, and neither of us had ever run a school. If a potential student was coming for an interview with her mother in tow, I would do the interview. At least I was thirty-five and had some history of business behind me to persuade the mum to part with the annual fee: five thousand pounds. (Today the price is almost twenty thousand.)

To attract male students, we advertised all-male evening classes: *The way to a woman's heart is through her taste buds. But can you boil an egg? Don't worry. In three hours you'll have mastered Coq au Vin.*

A guy rang up. 'Are you sure it's okay if I can't boil an egg?'

You'll be fine, I told him.

Confronted with the first instruction on his recipe, 'Separate the eggs,' he put one egg on the left of the board and the other on the right. He wasn't joking, either.

We ran the businesses – restaurant, school and catering company – separately, but sometimes they had to help each other out. The most stressful near-disaster was when the school had just opened and the catering company had got the contract for the Tate Gallery Candlelit Dinner. This was given annually for the grandees, sponsors and potential donors of the art world, the throng salted with celebrated living artists.

The Tate on Millbank had a great reputation for food, boasting the only decent restaurant in a museum, but it was too small to cope with a big banquet. Every outside caterer in town wanted the contract, and we were cock-a-hoop at landing it.

On the night of the dinner, I arrived at six o'clock. As I walked through the galleries, alive with barmen opening champagne and polishing glasses, florists arranging elaborate white and gold floral explosions on plinths, waiters setting chandeliers and gold-edged glasses on tables, my nose detected something horribly familiar. At first the smell was barely there – just a suspicion. Was I imagining it? And then as I got nearer the Tate's kitchen a whiff became a hefty waft, an unmistakable stink. Please God, I thought, let this not be what I think it is.

But it was. By the time I entered the kitchen I had no doubt. I went straight to the two enormous copper saucepans sitting on the hired stock-pot rings. The mussel velouté, made with fresh mussels, fish stock, white wine and cream was gently fermenting. Tiny pockets of air were bubbling on the surface on both pans.

I grabbed the chef's sleeve. 'The soup's off,' I hissed. 'It stinks to high heaven.'

'No. It's fine. I made it this morning.'

'I know you did. But I bet you let it cool in those great pans, and gave it plenty of time to . . .'

'It's fine,' he insisted. 'It's just the wine. Gives it a slight pong, I agree, but I've tasted it . . .'

'It's *bubbling*, Chef. It's off.'

'It's bubbling because it's heating.'

I put my hand on the side of the nearest pan. Stone cold. I took a deep breath and decided sacking the guy just before the dinner was not a good idea. I lowered my voice and said, 'Look, Chef, you get on with the rest of the dinner. I will look after the soup. Get four of your guys to carry the pans out to the van. I'll come back with more soup. Somehow.'

This was before mobile phones, and I couldn't summon help as I drove. But I did formulate a plan. No point going back to our catering business in the City – it was rush hour and the cooks would have left. No good going to the restaurant: it was fully booked and the chefs would be too busy and have no room on tables or stove. But I could go to the new school, which had no evening classes on a Friday. I'd somehow make seventy pints of soup in forty minutes and get back to the Tate by 7.45.

As soon as I got there I rang Caroline. 'Cal. I've got a crisis. Can you come to the school? And bring any of the teachers you can get hold of. And can you ask them to stop and buy anything white they can get: soup in cans, cream cheese, cream, anything at all.'

I rang the restaurant, half a mile away and asked them to send over in a taxi as much white stock, white sauce, cheese sauce and cream as they could spare. I went to Panzer's, the little deli next door, and bought them out of cream of artichoke soup, mussel soup, Vichyssoise, cream of onion soup and cream cheese.

Caroline arrived with two of her teachers. Between us we managed to lift the huge saucepans out of the van. Trying not to breathe, we poured the fermenting soup down the outside drains in the alley and scrubbed the pans out.

The school was well equipped but, as the students generally cooked for two, all the kit was tiny. Blenders whizzed a litre at most, and there was no getting our great catering saucepans onto the domestic cookers, or even onto the workbenches. We left them on the floor.

We put everything we had, half into one saucepan and half into the other. We didn't cook a thing, just strained the lumps out of the soups and whisked absolutely everything together.

About half way into the task we started to laugh. We knew we'd produce a soup of sorts, and in time, and our mix tasted surprisingly good. There is something exhilarating about a crisis, at least when you know it's going to be averted. I suppose it's the adrenalin. I don't manufacture crises (though I know some chefs who do), but I do rather enjoy a drama, especially if I am to emerge the heroine who pulled the fat from the fire.

I can't say our soup tasted of mussels. I tasted it often and I couldn't judge it at all. But it was silky smooth, savoury and very creamy. We raided the school larder for fresh tarragon, chives and parsley and chopped them up, put them in a plastic tub and loaded the soup, swathed in polythene wrap to inhibit spillage, into the van.

Leaving poor Caroline to clear up, I drove back to the Tate, getting there just before eight p.m. But dinner was not until eight-fifteen and there was a dinky little salad course to start. So we had half an hour to heat the soup. Then it was scooped into the silver soup tureens, a handful of chopped herbs on top, and the waiters sailed into the galleries, heads held high.

I had a letter from the Tate organiser congratulating us on a superb dinner and singling out the soup as 'unctuous and delicious'!

As for the chef, it was his swansong. Letting something go bad through not cooling it fast enough is one thing; we've all done that. But knowingly serving fermenting soup is quite another.

Leith's School was a triumph. In our second year we doubled our intake to the maximum of sixty-four students, and within five years we had moved into our own, much larger, building, an old primary school in St Alban's Grove behind Kensington High Street, which allowed us to increase the roll to ninety-six students. It had great wide stairs, high ceilings and huge windows. The ground floor had a late Victorian elegance but the top floor had been destroyed in the war and replaced with an ugly penthouse. So we rebuilt it as we thought it might have been, with a pretty gabled front in red brick. Up there the staff ate lunch together, family style, every day.

We commissioned the artist David Kindersley to carve the school logo of a plate of grapes flanked by knife and fork into the brick façade. When we'd almost finished the building, we discovered a roll of drawings in the basement, including one of the original nineteenth-century elaborate façade with gothic pointy roofs and much stone carving. I'm very glad we found it so late: we might have been tempted to restore it accurately, which would have cost a serious packet.

The school was the business that gave Rayne and me the fewest headaches – almost none, in fact. Education is generally a stable business – even in bad times people educate their children, and in a recession refugees from the City or business train for a hands-on cooking career. But the success of the school was mostly down to Caroline. She liked to run a happy ship, and she was a brilliant manager with a gift for figures and a reluctance to waste money. We needed no marketing or advertising because the students did it for us by word of mouth. We were paid for courses up front, which meant no cash-flow problems. The teachers (nearly always women) loved what they did and worked their socks off.

A highly successful sideline in publishing developed organically. I had written several cookbooks before, but after Leith's School opened Caroline and I collaborated on the beginner's, intermediate and advanced Leith's cookbooks, which were published by Fontana in 1979. They were followed by a composite large book, suitable for all levels of student, and one which we hoped would become for the next generation what *The Constance Spry Cookery Book* had been to ours – a big reliable tome in which you would find almost anything, and which mums would give to their daughters and sons when they went off to uni, got married, bought a new house, got divorced . . . The book,

Leith's Cookery Bible, first published in 1991, went on to sell a gratifying 350,000 copies.

Leith's went on to produce a *Fish Bible*, *Cake Bible*, *Vegetarian Bible*, *Techniques Bible*, etc. I occasionally 'co-authored' Leith's books, but I cannot claim to have done my fair share. I would write an introduction or chapter texts, but seldom the recipes, which were written by the teachers and repeatedly tested by the students. I believe that's one of the reasons the books have been so successful.

It's also a great way for ambitious teachers to get published. Getting a cookbook accepted if you are not famous – a telly cook, or at least the writer of a reasonably well-known regular cookery column – is almost impossible. But the Leith's name helped, and several successful cookery writers first got their names on a dust jacket under the Leith's banner.

In 1976 I was hired by John Junor, editor of the *Sunday Express* and my brother's father-in-law, to write the paper's cookery column. I've no idea why he chose me, but I suspected he enjoyed the idea of having his son-in-law's sister in his power. Certainly he detested the food I liked. He objected to garlic, onions, peppers, chilli, any herbs other than parsley, or indeed anything with any flavour as far as I could gather. He also wanted me to write in a more excited and overheated style, with lots of Oohs and Aahs, and Yum-Yums, which I could not do. He was a famously good editor and a famously difficult man, who did not easily brook opposition or even countenance debate. He was, however, the only newspaper editor I ever had who read the food pages, and he read my column to the last word, usually on Sunday mornings when he would ring me up to berate me for the garlic. But the exposure (the *Sunday Express* had a readership of three and a half million) was good for me and good for the cookery school.

We had a few students who didn't make the grade; they were anorexic or bulimic, on drugs or depressed. One day I heard Caroline being polite but unyielding with some titled captain of industry whose daughter was snorting cocaine and barely able to function. He must, she said, come to the school at once. 'No, she needs help *now*. Medical help. Psychiatric help. Support from you. No, you cannot leave it until the weekend. She needs you today, now.' He obeyed.

I remember only one horrible incident, and it was entirely my fault. My involvement with the day-to-day running of the school was limited to the occasional cookery demonstration or lecture, and the once-a-term exams where Caroline and I would taste our way through the separate starters, main courses, puddings and breads of ninety-six young cooks, marking each one on appearance, flavour, texture and skill.

But what I really liked to do, and had less and less time for, was to work with the students in the teaching kitchens. I find teaching more pleasurable and less stressful than demonstrating, which is more of a performance: trying to make sure the students understand what you are telling them without boring them to sleep.

One day, after a stimulating morning in the kitchen with a bunch of keen advanced students, I was having lunch with the staff and extolling the virtues of teaching as opposed to my usual office-bound life.

I then made a remark of exquisite crassness. 'The lovely thing about teaching here,' I said, 'is that it's so *mindless*.'

No one said anything, but the conversation stopped abruptly and two teachers simply got up and walked out.

Of course I had in no way meant to denigrate what they did. Food teaching requires ever-updated knowledge, careful preparation, organisation, skill, tact, personality, physical stamina, patience, and brains. It was too late to explain that that morning someone else had done the thinking, planning, preparation and organisation for my class, and all I had to do was turn up and cook things I knew backwards with a bunch of delightful students, and that I'd found it wonderful – both stimulating and relaxing.

I wrote the teachers a grovelling letter of apology, but I still remember the incident with a shudder. A searing lesson in thoughtless behaviour.

That sort of unthinking lack of tact is, alas, one of my besetting sins. Once, at a staff party attended by the combined employees of restaurant, catering company and school, I made a speech about how the backbone of our business was our food; how we were nothing without our reputation for good food, how everyone had to understand and care about food. I managed to imply that the cooks were more important than the secretaries, book-keepers, office staff, drivers, cleaners, wine waiters, directors, etc. In fact I upset a good half of Leith's, including my husband and partner.

London's top chefs were like bees round a honey-pot after graduation at Leith's School, snapping up the best students. So much so that my original idea of picking off the best for my own company's businesses proved harder than I'd thought. We had to compete for them.

One well-known chef was utterly unimpressed by Leith's School. Silvino Trompetto, the famous head chef at the Savoy, said no woman would ever work in his kitchens. He would not even have a female in the pastry department, where women had, in most hotels, begun to make headway. Nonetheless, I tried to persuade him to give a Leith's female graduate a try, a two-week trial. Absolutely not, he said.

I asked him why, expecting the usual nonsense about girls taking the men's minds off the job, or not being able to lift a full stock-pot. I was ready with my reply that if men managed to work with women in reception, why not the kitchen? And no-one, male or female, could lift a full stock-pot by themselves. But his answer almost left me speechless: 'Because, dear lady, at a certain time of the month, women cause the mayonnaise to curdle.'

'You *must* be joking. You can't believe that.'

'No, no, it's true. That is why women are not allowed into the mushroom sheds in France. They stop the spores germinating.'

I did finally get a woman into the Savoy, but not in the manner I'd have liked. Both Trompetto and I were judging a competition for third-year catering students and tasted their food blind. To my delight, and Trompetto's astonishment, the winner was a young woman. After the prize giving, I offered her a job. Trompetto overheard me and joined the conversation. 'Wouldn't you prefer to work for the Savoy?' he asked her.

Well, of course she would.

The most generous of chefs was Richard Shepherd, owner of a clutch of restaurants, notably Langan's. When, every year, he lectured at the school, he would offer the students an evening working in his kitchen so they'd get a taste of what a busy service entails. He didn't charge them (many top chefs charge for the privilege of a stint in their kitchens), and he gave them a complimentary dinner in the dining room on another evening. He said students needed to learn how to eat as well as how to cook.

Leith's School was steadily successful. Caroline ran the ship with her characteristic efficiency, economy, friendliness and high standards. In all its thirty-six years of existence I have yet to meet a student who did not enjoy the experience. Even the ones we failed or expelled would tell me that they wouldn't have missed it.

Quite soon Caroline (and William Waldegrave whom she had married in 1977) were making babies, and Caroline was as dedicated a mum as she was a school principal. She would take a few months off with the birth of each baby, but the school would still run like clockwork, with the senior teachers sharing the load and Caroline doing the books at home. But when baby number four, Harriet, arrived in 1988, we agreed she should hire a new principal to run it day-to-day and retain only her managing director role.

Our first appointment was a disaster. Kevin Woodford, then principal of the catering department at Sheffield University was an inspiring teacher, encouraging, good humoured and tough; and he wanted students to taste the food they cooked and to love the trade. He'd met our teachers and won them round, and I thought a male principal would put paid to any lingering idea that Leith's was a finishing school for dabblers rather than a serious school for chefs.

But the appointment turned out to be a big mistake, both for us and for Kevin. On Day One, with the assembled school waiting to meet him, he failed to turn up. Baffled, we tracked him down and he confessed to having funked it.

So Caroline stepped back into the job, any enthusiasm for male teachers evaporating. It took another twenty-odd years for change to come. Today about half the students and almost half the staff are men.

Kevin went into the restaurant business, became a TV chef of some fame and, I hope, lives happily ever after. Poor chap, I think he must be the only person who thinks of Leith's School with a shudder.

CHAPTER 11

HEAVEN LENDS A HAND

Li-Da

Having Daniel had satisfied some deep need in me to make a baby. Now adoption made more and more sense. I liked the idea of giving a home to a child in need of one and I wanted Rayne to be happy. I was also thirty-five, and after the scare over Daniel's navel I was less inclined to dismiss warnings of abnormalities in babies born of 'elderly' *primigravida* (pregnant for the first time) women – and thirty-five was considered elderly in 1975.

Adopting was, and I expect still is, a lot more difficult than the DIY method. And takes much longer. We were about as far from the ideal adopting couple as you could get. When we started on the quest, we weren't married, but I was pregnant. Rayne was over fifty and divorced. He smoked like a chimney. We both liked a drink. Neither of us believed in any god.

A year later we were no nearer adopting a baby. I wanted to renege on the deal, and take the risk of having another child myself. But I was persuaded by Rayne to at least investigate the possibility of a baby from Thailand first. He had seen how many unwanted babies there were in the country, and was enchanted by the nature of the people.

Not easy. The Thai government was opposed to foreign adoption because it encouraged the buying and selling of children. If we were not to get into the murky world of passing dollars under the counter, we needed a reputable lawyer, a genuine adoption agency, a proper orphanage. The best thing would be to go there and bang on doors ourselves, but Rayne's book about King Ananda was still banned and there was a good chance he'd be arrested if we turned up.

Then heaven lent a hand. We heard about a Cambodian child, Li-Da, sixteen months old, who urgently needed a home. Her story was heartbreaking: her mother had been killed by an American rocket, her father had been a soldier, loyal to the royalist regime which was losing the war. For months, needing to keep up with his paymasters, he'd followed the starving army, fleeing from the Khmer Rouge and carrying Li-Da on his back. By the time they reached Phnom Penh, he was wounded and despairing. He handed his six-month-old baby daughter over to an orphanage. Three days later the city fell.

The baby girl's saviour was an American economist, Meyer Burstein, who taught at the University of East Anglia, but was working for the US government on special assignment in Phnom Penh.

Before the Khmer Rouge overran the capital, all American military and civilian personnel were being pulled out of the country. Meyer and his English wife were childless and had been anxious to adopt a Cambodian baby girl. Without much hope, Meyer left some money with the orphanage with instructions that, if a healthy girl baby turned up, he would arrange her escape and he and his wife would adopt her.

Somehow it worked to plan. In the few days before the Khmer Rouge emptied the offices, the schools, and even orphanages and hospitals, and forced the city folk at gun point to walk hundreds of miles into the countryside to work the fields; before the systematic torture and murder of the teachers, doctors, or anyone who could read or even who wore spectacles, Li-Da, with nothing but the clothes she wore, a single bedraggled soft toy and forged papers, was flown to Bangkok by one of the last American pilots to leave the country. She travelled in a bassinet at his feet.

Meyer met her in Bangkok and took her back to England, to Norfolk, where he and his wife lived. Li-Da was briefly fostered by an English couple while Social Services checked out the Bursteins. And then she was handed over to them. Happy ending.

Except that when Li-Da had been with her new family for only a week, her prospective mother died. Mrs Burstein had had flu-like symptoms on the Friday and was advised by the doctor to take aspirin and not to worry. But it was pneumonia, and by Monday she was dead.

About a year later, my old friend and erstwhile suitor, the American lawyer Ed Gottesman and his girlfriend (my friend and literary agent Pat Kavanagh) were looking for a country house. They went to see a property in Norfolk, on the market because the American owner was returning to the States.

They didn't buy the house, but were intrigued by the seller. Meyer Burstein poured out his story: the loss of his wife; how US immigration would not give Li-Da permission to enter America because she'd not yet been formally adopted so was classed as an alien and as such a possible threat to US jobs; how, in desperation, he'd taken the child to Canada, where she stayed with a hired Scottish nanny in Toronto, while he, working in Chicago, crossed Lake Ontario at weekends to visit her; how this hadn't worked and the baby, now a toddler, was currently living with a Frenchwoman in Paris, a friend of his dead wife's who had intended to adopt her. But since her marriage was going down the tubes and her husband was claiming custody of their three children (and likely to get it in view of his wife's apparent irresponsibility in taking in a new baby when their marriage was so shaky), she was suddenly desperate to be rid of the child.

Ed and Pat knew about our quest for a new-born

Thai baby. They rang us up. Would a Cambodian toddler do instead?

I was immediately caught up in the idea of adopting Li-Da. Who could not want to succour a baby so ill-used by fate? Rayne was more cautious and my mother was violently opposed to any idea of a foreign child. 'It's bad enough for adopted kids anyway without having to cope with a new culture and a family of a different colour,' she said.

Our GP friend Jill Parker also questioned the wisdom of the adoption. 'There's no research into unnatural age-gaps in siblings,' she said. 'But imagine how hard it will be for Daniel. Bad enough to have a new-born sister, but at least she wouldn't be able to climb onto your knee or run to you, or push him out of the way. But a girl six months older than him? It could be damaging. We just don't know.'

Most of our friends could not understand why we didn't just have another natural child and lessen the risks.

In the face of so much negative advice, we went to see a Harley Street psychiatrist. We explained Li-Da's history to the doctor while Daniel crawled happily around, pulling papers out of open drawers and banging things about.

'Will he be damaged, do you think?' I asked.

The doctor looked at the havoc our eleven-month-old was wreaking and said, 'I'd say this little bruiser will be fine, but I would not adopt the girl. The risks are just too big.'

He explained that anyone who had gone through the events and repeated loss that Li-Da had, could not remain un-traumatised. 'She has been trying to learn three successive languages just at the point when language forms. I would not be surprised if she doesn't speak until she's five. She may never speak. Counting the foster mother, she has had four "mothers" and lost them all. She may never be able to love anyone. For sure, something will out. She may be fine at first, but when puberty hits? I would think very carefully before you consider adopting this little girl.'

Despite the warnings, we decided that a home-made teenager might cause us grief too. And anyway, Li-Da needed a home. If she didn't find one at once, she'd be put into a French orphanage and then we'd never get her out. If Rayne was too old to adopt in England, I was too young to adopt in France – babies at that time went to barren women over forty, not fertile younger ones.

I flew to Paris with the infant Daniel to meet Li-Da and see how my son would react to her. I was both excited and fearful. Somehow we'd become committed to a child we had not even met: we'd talked to friends, met her present 'father', seen a psychiatrist, raised expectations all round. Rayne wanted to adopt. What if I didn't warm to her?

We checked into a small hotel in the 16th arron-dissement and set off for Madame le Blanc's apart-ment. It was close to the Bois de Boulogne and infinitely respectable, but dark, stuffy and smelt of furniture polish. I can't swear to the tick-tock of grandfather clocks in the otherwise silent hallways, but in my memory that is how it felt. You would never have guessed children lived in that flat.

It was immediately clear I'd misjudged matters. It was afternoon-nap time, not time for visiting. I left Daniel sleeping in his buggy in the passage, and was led, heart banging, into a gloomy room in which three children lay asleep: two in cots, and Li-Da on the floor. She was on a mattress inside a playpen, and her face was pressed against the bars. Her cheeks were tearstained and greasy, her mouth was open, slightly dribbly, and she snuffled rhythmically.

She looked sweaty and uncomfortable and singularly unappealing. And yet my heart lurched for her. Poor little tot: she'd been put to bed in a centrally heated room in her outdoor coat, hat, boots and gloves, even her walking reins.

And when she woke, and I took her and Daniel for a walk in the park, she completely won me over with the personality and character that have never left her: her interest in everyone and everything, her generosity – even then she'd as soon push a sweet into Daniel's mouth as her own; her childish solemnity, her merriness, her tragic crying as if the world was at an end, with the perfect round of her mouth taking over her face and displaying her tonsils like a cartoon character, her almost hysterical pleasure in everything. And of course her chubby Chinese-doll looks.

But I was determined to be rational, unemotional and grown up about the situation. I took her to a doctor to check her out: he declared that apart from nappy rash and the fact that the circumference of her head was very fractionally smaller than the average European's ('but then maybe that's normal for Asians'), she seemed fine.

Madame le Blanc, Li-Da's would-have-been mother, had some strange ideas. A classy Parisienne, slim as a *Vogue* model, she worked in the Bibliothèque Nationale. She thought children caught cold if their outdoor clothes were removed too soon. She thought the way to potty-train a baby was not to change its nappy, with the result that Li-Da's bum was a sea of rash. She said the only way to get Li-Da to sleep was to leave her to cry, and I am ashamed to say that I didn't challenge her. I so wanted to get my hands on this cheerful, adorable child, and I needed Mme le Blanc's approval, so I didn't dare. She warned me that Li-Da was difficult: she liked to drink her bath water, she ate a lot, and cried at loud noises.

Well, so would you, you air-brained French clothes-hanger, I thought but did not say, if you were thirsty, had been half-starved and your mother was killed by a bomb.

She also declared that Li-Da would never take to us: she hated to hear English spoken, and she had a pathological fear of men.

But when Rayne, summoned by me, arrived the next day, he opened his arms to Li-Da across the sitting room, and, smiling confidently, she toddled across the carpet into them.

That night, when she was put to bed in the playpen she set up a heart-rending wail, raising her arms to be lifted out again.

'Darling, we have to leave her,' I whispered to Rayne, 'She says it's the only way . . .'

By way of answer he picked her up, hugged her briefly as he walked to a daybed, lay her face down on it, and put his large hand in the small of her back to rhythmically rock her. 'Ssshhh, ssshhh, little one,' he said. She went out like a light.

Rayne took Daniel home with him and I stayed on with Li-Da. We needed a visa to get her into England. I was terrified I wouldn't be given one, and I'm ashamed to say I began to consider how to cheat the system. I thought, if possession is nine-tenths of the law, the trick would be to have Li-Da physically living with us when we applied for adoption. Daniel was on my passport, and I thought I would just smuggle Li-Da in as Daniel, but Rayne sensibly vetoed this – apart from the dishonesty it would complicate matters later, since we would need to explain her presence when we applied for adoption.

When my more honest husband had left, however, I had what I thought was a brainwave. I would just say I was acting for Meyer Burstein, and, as his wife was now dead, I was collecting her on his behalf, and taking her to him in England.

But I still needed papers for her. I went to see the British Consul, a man of my age, but sitting behind an intimidatingly large desk. I explained my mission as Burstein's emissary. Under his questions (Why was Burstein taking her to England? Why was I acting as his agent? Was I a nanny? A friend? A relative?) I got more and more muddled and distressed and babbled about the importance of taking Li-Da away before she was put into an orphanage, about her present situation as the unwanted cuckoo in an unhappy nest, about the horrors of her life so far, and finally I burst into tears. Whereupon the consul gave me a large white handkerchief and said, 'How about we start again, Mrs Kruger? Is it not the truth that you want to adopt this baby yourself?'

Before I left his office he had telephoned the Home Office, explained the situation and arranged for Social Services to check out Rayne, the year-old Daniel, our flat, and our suitability as adoptive parents. By the time I got home three days later Li-Da had permission to live with us, she had a guardian *ad litem* (her official carer) and the adoption process had begun. I have forgotten that consul's name, and lost the relevant documents, but I shall be grateful for his kindness and compassion for ever. Li-Da was, and is, a joy.

Of course we were anxious about having taken such a big step, but Li-Da overrode all doubts in her first twenty-four hours with us. To win my mother over, I had planned to give both babies lunch and a sleep and then dress Li-Da, washed, refreshed and fed, in pristine white dress and frilly knicks to greet her grandmama.

Li-Da ate the fish fingers and sausages with speed and concentration. But when, her tummy tight as a drum, both cheeks stuffed like a hamster and unable to swallow a mouthful, I tried to lift her from the high chair, she screamed. I took advantage of the open mouth and hooked out the food. Louder screams. So I put her in the cot with tear-stained greasy cheeks, filthy Babygro, sausage in one hand and fish finger in the other.

Which is how her grandmother, arriving early, first saw her. And fell for her.

But it wasn't just Peggy she had to seduce. It was me. That first night I went into the nursery to have one last look at the two of them tucked up in their side-by-side cots. As I opened the door, I was suddenly aware of an emotion somewhere between panic and horror. The nursery smelled different, not like Daniel, not right. Li-Da had changed everything. For a split second – and it *was* only a second – I wanted Li-Da gone, out of the nest. I started to cry, wailing to my husband that we should never have done it, that it would never work. He just held me and said I was exhausted. Things would look different in the morning.

And, next morning, when I went into their room,

the alien smell had gone. There was just the warm, lovely smell of baby. Babies. *My* babies.

I imagine all adoptive parents who already have children of their own worry whether they will love an adopted child as much as they do their own flesh and blood. But after that first panicky night, I always knew who I'd save first in the sinking boat or burning house. Whoever was nearest.

Li-Da's arrival woke her lazy brother up. Daniel was a year when she arrived, but showing no signs of wanting to talk or walk. He hardly crawled, and when set up on his legs, would curl them up and insist on being carried. But Li-Da, seven months older, could run. He soon rumbled the advantage of this, and stood up and walked.

And they were soon chattering like magpies. For a few brief weeks they spoke that curious gobble-degook language that twins sometimes develop before they learn to talk properly. It's disconcerting to see your babies having a conversation you don't understand. Once, sitting on the carpet, Li-Da pointed at me, said something to Daniel, and then they both laughed so hard that Daniel toppled over backwards.

It wasn't all plain sailing for Li-Da. On arrival she had a few words of French. One night she had a bad dream and started screaming. I ran into the nursery to hear her, still asleep, calling, 'Maman, Maman.' As I picked her up and she woke, her wails changed to 'Mummy, Mummy.'

She was terrified of rat-a-tat noises, I imagine because they sound like gunfire. She was only six months old when she left Cambodia, but I'm sure some memory of war remained. She would not pass a workman with a pneumatic drill. And one day in Kensington Gardens, Princess Margaret's bright red helicopter came in to land at Kensington Palace. I pointed to it, telling the children to look up. Daniel was fascinated, but Li-Da screamed and dived between my legs to cower under my coat.

Babies loosen the tongues of complete strangers. One day our two were playing in the park sandpit while I watched, sandwiched between two other mums on a bench. One said, 'I'm sorry, but I have to say this: I think it is morally wrong to pluck a child from its roots, and force it into a different culture . . .'

I was just about to squash her flat with Li-Da's background of genocide and culture of war when the woman to my left jumped to my defence. 'On the contrary,' she said, 'I think you are just wonderful to adopt a baby from one of those countries – especially when she is so plain and so black.'

CHAPTER 12

COUNTRY WIFE

Home life

Even before Li-Da arrived, we'd begun to think of a house in the country. I still marvel that we were able contemplate this, but all the businesses were doing well and we told ourselves we could always sell again if times got tough.

I had long cherished the idea of a duck farm. Every night we sold, on average, sixteen portions of our speciality, Leith's duckling – a version of *canard à l'orange* with braised celery and fried almonds. That's eight ducks a day, fifty-six ducks a week, upwards of two hundred a month – and that was just the restaurant; we'd need more for the school and catering company. It must make economic sense to raise them ourselves, I thought, but I turned out to be totally wrong. Further research revealed the depressing fact that few people make any money with ducks. They are hell to pluck, and dry-plucking machines are only worth it if you're plucking all day every day. Amazingly, we would have lost £1.50 on every duck.

Still, by moving away from London, we could

grow herbs, vegetables and flowers for the business and, more important, Rayne would have peace to write, and Daniel (and any future sibling) would grow up in the country.

We started spending weekends house-hunting. Driving round England, babe in the back, lunch in folksy inns, nights in B&Bs, fantasising about living in mansions way beyond our means, was my idea of heaven. Eventually I found Chastleton Glebe, a Cotswold house overlooked by no other, but with a view (Rayne's stipulation) and stables, and a bit of land (my stipulation).

When Rayne came to see the house, it was so cold inside that a vase on the mantelpiece of the unused drawing room had frozen water in it, and we had to go outside and stamp our feet in the snow to warm up. But Rayne saw at once that he could have his dreamed-of study at the top of the house, overlooking his dreamed-of pond at the bottom of the field; that we could lose a couple of rooms on the first floor to make a double-height entrance hall and a wide landing, and we could still have six bedrooms even if we added bathrooms for every one of them.

Once we had bought the place, I couldn't stay away. Through the summer of 1975, before Daniel could crawl and before Li-Da had arrived, I would sometimes drive down for the day. Daniel would sleep or gurgle in his bassinet under a tree while I dug up Jerusalem artichokes or picked spinach or beans planted by the previous owner.

One night I was washing, blanching and freezing vegetables in the London flat, when Rayne came home after playing chess with a friend. I was exhausted and burst into tears.

'I can't cope. I've still got the rhubarb to do and the peas aren't even podded and . . .'

Rayne put an arm round me and looked at the mountains of produce. 'How much is all this stuff worth?'

'I don't know, not much. But that's not the point. It's a sin to let it go to waste.'

'No it's not. It's a sin to let it exhaust you so.'

We binned it all and went to bed.

Li-Da arrived in September and by now Rayne was supervising the building operations. One day, when the house was nearly finished but still lacking a staircase to the top floor, we'd all climbed up a vertical ladder to what was to be Rayne's study. It was empty except for some painter's paraphernalia in the corner. The children were running around excitedly in the big open space and I was guarding the hole in the floor through which we had ascended. Suddenly Li-Da was screaming and Daniel was standing stock still, a big paint brush in his hand. He had picked it out of the white spirit tin in which it was soaking and, waving it about, had sprayed Li-Da's eyes.

Rayne and I went into automatic parental crisis management mode. Rayne scooped up the screaming Li-Da, I grabbed Daniel, and we got down that ladder like trained navvies. Rayne was down first and I shouted after him, 'There's a tap in the veg garden. It's the only one working.'

We got there together. I dropped Daniel, Rayne held poor Li-Da face up under the tap and turned it on full blast. She yelled her head off, poor mite, but she was fine. Poor Daniel was frightened and bewildered.

Rayne declared himself hopeless at all domestic tasks. This was not strictly true: he and I had once helped Jane bash a hole in a wall and put a door in. And he'd assembled all my flat-pack furniture and shelves at Upbrook Mews. But by the time we married he had decided that the tool box, along with the washing-up stuff, the car jack and much else besides, would be *terra incognita* to him. So fixing things fell to me. At Upbrook Mews this seemed fair: it was my house and I'd lived there for years so I knew how to relight the boiler and change the fuses. But when we moved to the Colonnades apartment I was slightly put out that somehow it was still me lying under the boiler or teetering on ladders.

So, when we finally moved into Chastleton Glebe, I decided to have nothing to do with the boiler, fuses or anything else. Your job, I said to Rayne. Fine, he said, and agreed that whenever anything went wrong, he'd cope. Which he did. By ringing up the boiler man or the electrician.

I could hardly complain. I knew when I married him that he wasn't going to do any washing-up or cooking. And indeed, twenty-five years later he still didn't know where the tea-towels lived, though they'd been in the same drawer all that time. But I did discover, more to my amusement than chagrin, that during his equally long marriage to Nan he had cooked eggs and bacon for breakfast almost every morning. Somehow he lost the skill when he married a cook.

I love planning things, especially kitchens. I commandeered the former dining room for the kitchen. It faces south, with a big bay window which we turned into a breakfast area.

We designed a central circular unit with drawers and shelves underneath and a revolving structure in the middle of the table top that took all my spice jars and bottles, with a ring of knife-slots to keep the knives out of reach of children, and a pot on top for kitchen tools and rolling pins, etc. It was made for us in cherrywood by a friend, Michael, who had been the *Sunday Telegraph* picture editor but had given that up to make exquisite inlaid harpsichords. Luckily for us, if not for him, Michael was a bit short of commissions at the that time so had agreed to make our table.

My mother and I came down to the as-yet-empty house the night he was to deliver it. He didn't arrive until two in the morning. We had no food or drink and we got so hungry waiting that we picked apples from the orchard and blackberries from the hedge and pinched some of the builders' sugar to make a compote in the microwave – the only piece of kit as yet working. It was simply delicious and seemed like an omen of many happy meals to come. Michael finally arrived with his hugely heavy island unit, which he then had to assemble for photographs by morning – or, should I say, later that morning – because the *Sunday Telegraph*, his old paper, was doing a feature on the kitchen.

Into the huge fireplace we installed a spit, made by the local blacksmith and powered by a second-hand central heating motor. We only cooked on the fire a few times, roasting a whole sucking pig or a spring lamb on the spit for big parties, or for more ordinary barbecue fare cooking on a Victorian brass clockwork jack, on which we'd hang a chicken or a ring of sausages and which rotated in front of the hearth. It was fun.

Once we had a party, mostly for the children, which was a sort of cross between Halloween and Guy Fawkes, with the children's carved pumpkins for decorations and a bonfire in the courtyard outside. Daniel, aged about five, was almost as nervous of the fireworks as our new mongrel dog, Mollie. When a particularly high rocket exploded in the sky, he said, 'Dad, will God be alright?'

I was very conscious of my amazing good fortune. I was only thirty-six when we moved into Chastleton and the children were two-year-old toddlers. And yet we had a six-bedroomed house, barns and stables, soon to house ponies and donkeys, a five-acre garden surrounded by our own fields with space for a future lake and tennis court, plus three cottages, one of them occupied by a housekeeper and gardener. Such privilege still seems, after nearly forty years, unbelievable.

I felt I was living a dream life. Rayne was happy in his study, reading and writing, coming down like clockwork at one for lunch, sharing a teatime biscuit with Mollie the dog, spending the late afternoon watching *Countdown* or sport. I had a job I loved. Weekends were for family and friends and on Mondays, once the children were at school, I would cook for the week, work in the garden and do domestic stuff, which I have always enjoyed. On Tuesdays I would wake at six and spend an hour picking and packing the flowers we grew for the restaurant into cool boxes in Rayne's car. Then he would drop me at the station. I would work on the train journey while he drove to London, listening to the *Today* programme. He would drop the flowers at the restaurant and spend half a day in the office. We'd eat together in the restaurant and he would return home next day, while I would stay on till Thursday evening working in the business.

On Fridays I would work at my desk at home on cookbooks or journalism. By my mid-forties, I'd graduated from both the *Daily Mail* and the *Sunday Express*, at each of which I'd worked for four years. John Junor was furious at my departure from the *Sunday Express* to work for the *Guardian*. He was famously angry with any journalist leaving his employ: you had to be very sick or retiring not to incur his wrath. He rang me up and ranted about disloyalty and betrayal.

'The *Guardian*! They cannot be paying you anything like I'm paying you.'

'No, JJ. They're paying me much less. About half in fact.'

'How *can* you? I *made* you. Who had ever heard of you?'

'I was the cookery editor on the *Daily Mail* for four years before I came to your paper.'

'The *Mail*!' He snorted derision.

I stayed at the *Guardian* until 1985, loving the freedom to write what I wanted. Nouvelle Cuisine was all the rage, and it was a chance to write about the great French chefs who were leading the movement, and include recipes for fresh food, cooked at the last minute, with exotic ingredients hitherto rare in French and British cooking: raw tuna, chilli and lemongrass, mangos and passion fruit. At first I wrote a weekly column, but I was horrendously busy with my company at the time and managed to negotiate a drop to fortnightly, and finally to a monthly column.

Then someone in the hierarchy noticed that I was being paid almost as much for a monthly column as Matthew Fort, who had replaced me as overall food editor, was getting for three columns and the editorship. So that was the end of me. Quite rightly. Matthew, now a good friend, denies his hand in my demise, but it amuses me to think that he sacked me and then hired my brother Jamie, who did a series of very funny and informative articles on growing vegetables.

At the time, I was also freelancing occasionally and had written a few pieces for the famous and charismatic Harold Evans, then editor of the *Sunday Times*. One day he asked me to lunch. I arrived at the *Times* building and his secretary told me to go straight into his office. I opened the door to see Harry facing the window, doing star-jumps.

'Harry, what on earth are you doing?'

He turned round, shook out his arms and legs and said, 'Oh, I just have to get rid of some energy.'

He was prodigiously energetic. He'd recently learnt to ski and was obsessed. He was on a mission to get the world to ski, especially anyone over forty. To this end he proposed to send half a dozen forty-something journalists, including me, to learn to ski, and to write about it.

Promptly giving up my vow never to ski again after my shameful performance twenty years before, I agreed at once.

We went to different ski resorts and were taught by different methods. I was sent to Wengen, where I had old-fashioned long skis (short ones were a very new thing then) and a private instructor, who I shared with my friend Annie Sarsen. Other journalists went to different countries and learnt by different methods, in ski school, with short skis, or *langlauf*-ing across country.

There were no nursery slopes that year at Wengen, but my instructor, a terrifyingly athletic, seventeen-year-old blonde Valkyrie, would shout encouragingly when I froze at the top of some horrific slope, 'Go on, go on. You can do it. You are not so old!' I wanted to whip out my passport out and shout, 'I am, I am, I'm much too old.' Annie managed much better and the Valkyrie loved her. I felt like the dunce.

What finished me off was a day that included a long steep descent to a bridge over a frozen stream. I just knew I would go down on my bottom, head and tummy, but not on my skis and, indeed, after launching off, I tumbled down, skis all over the place.

At the bottom we had to stamp sideways up the other side, which, though less terrifying, was utterly exhausting. Then, to my huge relief, a ski-lift hove into view. It would take us to lunch – the only part I enjoyed.

But how to get on it? Annie jumped onto one of the little chairs whizzing past, but I missed a few before I eventually got myself onto one and busied myself with trying to fit the bar across my middle. When I looked up I saw the empty chairs ahead swinging round to go down the mountain again and I realised I had no idea where to get off. My Valkyrie was now shouting at me from behind, 'Get on, get on,' but did she mean get OFF or GO on? I hesitated and was lost. I'd missed the spot and was rapidly being swung into the air.

So I leapt for it. Staggering and furious I turned to berate the poor girl, only to get clobbered by her now empty chair swinging past.

At last I tottered into the restaurant at the top of the mountain, drank a great deal of gluhwein and swore never to ski again, a promise I've found very easy to keep.

Rayne spent most of his time in his top-floor study, from where he could see the vista he'd designed: the lake, island, Chinese bridge and pagoda. He'd insisted on a huge modern picture window, which caused a bit of friction. The top floor would have originally housed the servants, and the dormer window was tiny. We agreed to enlarge it, but I thought we should copy the other large windows, with stone mullions between traditional windows of eight large leaded panes. Rayne, however, was determined on his picture window, and since it was to be his room after all, he won that battle. Over the years, countless visitors, especially groups visiting the garden – which we opened every year for the National Gardens Scheme charity – have remarked at the crass insensitivity of ruining a beautiful façade with a modern window!

One day I overheard a woman saying, 'Can you believe it? Just look at that awful window. What philistines.'

I relayed this to Rayne.

'Yes,' he said, 'but just think what pleasure her superiority gave her. And anyway I have more pleasure looking out than she, or you, have pain looking in.'

I used to threaten that when he'd departed this life or left me for a twenty-year-old, I would change the window, and as I write I am doing just that – but not without a pang of regret at demolishing my husband's window on the world. As he got older he spent almost all his waking hours, and a good few sleeping ones after lunch, in that room. It is still full of his books and has the same familiar smell and feel: male, bookish, quiet. Li-Da and I try to insist it is the family library, but somehow Daniel has gradually taken it over and it's become his study.

Right at the start of our house-hunting Rayne had said he wanted to look out on water, but I was adamant that there would be no pond until the children could swim. Even then, I was reluctant.

When we finally dug the lake (technically, having a water surface of an acre, we could grandly call it that) at the bottom of a large field, I was terrified of children falling through winter ice, so we made a rule: the ice had to be solid for five days, or five inches thick, before they could play on it. In the Seventies and Eighties most winters were cold enough to achieve this at least once or twice a season.

One day I was pulling the children, then perhaps four or five, along the ice in a bread crate attached to a rope. Foolishly, I was in wellies and slipped backwards, cracking my head on the ice. Just as in a cartoon, I saw stars, and felt myself teetering on the edge of consciousness. Aware that Rayne would not know if I fainted unless he happened to be looking out of his distant study window, I made a huge effort to stay in this world and said clearly, 'Call Daddy.'

What stopped me passing out was Daniel's piping little voice, wobbling with anxiety, calling 'Daddy, Daddy.' What I *should* have said was *go and fetch Daddy*. I somehow pulled myself together and got up.

From the age of four the children went to a primary school two fields away. Occasionally we'd take them there on Gentle or Silver, our donkeys, and give the other children a ride round the school drive, a pleasure that Health and Safety would never allow today.

We had another succession of nannies in the country, with the usual mix of good and bad. Among the bad were the first – a pair of middle-class sisters. They had no qualifications and were not very bright and I suspect their parents had pushed them into applying for the job. One was to look after the children and her younger sister the house and animals. They didn't last long. The younger one, longing for us to have smart horses she could ride, didn't think much of mere donkeys. She was extremely decorative as she taunted the remaining builders still on site by gyrating her bum as she cleaned the windows – and made a rotten job of the windows.

Her sister's faults were more serious. She didn't like children and she had a very short temper. One day I caught her smacking two-year old Daniel – which made sacking her easy, and instant.

They were followed by rather more professional nannies, but they were young and didn't stay long enough to turn into the legendary nanny to whom their charges are devoted to for life. I am grateful for this. It must be so hard for a mother if her child turns to Nanny rather than to her.

I still, though, carry a residue of guilt, the price all working mothers pay. Both Daniel and Li-Da have told me horror stories of their childhood, which they never said a word about at the time: weeping with fear on a pony; made to take long walks in the freezing mud, being forced to sit in front of food they didn't want.

But most of such guilt as I have is for things *I* did or failed to do, rather than what others did. I once got so angry with Li-Da I chased her round the playroom, wanting to whack her to kingdom come. When I caught her, I took her by the shoulders and then, suddenly scared of my own fury, I took a deep breath and hugged her instead. She burst into tears.

'Why are you crying?' I demanded. 'I just kissed you, didn't I?'

She looked up at me, eyes spilling over. 'But Mummy, it wasn't a *nice* kiss.'

And once I did smack Daniel. I can't even

remember why, but I whacked his bare bottom in the bath. Immediately the imprint of my hand glowed red on his skin. And then we were both crying.

He doesn't remember this any more than Li-Da remembers the playroom chase. I'm ashamed of these outbursts but I refuse to believe that such isolated incidents are damaging for life. And anyway, parents can only do their damnedest. Few of us are paragons.

Far more serious I think, was Li-Da's long struggle with her dad about her weight. He had spent time in the Far East and was anxious lest Li-Da go the way of so many young Asian women in getting fat as butter as they grew older. And it was true that Li-Da had what today is called 'an issue' with food. For months as a baby she would have been starving, so it is hardly surprising that as a little girl she would hide sweets and be keen on second helpings.

She was not in fact an overweight child, but she was more rounded than Daniel and Rayne began to fret about her weight. He would watch her while she ate, and she felt he counted every mouthful. This led to her consuming very little at meals and then surreptitiously tucking into left-overs in the fridge.

But still she was not fat, and it became a problem between me and Rayne. I would intervene in Li-Da's defence, try to stop him making remarks about her eating during meals, and would earn his disapproval by offering her second helpings along with everyone else.

Eventually I decided to prove to Rayne once and for all that Li-Da was not overweight. I insisted we take her to a specialist who measured her BMI and charted her weight, etc. She came out well within the normal range, but just above the median line. For me this meant Rayne should relax, she was normal. But to him her position just above the line meant we should be ever vigilant. So nothing changed.

Li-Da found the whole thing, and the visit, traumatic. It made her feel there was something wrong with her. And she began to believe that she was second best in her father's eyes. Sadly, she had a point. As Daniel grew up, he and his dad had more and more in common. They both preferred solitary reading to anything, and were interested in history, politics and literature. Both played very good tennis, both were self-effacing and clever. They enjoyed each other's company.

Li-Da liked all the things that Rayne regarded as, if not exactly trivial, certainly as less important: food, friends, and, as she got older, fashion, film, fun and pop music. She did play tennis, but not as well as Daniel. She once said plaintively, 'Do you know, Dad has never, ever asked me to play tennis with him. Not once.'

Occasionally, my attempts to mediate between Rayne and Li-Da led to mighty blow-ups. The first time was when, aged four, she had reached for the Smarties on the Christmas lunch table. Rayne barked at her and she burst into tears. I blew up, scooped up the child and the Smarties, and disappeared to feed them to her. But we were both crying and she wouldn't have them.

Another time I was so angry at breakfast that I picked up my bowl of muesli, and, just managing not to hurl it at Rayne, hurled it instead at the ceiling – to the stunned astonishment of my niece and nephews who had never witnessed such a thing in their better-mannered family. The stain remained on the ceiling for years.

My quarrels with Rayne were very few, but nearly all were triggered by my defence of Li-Da. Once, I forget why, I lay in bed, first seething, then wretched, while Rayne contentedly slept beside me. So much for not going to sleep on a quarrel, I thought. Unhappy and unable to sleep, I went downstairs and out of the house. I walked round the dark garden, but it was cold. I wanted to go back to bed but refused to let myself. I ended up in the stable, weeping on the warm neck of my horse Russ, a three-year-old chestnut I had unwisely bought – I was still falling off him, and still adored him, fifteen years later. I tried to get Russ to lie down so I could tuck up beside him, but he wouldn't. So in the end I did go back to bed. Rayne, of course, had not stirred.

Another time I slammed out of the house, jumped

into the car and set off, never to come back. I ran out of petrol before the first village and had to ring Rayne to come and rescue me.

I loved Rayne utterly, but he was not the easiest of men. And there was one thing that I dared not discuss. His smoking. He had smoked all his life. He famously set the bed on fire on his honeymoon night with Nan in the Savoy. He often sang the hotel's praises because, since he and Nan had spent all their savings on this one night, he was terrified he'd be charged for the damage, but the manager said, 'Think no more of it, sir,' and sent them up a bottle of champagne.

By the time we moved to Chastleton he was smoking eighty cigarettes a day, twenty of them during the night. Our woollen blankets all had holes in them and the carpet by his bed was spotted with burn marks. I would often wake in the night to see the glow of his cigarette. He used to wake up because he needed the nicotine, and the cigarette would relax him and help him get back to sleep, until a couple of hours later when he needed another drag.

In 1970, Rayne had his first operation on the furred-up artery in his abdomen which bifurcated to feed his legs. Although he had a private room in St Mary's Hospital in Paddington, of course he wasn't allowed to smoke. But he did, and pitched the dog-ends out of the window. They landed just where the nurses, also banned from smoking in the hospital, were congregated outside having a fag. One of them was the matron in charge of Rayne's ward, so he was rumbled.

I think, being such a strong character, he was deeply ashamed that he could not kick the habit. There were several more abdominal operations, each procedure more dangerous and scary than the last. I remember one of them when the children were about five, which lasted several hours, and when they were done and he was in intensive care, it was thought he might not live. I walked up the road from the Wellington Hospital to the Parkers' flat, and Jilly gave me a hug, smoked haddock cooked in milk and a whopping great whisky. And, because she was a doctor, she could get truthful bulletins rather than anodyne answers out of the medics. After an hour or two, she reported, 'He's fine. You can go and see him.' I did. His face looked sunken and grey, and I thought he was still unconscious, but he gave my hand a little fluttering squeeze.

The next day he was back in his room, pinker and stronger, and, still under the influence of the anaesthetic. The drip machinery held his hand up in front of his face, exactly where he would hold it if he had a cigarette in it. He kept trying to smoke the drip, which would have been funny if it was not so tragic. What I did find funny were his ramblings – the drug had made him unusually talkative:

You know darling, we should go into the flavoured medical drip business . . . This drip is entirely tasteless,

*and it would fit in very well with Leith's Good Food
...When you are approaching your doom you don't
want to lose concentration and end up on a tram track
to Doncaster.*

I think this operation, and the growing evidence
of the dangers of smoking, plus the example he
was giving to the children finally made him determined to stop. But, to my real distress, within a
very few months, he was smoking again, only now
in secret.

Everyone knew he smoked. His study was a
friendly fug and I could smell tobacco on his
breath from yards away, but we all went along with
the pretence. No one wanted to challenge him,
and I knew he was just unable to stop and to
torment him with the fact seemed cruel. Besides,
I reasoned, at least if he had to refrain from
smoking when we were around, he would smoke
less, which he did. At least he no longer smoked
in the night.

I have a reputation for both bossiness and
doggedness, but in this matter I seem to have been
extraordinarily feeble. I think there are two reasons:
one is that I am by nature tolerant, inclined to see
things from the other point of view and sympathise
(or you could say, easily persuaded and without a
mind of my own), and the other is that in our
relationship Rayne wore the trousers. I think he
did so in all of his relationships, without ever being
overbearing. If he didn't want me to lecture or
insist, then somehow I lost the will to do so. And

he managed to make that alright too – I seldom felt resentful.

But for all the worries about Rayne's health, the occasional blow-ups, and the recurrent dream that he would leave me, the best time in my life was the decade between 1975 and 1985. Rayne was well enough to be active and fun, I was in my prime, and our children were young enough for home to be the centre of their lives.

At about this time the BBC decided to make a programme, *The Best of British*, profiling half a dozen people in different professions and they proposed me as one of them. After my Tyne Tees TV baptism by fire I was nervous, but I was too much of an egotist to resist, and found to my relief that not all directors made you read everything off an autocue.

Then along came another, more successful, BBC series called *Take Six Cooks*, also profiles, but this time all of cooks, presented by Kay Avila. The film portrayed me as a young, successful, happy woman, who had just about everything. It is an enviable picture of a dream lifestyle – the garden looking glorious in the sun, me cantering round the paddock on my horse, Russ, and sitting under the vine-covered pergola with my toddlers eating 'stripy supper' – a large Matzos crispbread spread with narrow rows of cheese, ham, tomatoes, fish paste, cottage cheese, etc, and ending, by way of pudding, with a line of honey or jam.

★　　★　　★

Holidays were mostly spent at home, but almost every year we would take a fortnight at the Cape in South Africa staying in a glorious beach house in Plettenberg Bay that belonged to our friends Michael and Phyllis Rapp. I loved that place. Daniel was conceived there, and most of Chastleton was designed there, with Rayne and I poring over plans while the babies slept.

Every year I would worry that there would be trouble at South African Immigration. Li-Da was most definitely not white and apartheid was still the law, but no one was ever anything but delighted and intrigued by her. As a toddler she would run about on the beach, the only brown child, digging sandcastles or shrieking in the surf.

The children's school, Kitebrook, took girls to the age of twelve and boys to the age of eight. The children were happy there – no clinging and crying on Day One – and made friends they still have thirty-four years later. Of course there were occasional blips. One day Li-Da, five at the time, came home miserable.

'What's the matter, darling?

'Lucinda is so mean to me. She says I'm black.'

My over-sensitive antennae, always alert for racial slights to my dark-skinned daughter, prompted instant thoughts of storming the headmistress's study with complaints. But I made an effort at control and said calmly, 'Well, darling, what colour do *you* think you are?'

'I'm brown, of course.'

'And what colour is Daniel?'

'Pink.'

All she was concerned about was accuracy. And there was I panicking about racism.

One day, when the children were about five or six, I went to school on a parents' day and the class all had their paintings exhibited on the wall. The subject was 'What I learnt in the holidays.' Daniel's picture of Ian Botham with an enormous cricket bat was there among the twenty-odd pictures. But nothing by Li-Da. Instantly indignant, I went to the form mistress and protested.

'Come with me, Mrs Kruger,' she said. She took me to her desk and extracted Li-Da's picture. I recognised it at once. It was a reproduction of a picture in a book called *How a Baby is Made* that we'd been reading at bedtime. My daughter's picture had a bosomy lady lying on her back with a bearded man on top of her. What was going on inside was represented in dotted lines: Li-Da had given the man a phallus that stretched to the woman's throat.

'It's very good,' said her form mistress. 'You can see I gave her a star.'

'And *I* can see why you didn't put it on the wall.'

CHAPTER 13

GROWING PAINS

Family fortunes

My mother's marriage to Robert Langford was in trouble by 1980, and after seven years they divorced. Poor Robert, he never had a hope in hell of filling the gap my father left. And while Peggy could be bossy and demanding, he was touchy and selfish. She was almost exclusively interested in the theatre but Robert, though a good actor and producer, would have been much happier as a racing driver. He worried and infuriated Peggy by disappearing to the race track whenever he could.

When Peggy left him, she came to England, staying for a while in a little studio flat above Leith's Restaurant. None of her three children, although all living in England, wanted her to leave South Africa. She was at the top of her theatrical game and could work pretty well as much or as little as she chose. She knew everyone in the theatre and was something of a Grande Dame in South Africa. In England she was unknown, the competition was fierce, and if it was difficult for leading actresses of her age to get parts, what chance would Mum have?

But come she did, and instantly set about starting a career afresh. She never achieved fame in England, but she worked more than most actresses of her age. She was never too grand for any part, nor for any company. She would tour the provinces in B-list theatres, in plays like *Boeing-Boeing*, be paid peanuts and stay in cheap theatrical digs. I used to beg her to stay in a decent hotel – she could afford it – but she said no, it would ruin her relationship with the rest of the cast, and besides, she was fine. It was fun. She was a true actress, only happy backstage or on stage.

She said her favourite job in England was in *The Mousetrap* because her character was bumped off in the first act and she could do her knitting in her dressing room until it was time to go home. And she liked playing Mrs Pinfold opposite Michael Hordern in Waugh's *The Ordeal of Gilbert Pinfold* in spite of it being the dullest of parts, because it was at the Roundhouse and she could walk to work from the studio house she rented in a Primrose Hill courtyard.

Peggy and Robert divorced but remained on good terms, and a few years later Robert came to England too and rented the studio opposite her. She resumed her expectation that he would mend her fuses, fix her TV and climb on a ladder to change her lightbulbs. Meanwhile, he was glad to take a six-o'clock whisky off her every evening.

When Daniel left Kitebrook School at the age of eight, he went to Arnold Lodge Prep in Leamington Spa, for which he had to write an entrance exam. When Rayne and I went to collect him afterwards, Daniel wasn't with the others and we spent an anxious twenty minutes searching the grounds with the headmaster.

We found him, tearful and distraught. Ever a bit dreamy and easily distracted, he'd got lost on a tour of the school. He and I both controlled the impulse to run into each other's arms. I said, 'Oh, there you are darling,' as calmly as I could and he wiped his face with this sleeve. As we walked back, Daniel still sniffing, the Headmaster said, 'That's a rotten cold you've got, young man,' and handed him a handkerchief. What an intelligent man.

When Daniel was nine or ten he developed a short-lived enthusiasm for fishing for trout in our lake. Two things put paid to his zeal. First, I insisted he gut and scale anything he caught, and he was very squeamish. The other was an incident when he was fishing alone from the rowboat. I heard his screams from the kitchen and at once thought he'd hooked his eye. I tore down the field and over the bridge to find him standing in the boat, tears streaming down his face. He'd forgotten the priest (the weighted cosh for despatching fish) and he'd tried to kill his trout by hitting it with his sneaker but the fish had just bounced, and then gone on flapping. Daniel could not beat it. Poor fish. Poor lad.

Soon Li-Da joined him at Arnold Lodge, to the distress of the headmistress at Kitebrook. She tried to persuade me not to remove her, but I was worried that, being the only non-white child in the school, Li-Da was becoming the school's multicultural mascot. She seemed to get all the best parts in the school plays and featured at the centre of school photos and brochures. I thought she should go to a school with a few black or Asian children.

Within a year both children had somehow got the message that boarders were the elite, had more games and more fun, and they wanted to be weekly boarders.

I was against it, but Rayne persuaded me with talk of road accidents – we had already twice skidded into a ditch on icy roads. But I was convinced that Daniel, less gregarious than Li-Da, would be miserable.

On their first night at school, the phone rang. Rayne picked it up, and said to me, 'It's the school matron. Daniel wants to speak to us.'

'Oh God, I told you,' I cried, 'He's wretched. He'll want to come home. We should never have . . .'

I snatched the phone and Daniel came on the line. 'Hi Mum.'

'Darling, are you alright?'

'Sure. Mum, it's brilliant. Can I stay the weekend?'

'No,' I said firmly. 'We'll miss you too much.'

Even when at home the children were now big

enough not to monopolise all my free time and I became obsessed with our five-acre garden and spent many happy hours and buckets of money on it. My husband didn't care for flowers, except in the cutting garden, so from his study window only trees, grass and water were visible.

He tolerated my extravagances with wry remarks about how much cheaper it would be to have all our vegetables delivered from Fortnum's in a Rolls Royce rather than growing them, and how erecting our stone, vine-covered pergola had been so expensive we'd have been better off flying our friends to the Mediterranean for al fresco lunches. But, though Rayne refused to share my obsessions, he knew how much pleasure it gave me to feed people with veg from our garden, to sit under the pergola with the extended family, eating simple, delicious food. A lot of my best memories are of meals under that pergola.

Having the children at boarding school, I reluctantly admitted, had advantages. It allowed me to concentrate on the Leith's businesses during the week and give home and family full attention at weekends. Being my own boss meant I could take holidays and half-terms off too, and generally fool Daniel and Li-Da into thinking I was a full-time mum.

This worked well all through their schooldays. When I won the Veuve Clicquot Businesswoman of the Year award in 1990, Daniel, then fifteen, read the press coverage and said, 'Hey Mum, this

267

isn't true is it? You aren't the hot-stuff business-woman they say, are you?'

'Well, all that article is true. That's what my work is. You know that.'

'But it can't be. You're always at home.'

I think I'm prouder of this little exchange than almost anything.

During the Eighties – my forties – the house was often full, especially at weekends. My mother came down a lot and so did Nan. Friends would some-times remark on the oddity of Nan remaining such close friends with Rayne, and even more oddly, with me. But the simple fact was both Rayne and I loved her and Rayne was still her best friend if not her husband. She once told me that now, married to me, he was much nicer to her, and that she saw much more of him at our house than when he had been married to her and shut up in his study all the time. Of course I cannot know if this was true but she certainly behaved as a friend, continuing to invite me, with or without Rayne, to lunch or supper. When she and I were both, separately, asked to a garden party at Buckingham Palace, we went together and had a very merry time.

Nan's daughter, my friend Angela, her husband Donald Douglas, and their three girls, Amy, Eliza and Jodie, much the same age as our two, had a cottage in our field for weekends and holidays so we saw a lot of them.

The Jamie Leiths and I took it in turns to have

268

both our extended families for Christmas. On 'our' years, Nan and the Douglas family often came too, and we would sit down twenty or more for lunch.

Rayne, in his sixties, was still well and active. We built a tennis court and all of us, except Rayne, rode, though not seriously. Shortly after we'd moved to the country, I'd struck a bargain with him: we could have horses, but we'd not hunt. He was not particularly concerned for the foxes, though he agreed with Shaw's dictum about the unspeakable in pursuit of the uneatable, but he thought charging over stone walls and five-bar gates suicidal. So we just hacked around the fields and lanes.

If I had that time again I don't think I'd suggest ponies for the children until, and only if, they begged for them. But I loved riding so much myself, I forced the pace.

But I never did get the hang of life in Heythrop Hunt country. The first neighbour to come and say hello was an eighty-year-old horsewoman whom I afterwards learned still rode side-saddle to the hunt! I was mucking out the donkey's stable when I heard a corncrake female voice behind me.

'No, gel, you just haven't a *clue*,' she shrieked. I turned round as she barged into the stable, took the pitchfork from me and gave me an excellent demonstration of mucking out.

'You must go for the manure first, and toss the clods up and down on your fork a bit so the dry straw falls off. You pitch the wet straw and the manure into the barrow, and keep the dry straw. Too wasteful for words, what you were doing.'

Only then did she introduce herself and explain the white collar-bandage round her neck. 'I'm orf games you see. Blasted horse pitched me orf. Cracked my neck. Not serious. Be right as rain for the season.'

When Li-Da, aged about twelve, was invited to a hunt ball, I had no idea that children had to go in ball gowns. I sent her off in a pink jump-suit. She looked adorable, but suffered utter humiliation as all her friends were in silk or velvet down to the ground.

It was not just the horsey crowd that Rayne wished to avoid. He was reclusive to the point of obsession. When a formerly invisible house a quarter of a mile away was enlarged and renovated in bright new stone, I had to plant a tree to shield it from view.

One day as we were driving out of our lane, I waved to a couple walking their dogs.

'Who's that?' Rayne asked.

'Darling, they live across the road. He's been your neighbour ever since we've been here.'

Our neighbours recognised us as little as we them. One blazing summer day I had taken the children to play in an abandoned quarry belonging to one of them. It was in the middle of the field and secluded so while the children skidded up and down the gravelly slopes on their bottoms I stripped off to my bra and knickers to sunbathe. I was half asleep when I heard an indignant voice asking me what the hell I was doing. I sat up and recognised my neighbour, Mr Freeman, at the same time as he recognised me.

We were elaborately polite to each other, me apologising for not asking if we could come in advance, and he saying, 'No, no, it's perfectly alright, Mrs Kruger. It's just that sometimes we get hooligans in the quarry and they break the windows of the old buildings down there, and it's dangerous. But, with your children, no problem.' And off he went.

A few minutes later Daniel and Li-Da arrived, breathless with excitement.

'Mum, it's just great. There are these old overgrown greenhouses or something down there, and if you stand on the top and lob a rock onto the roof, ker-pow, it's fantastic, the explosion is amazing.'

Since both children had been happy weekly-boarding at Arnold Lodge, I had fewer qualms about full boarding but I was still reluctant. I wanted them home at weekends, something the best schools did not allow. I was persuaded by Rayne, who wanted the best schools, and said if it didn't work, we'd think again.

Li-Da went to Headington, a girls-only school in Oxford. We'd been charmed by the eccentric headmistress, though mildly alarmed when she showed us a smoking room.

'Smoking room?' I asked. 'For the staff, presumably.'

'Oh no,' she said. 'If the seniors are allowed to smoke for an hour a day, they won't be off down the hockey pitch, smoking in secret.' Sadly for Li-Da perhaps, but to my relief, the smoking room had gone by the time she started at Headington.

Eton was the last establishment we visited in our search for a school for Daniel. The local comprehensive had a poor reputation so I'd wanted him to go as a day boy or weekly boarder to the minor public school in the next village, but the headmaster was suddenly sacked and the school seemed in disarray. So we started on a tour of all the independent schools within easy reach of home. I hated them all. Malvern felt like a military camp, all discipline and no fun, while Marlborough was so *laissez-faire* that three children had recently gone AWOL for days without anyone noticing.

We arrived at Eton full of prejudice about toffs and the super-rich – and were immediately bowled over by everything: curriculum, staff attitude, facilities, the lot. The place was beautiful with its river, playing fields, woods and ancient buildings. And the opportunities were endless: there were clubs for every hobby imaginable, facilities for everything from print-making to silversmithing, with specialist teachers on hand. I defy anyone to visit Eton and hang on to their prejudices.

But getting Daniel into the school was something else. We had not put him down for Eton at birth, so he went on a general list which would mean he'd make the grade only if he did extraordinarily well at the entrance exam.

Daniel was a year younger than most of the boys in his class at Arnold Lodge and we had decided that he should stay on there for an extra year. That way he could grow up a bit, and be top-of-the-heap for a year before facing being bottom of it at a new school. Meanwhile, he would take the Eton entrance exam in the hope of securing his place for the following year.

On the day, Daniel was the only child at the school sitting the exam. After twenty minutes he hadn't written a word. Daniel should always be grateful for what followed. The invigilating master told the headmaster, who sent Daniel to the matron with instructions to relax and have a sleep. The head then rang Eton, explained that Daniel was a clever boy, but had somehow locked down. The admissions tutor at Eton told him to keep Daniel isolated so he couldn't look up answers or get help, and then present the paper again. The second time round Daniel had no problem.

I rang Eton to ask if he was in or out. I was told he was in, but he had to start that October (1987) not the next year, for which we'd applied.

'But why?' I asked. 'If he's not good enough for the next intake, when he'll be more mature and have an extra year's education behind him, how can he be good enough now?'

'The problem is that we have had exceptionally

good applications for next year and less good ones for October.'

So Daniel went to Eton aged twelve. The school treats the boys like university students from day one. They have their own study-bedrooms and they have to work out their own timetable and find their way to their classes all over the town, with few boys in the same house being in the same stream for every subject. Daniel got lost and was late all the time. The boys live in houses of mixed ages, and it is up to them to decide what sport, clubs, and extra-mural activities to follow. Daniel was too homesick to join anything he didn't have to.

We took him to tea at the Castle Hotel in Windsor, where he sat, woe-faced, trying to be brave but actually silent, wretched, and unable to eat anything. One day we got a letter describing his miseries and including the line, 'I just want to run and run and never come back.'

I picked up the phone to his housemaster, who was also his English tutor. I started to read the letter and after a few words he stopped me. 'Hang on for a minute, Mrs Kruger, would you?' I heard the rustle of papers and then he said, 'I'm sorry, go on, I'm listening.' After a few more words, he started to say them with me. He had the same letter in front of him.

'I asked the class to write a letter about their new school as a homework exercise. Daniel must have thought his letter too good to waste. And it *is* very good. He got top marks for it.'

I wasn't convinced. Perhaps he'd written the letter to us, and wanted his housemaster to know, indirectly, how unhappy he was. Either way, to me it was a cry for help. To his housemaster it was a canny bit of economy.

Rayne and I discussed it and we told him he could leave Eton if he wanted to. I remember saying something like, 'Darling, you are a bright boy. I'm sure you'd get into Westminster. You could be a day boy and I could stay in London with you during the week.'

'No, Mum,' he said, 'I don't want to. I'm not going through this all over again at a new school. Especially as Eton is the best school in the world.'

Wow, I thought, what a marketing job. The lad is utterly miserable, but in three weeks they've still managed to convince him of the peerlessness of Eton. Of course Eton *is* a good school, but for a boy like Daniel, who would always retreat into a book and shut himself up in his study rather than join in, it was initially disastrous. He only began thoroughly enjoying Eton in his last three years, when he was allowed to confine himself to English, politics and history, and when he edited a subversive newspaper suggesting that the school change its ways!

Fortunately, unhappiness is like any pain: one doesn't fully remember how it felt, and Daniel makes light of the unhappiness I know he went through. I'm probably being unfair to Eton, but I found the change in my son hard to bear. He went off to school an affectionate twelve-year-old who would climb into our bed in the morning and read poetry with his dad, and who would rush into my arms and kiss my cheek. But within weeks he had been Etonised. He didn't quite say, 'Good Morning, Mater,' and stick out a stiff little hand, but there was no more kissing – especially no more kissing Rayne – though he still just about tolerated a kiss from me.

Only once in that first term did he revert to the Daniel of old. We were at the Eton carol service, where he sat between Rayne and me, warm and cosy, behind the tall backs of bigger boys. Suddenly, while a boy was reading a lesson, Daniel reached up and kissed my cheek. I gave him a discreet hug, hoping he wouldn't realise what he had spontaneously done and feel mortified. No one saw, and I felt a glow of gratitude. Underneath this buttoned-up little person was the boy I knew.

Eton was undoubtedly a sharp lesson in stiff upper lip, but home had pressures of its own. On Daniel's first half term at Eton, I collected a carload of boys from school. Daniel sat silent next to me while the boys in the back were discussing the coming week.

'Oh God, and Mum will insist I ride my pony.'

'Mine too. And isn't it just awful when you fall off and she makes you get on again.'

'And the worst is my sister is so good at it. She's not chicken at all, she can jump anything.'

'And when it's not scary, it's so *boring*. All that catching and grooming, saddling up . . .'

'And brushing down, and feeding and lugging buckets and mucking out . . .'

'Is that how you feel too?' I asked Daniel.

'Pretty much.'

Rayne refused to have anything to do with horses. He said they were dangerous at both ends and uncomfortable in the middle, and he looked on the rich horsey crowd as creatures from another planet. They scared me too, but I did my best to look cool.

Li-Da rode well, but I was an embarrassment as a pony-club Mum. I could not back the horse trailer for love or money, and the children would pretend I was nothing to do with them as I asked some exquisitely jodhpured mother or Barbour-clad father to park the thing for me.

Optimistic, friendly Li-Da did well at Headington in spite of a tense start. She arrived at her boarding house on the first evening with her face swollen to a moon, her Oriental eyes scarcely visible above her purple cheeks. She had been playing with her cousins in the bracken, and turned out to be violently allergic to it. But she insisted on going to school, saying arriving late would be worse.

Her co-operative and gregarious nature served her well, and she was happy at Headington until, at fourteen or fifteen, the old-fashioned rules began to chafe. She wanted to go to a school where boys were not regarded as mad, bad and dangerous to know.

She had a point. One day her housemother rang me: 'Mrs Kruger. I thought I should tell you that Li-Da has been receiving telephone calls from a boy.'

'Isn't that allowed?'

'Well, let us say it is not encouraged.'

'Any idea who the boy is?'

'Well, he *says* he's her brother.'

'Perhaps he is. She does have a brother.'

I could almost see her shaking her head in disapproval and scepticism.

So Li-Da opted for St Edward's in Oxford (known as Teddy's, a boy's school that had begun taking sixth form girls) where she was popular, happy, and learned to row. I think she chose her university – Strathclyde in Glasgow – with some vague idea that, since it was on a river, it would be great for rowing – which it may be, but by the time she got there she'd given up the sport.

As Rayne got older he became more impatient and anxious, and by the time the children were teenagers, travelling with him was purgatory. He would declare a departure time by which we were all to be ready and in the car, but twenty minutes before the time he would be harrying and barking at everyone. Plane trips were the worst because he could never accept that being a difficult customer gets you nowhere except to the back of the queue. It reached a point where it would be a minor miracle if we completed a journey without Rayne quarrelling with someone, and my being furious with him. So I took to dosing him with Valium, which worked a treat. I would crush a tablet and put it into the icing of a piece of carrot cake or the marmalade on his toast, and he would be as calm as a cucumber, his old charming self, relaxed and engaging.

Once, on arrival in Cape Town, he said, 'There you are, I'm not ratty and difficult. I've been nothing but sweetness and light.'

The temptation to tell him why was strong, but I wisely – if a little deceitfully – kept my counsel.

I confined my drugging activities to long-haul flights, though sometimes the temptation to get him to relax on other occasions was hard to resist. Once in the Cape, he couldn't bear to see Li-Da climb the rock cliffs at Plettenberg Bay, and all the time the children were in the sea, he would pace anxiously, fretting about undercurrents, freak waves, jelly fish, running tides.

One day, after a night of high anxiety because the children had gone out to a disco with some friends and were to be given a lift back by parents we did not know, he declared family holidays were over. I had great sympathy for him. He'd loved holidays when the children were little: he dug forts and moats in the sand with them, we went for long lonely walks on the deserted beaches, and I cooked simple suppers for the four of us. But now the children were growing up and needed more exciting company, and the last thing Rayne wanted was to join in some other family's barbecue, or beach game. And the dangers of boys and cars and discos worried him sick.

Being fourteen or fifteen is famously difficult, for parents as well as for children, and we had the usual minor anxieties with ours. When they were fifteen they had a party, which they insisted be held in a shed, not in the house. Why, we asked.

'Because they'll trash the place. Break things, get drunk, throw up.'

So we were warned, especially by Li-Da's housemaster, who told me to search the Teddy's contingent for bottles as they got off the train. But the boys were too clever for that. They arrived with the booze in their bellies, as did the Etonians. The reek of alcohol as I loaded them into the car was overwhelming.

All we were offering was a mild punch, so, with only a smashed window and a smashed light bulb, I guess we could count ourselves lucky. But our gardener, whose stepdaughter, Sarah, was invited to the party, came up at about ten p.m. to check on things and was so shocked at the public-schoolboy obscenities and adolescent roaring emanating from the shed that he took Sarah home.

Next day our children, miraculously, were up before us. I'd imagined they'd not stir until lunchtime. Why so, I asked.

'We had to clear up the mess in the garden and

down by the lake before you found it.' I didn't ask what mess. Better not to know.

One day, just after her seventieth birthday, Peggy announced she was going to have breast reduction surgery.

I was aghast. I think I said something horribly insensitive, like 'A boob job? Whatever for Mum? Who's going to see your breasts?'

'I'm doing it for *me*,' she replied. 'I've lugged these great things around with me ever since I was fifteen, they weigh a ton and I'm sick of it.' She pulled her bra strap off her shoulder to show me the red weal under it. 'I only kept them because your father was so fond of the things.'

She went ahead and did it. She was very overweight at the time, but because she immediately felt lighter and happier, she went on a diet, lost a couple of stone, got offered a good part, and attracted two would-be suitors, both of whom she spurned.

So, when I was fifty and saw a photograph of myself looking a hundred, with double chins and wrinkles, I decided on a face-lift. Why not? Plastic surgery had done my mama a power of good. I expected a lot of opposition from Rayne but all he was concerned about was that I should find a good surgeon who wouldn't make me look like someone else.

I had it done in South Africa. Dr van Niekerk told me firmly there was no way he could make me emerge with a swan neck. Instead, he concentrated on lifting my top eyelids, which sometimes looked like great drapes hanging over my lashes, and getting rid of the bags underneath. He did it while I sat up in a chair and self-administered the anaesthetic. In between nodding off, I quite enjoyed it. It hurt a lot afterwards, and my cousin Lee and I went off to her beach house for a week to hide. Face lifts were not as common in 1990, and kindly people in the pub assumed my black eyes were the result of a car crash.

I did look pretty awful. Apart from the bruising, I had purple-black cheeks as a result of the laser treatment to rid me of all the little red veins that had broken – said Dr van Niekerk – from years of standing over too-hot stoves or riding in the freezing wind.

But the swelling and bruising slowly vanished, and for the first time I could remember I could see my eyelids, the saggy bags had gone, and so had the broken veins. I was thrilled with the result.

Going to South Africa 'for a holiday' had proved an excellent idea. When I got back, I had a good deep suntan and I'd streaked my hair blond, so everyone attributed my looking ten years younger to sun and hairdresser. Only my canny sister-in-law rumbled the truth.

Li-Da was growing up and, as Rayne had predicted, would prove to be more resilient and able to hold her own than I had feared. And she had a sense of humour. When she was in the sixth form, Rayne made his oft-repeated complaint that he never saw her with a book. Instead of protesting or sulking, she replied, 'Dad, I'm sixteen. What do you expect? All I think of is sex and shopping.'

I could have clapped. And he roared with laughter.

When she was very young I'd tried occasionally to interest her in the land of her birth, but during the Seventies and Eighties there was little available that was not mind-crushingly boring to a teenager – articles in the *National Geographic* about traditional dance, for example. The only alternative had been the horrors of the country's recent killing-fields history.

But as she grew up, like most adopted children she wanted to know more of her birth parents and background. And of Cambodia. When she left school she went off to Thailand with a girlfriend to hang out on Phuket beach. Rayne gave his permission but said, 'You are not to go to Cambodia. It's too dangerous.'

I remember thinking Phuket Beach was probably just as dangerous for a seventeen-year-old up for adventure. But Rayne was right. Cambodia was still largely dominated by the Khmer Rouge and was far from safe. The papers had been full of a story of three foreigners who had been kidnapped, held hostage, then decapitated, the bodies left on the roadside.

Then Li-Da rang from Phuket. 'Mum, I'm going

to Phnom Penh tomorrow. But don't worry, it's safe there. I'll be fine.'

'Darling, you can't. It's *much* too dangerous. Anyway, you haven't enough money.'

'I know, but it's cool. I borrowed some from a guy on the beach.'

'What guy? Li-Da, this is mad, you cannot go off with a strange man.'

'No, no. I'm not going with him. He's just lending me the money.'

'Oh God, are you going alone then?'

'No, I'm going with someone else, another guy I met on the beach.'

Of course Li-Da was fine. She paid back Boy One, Boy Two drifted off and she came home full of excitement about Cambodia.

Li-Da was adventurous, but there is such a core of responsibility and kindness in her that she spared us much of the teenage hell many parents suffer. She never ran away, dropped out, got hooked on drugs, broke windows, came home covered in tattoos, wanted to die or spurned us.

She attributes her goody-goody (well, fairly goody-goody) behaviour to her gratitude to us for saving her from her nightmare babyhood and giving her a loving childhood. And I think she does suffer 'survivor guilt' and the burden of somehow paying back her good fortune by not giving us pain.

Of course *we* didn't save her, Meyer Burstein did. We just had the massive good fortune of finding her. And adoption, as I have told her many times, is a selfish act. People don't, I hope, adopt out of nothing but philanthropy, but out of a desire to have, to love, cherish, bring up, care for a child. It is because they want a child, not because the child needs them. We owe her more than she owes us.

She is a film-maker now. Her debut film was a documentary called *Belonging*, showing her efforts to trace her origins in Cambodia. It was a finalist for the Grierson Award, the 'Oscar' for documentaries.

The film follows Li-Da's search for her birth family. We meet hopeful mothers who desperately want her to be their daughter lost twenty-five years before, and she travels the country following dud leads and meeting ordinary Cambodians living pretty hand to mouth.

She manages to hunt down the official who signed her exit papers when she was flown out of the country at the age of six months. Since they included her parents' names and the district where she was born, she'd hoped they would lead her to remnants of her family, but the official admits he forged everything, making up names and districts at a time when the country was full of nameless orphans to deal with.

And so she ends up with less information than she started out with, but she has fallen in love with Cambodia.

She also fell in love with Sonny, a young

Cambodian who has had, like almost everyone his age, a childhood dominated by brutality, loss, death.

Li-Da's romance with Sonny – she came home wearing an engagement ring – didn't last, but he is a wonderful man, who has supported his mother, five siblings, granny and aunt since he was twelve. He and Li-Da are still friends, and she goes to Cambodia as often as she can. Occasionally I go too.

Though I never for a moment thought that Li-Da would turn against us, her adoptive parents, her wild streak did worry me. In her gap year, working in a school in South Africa, a riot broke out in Cape Town with crowds chanting anti-apartheid slogans and breaking windows. Li-Da rang me, her voice high and breathless with excitement. 'It's fantastic, Ma, I joined the protesters and we toi-toi'd' (that singing and stamping dance Africans do) 'down the street. I got right up close to a burning car and got some amazing photographs.'

When I told Peggy about my fears for Li-Da, she reminded me how I'd put her and Dad through hell when I was Li-Da's age.

'Yes, but that was all about boys. It's her lust for danger I worry about.'

'Better a lust for danger than no appetite for anything,' she said. That from a woman in her seventies.

Daniel was never a tearaway, or if he was, he hid

it successfully from his parents. He did well at Eton and applied for a place at Oxford. He had been thinking of Wadham College, but one day Harvey McGregor, the Master of New College, came to lunch and persuaded him to switch to New.

I took Daniel to his interview and was astonished that he was only in there for twenty minutes, not the forty or so expected. He didn't think it had gone well.

Next day his Eton tutor was on the phone, furious. 'You idiot, Daniel. Of course they chucked you out. You failed to deliver your written work.'

'But I did. I delivered it to the Porter's Lodge.'

'You did?'

'Yes, and got a receipt for it too.'

New College had a look and duly found the papers, but it was too late. All the places had been allocated and there was no room for Daniel.

I was the incandescent mother, prepared to tear the place down, insist on justice, retribution, whatever. Harvey MacGregor's attitude was of the 'Ah well, that's life, get over it' school, and Daniel rather agreed with him. He decided Edinburgh would be better anyway, and accepted a place there.

I'm glad to say that when he pulled off a first class degree and won the Kirkpatrick Prize for the best history student, he applied to Oxford to do a PhD and went to Lincoln College, not New.

It seems something of a cliché to say that my

children are the greatest satisfaction in my life, but it is true. To see them safely through childhood and youth is a blessing so many parents do not have. When they graduated from university I said, somewhat smugly, to my mother, 'Well Mum, we did it. Daniel and Li-Da are healthy, happy, and independent.'

'Don't count your chickens,' she said. 'May I remind you that your elder brother, at fifty-eight, is currently living with me.'

David had left Mary, and was camping on his mother's sofa for the time being. He and I remained close while he ran Leith's Good Food, and while he was married to Mary, but sadly, after he left her, and the job with Leith's, he returned to South Africa and the old adage about out of sight, out of mind, kicked in. We saw each other perhaps once a year, when he and his new wife, Lorna, came to England or I visited the Cape. At every reunion it would be as though he'd never left: we'd fall back into the old family jokes and I'd wish I saw more of my big brother. And then we'd part and promptly forget each other again.

Peggy was beginning to lose her memory. By her eightieth birthday, in 1982, it was shaky, but still good in patches. Leith's had the contract for the catering in Hyde Park and we gave her a party in the Serpentine restaurant. I had offered her a *Thé Dansant*, with Palm Court musicians playing Cole Porter as befits an old lady, but she insisted on 'a proper dance, in the evening'.

She had her party on the Friday, and Daniel and Li-Da had a combined eighteenth birthday party on the Saturday. My mother was last off the dance-floor at hers and first on it at the children's.

My mum lived the last fifteen years of her life with little idea who anyone was. She had two excellent carers, Alison and Cathy, whom she resolutely called Elaine, as she did almost everyone – even me at the very end. (Elaine had been her neighbour and great friend, but had long since left to live in South Africa.)

As David was now living in South Africa, it fell to me and Jamie to look after her. I concerned myself with her health, clothes and domestic arrangements and, since I worked in London, I managed to visit her most weeks. Jamie looked after Peggy's finances, did battle with the landlords and the Council, and visited her when he could. We would find her reading the same picture book over and over again, but with all the pleasure of the new. Before she became totally deaf, you could cheer her up by telling her some good news; never mind if it was years old or she'd been told it yesterday. I would tell her that Sam, Alex or Daniel had got firsts at university, or that Li-Da had made a film about Cambodia, and she would be thrilled all over again. And conversely, she would suffer repeated unhappiness if told of some sadness. We learnt just to lie.

One sad day in 1992 I had to break the news that Nan had died. I'd taken her to see Nan a few weeks before, but she had forgotten this in spite of their having had a rather jolly and animated conversation. Peggy was deeply distressed, repeatedly saying she should have been told, she hadn't known Nan was ill. Of course she had, and she did.

Nan was by then in her nineties and very frail, but she would make a supreme effort for visitors and exhaust herself, suffering horribly the next day. Eventually Angela had to ask me not to visit her, and to keep my mama away too. But Rayne continued to see her every week until she died.

Nan's death affected everyone. Peggy would forget, mention Nan, be told she was dead, and suffer all over again. Rayne just shut down and stopped talking altogether for a while. He did the same thing when his mother died: just retreated to his study, said nothing to anyone, couldn't share his grief at all. I myself felt real sorrow: sorrow for everyone, for all that had been, and for the unhappiness Rayne and I had brought her.

One of my mother's pleasures outlasted all others. Frankie and Johnny were a pair of identical tabby kittens that I'd given her and which no one could tell apart. She had them for ten years or so. When Johnny died, we just pretended he was outside, and the present one was whichever cat she thought it was. When the second tabby died, we got another cat – a big black bruiser with white markings, nothing like Frankie or Johnny, but she thought he was Johnny too.

Senility is a horrible thing, but it's not all tragedy. Some of it is serious comedy. Once I'd spent all day weeding Peggy's little garden in the rain. And she'd spent all day telling me not to: she didn't want the place weeded, I must come in and have lunch – which we'd already had – I was not to throw away the rusted and broken table and chairs because she felt sorry for them and was going to fix them and paint them.

Finally she fell asleep in her chair, and I quickly got a taxi to come and collect the dilapidated furniture to take it to the dump. While we were struggling to unscrew the rusty legs to get the table into the cab, Mum woke up and caught us at it. Genuinely upset at my cruelty in rejecting her table, and my bossiness in doing it without her say-so, she insisted we reassemble everything and put it all back in the garden, which we did. I gave the taxi driver a massive tip for his pains, but when she'd gone to bed, I took advantage of the long summer evening to have another go. I called another taxi and took the broken ones to the tip, then went to Homebase and bought six new chairs and a table. I took them back and assembled them in her garden. It took me until ten o'clock and I went home reeling with exhaustion.

Next day, I arrived with some Pathclear to keep the weeds at bay on the paving slabs where I'd weeded. A happy Peggy greeted me at the door with, 'Oh, you must come and see the garden, I want to show you what your darling brother has done. It looks so beautiful. All weeded and clean. Isn't he wonderful?' We surveyed my handiwork. 'And look, he bought me these wonderful new chairs and table.'

One New Year's Day I made lunch for everyone in Mum's house. It was a simple but delicious salad with hot grilled chicken that had been marinaded in a soy and honey mix. We were all tucking in when she pushed her plate away.

'Darlings, I am so, so sorry,' she said. 'I am a perfectly dreadful cook and this is disgusting. Leave it. Come on, we're going out to a restaurant.' Everyone protested that it was delicious, we all refused to budge, and quite soon, Peggy said, 'This is delicious. Penny, you are such a clever girl.'

And then there was the time she got stuck in the bath. Nervous that she might slip, Jamie had installed a phone with huge numbers next to the bath so that she could dial without her glasses. He stuck a notice next to it with his, my and the police numbers in giant print. Seeing the phone and numbers would often prompt her to ring one of us. One day it was my turn.

'Do you know darling, it's most odd, but I cannot get out of the bath.'

I started to tell her to turn over onto her knees, but she lost interest and started talking about something else.

'Pegs, you need to get out of the bath. I will tell you how. Listen.'

'What nonsense darling. Of course I know how to get out of the bath. I do it every day.'

'Okay, then, do it now.'

'Why? You are so *bossy*. Why should I get out of the bath? I'm very happy in it. I will get out in my own good time.'

I gave up, but a few minutes later the phone rang again. 'Darling, it's most odd, but do you know, I can't seem to get out of the bath.'

She was perfectly cheerful about it, but I began to fret and finally rang first her carer, who was out, then her neighbour, who didn't have keys but said she would go and talk to Peggy through the window, and finally the fire brigade, who promised to send someone.

Peggy was back on the phone. I said, 'Don't worry darling, the fire brigade are going to come and get you out.'

'What do I need the fire brigade for? I'm fine. Just thought I would ring to find out how you all are.'

And then I heard her neighbour calling outside the window, and Peggy said, 'I have to go. So sorry, but there's someone at the door.'

'But Peggy, you're stuck in the bath, remember?'

'What nonsense . . .'

And so it went on.

I kept her on the phone, sometimes having to ring her back if she put the phone down to 'get out and deal with the door'.

After about ten minutes she exclaimed. 'Good Lord, there is a policewoman in my bathroom!'

The fire brigade had come mob-handed. Two burly guys, and a skinny policewoman who had managed to climb through the bedroom window.

Peggy was delighted. When I rang a little while later she said, 'Darling, I'm having a tea party. There are two very handsome chaps in uniform and a woman police officer. I have no idea why they are here, but Elaine' (that time Elaine *did* mean Elaine, her neighbour) 'has made us tea and we are having a lovely time. Come round, darling, do.'

Until she turned ninety, we would joke that Peggy would outlive us all, she was so physically well, if mentally away with the fairies. But after ninety she deteriorated and had a couple of falls, with consequent stays in the Royal Free Hospital. One day she looked out at the tree-tops of Hampstead and said, 'The Karoo looks very green this year, doesn't it? But this is a dreadful hotel. The service is appalling and the food uneatable.'

Soon, we realised she could die at any time and we decided we wanted her to do so at home. Hospitals confused and upset her, and over-stretched medical staff can't be trusted not to over-tranquillise old ladies to stop them falling out of bed or anxiously wandering the wards. And they're not great at listening to the patients or the relatives either. I had the following conversation with a doctor.

'Your mother has pneumonia. We need to give her antibiotics.'

'Please don't. She does not want intervention.'

294

'Are you saying you don't want your mother to live?'

'Perhaps I am. I don't want her to go on having the life she has now, in and out of this place and no pleasures at all. She cannot get out of bed. She cannot walk. She is incontinent. She can hardly eat. Or see. And she is profoundly deaf. She doesn't know who anyone is or *where* she is. Can't you just give her pain relief and let Nature take her course?'

I got a lecture on the Hippocratic Oath. And Peggy got the antibiotics.

Peggy had written a 'living will' specifying that she was not to be artificially revived or kept alive if she had a heart attack or stroke and her quality of life was judged by us not to be worth living for. But such pieces of paper are useless if they are in a safe, a desk or with a lawyer. Her carer Alison wisely said we needed a copy at her bedside or in the hall. That way, whoever was with Peggy could brandish it at locum doctors or paramedics in the faint hope that they would use their judgement rather than follow the hospital protocols. But we knew our best hope of preventing over-zealous medication would be to keep her out of hospital. If Peggy was dying peacefully, we would not call an ambulance.

In fact, she died in April 2010, when Jamie and I were on a canal boat in France. Alison, aware that Peggy was dying, sat with her, holding her hand, but unfortunately one of the Council's nursing assistants who came in the morning to help get Peggy turned over and washed, saw that she was dying. The woman became hysterical, called on God, the Virgin Mary and all the saints, and, ignoring Alison's protests, called 999 as well.

But Peggy, her actress's timing perfect to the last, made her exit just before the ambulance got there.

She was cremated at Kensal Green cemetery in London, where we stood around mournfully. I felt sorriest for Alison and Cathy, who had devotedly cared for her for many years. Their lives would change more radically than any of ours. Li-Da and I scattered primroses and crocuses from Chastleton on her coffin.

In January 2011 the whole extended family travelled to South Africa to scatter Peggy's ashes on the same hillside plot on which we'd scattered Dad's gritty and greasy ashes fifty years before. This was an altogether happier occasion, and hers were light and floaty.

It was a still, sunny, day. The cemetery is no longer used, and there was no one else there. The grey, granite gravestones were softened by knee-high spring grass and we were cheered by slanting sun, dappled shade and deep blue sky above the pine trees. We just stood round and talked about Peggy, and some of my cousins talked *to* her. And then we went to my cousin Paul's for a rather merry wake.

CHAPTER 14

CONFERENCE CALL

And tea for the Queen

Leith's catering company had a great reputation, but it didn't start making serious money until we landed some long-running big contracts.

The contract that put us on the map was with Orient Express. It was to feed the passengers on the British Pullman train that ran from Victoria station to Folkestone harbour. From there, the passengers caught the ferry to Boulogne to meet their Orient Express train, bound for Venice or Istanbul. We had to provide lunch on the way to Folkestone and tea for returning travellers on their way back.

Someone had recommended us to James Sherwood, the extraordinary American who had started what became the worldwide Sea Containers company. As a sideline, he'd bought and restored some of the original Orient Express coaches. His love of historic trains and beautiful old buildings eventually led to the luxury hotel and travel company that Orient Express is today. When I first met him in 1982, however, the train was yet to do its maiden run to Venice, with the world's press and a galaxy of A-list passengers on board.

We were invited to prepare a test lunch for Mr Sherwood and his wife, Dr Shirley Sherwood. Because the passengers' dinner on the continental Orient Express would be classic French cuisine, including a meat main course, we decided on a summer lunch menu for the English Pullman of chilled watercress soup, salmon, and Eton mess – a mix of strawberries, meringues and cream. But how to make it out of the ordinary? Better than anyone else's? For all we knew, the Sherwoods might be having trial lunches delivered by half the caterers in town.

I hit on the idea of shaping the croutons for the soup into little steam engines with puffs of smoke (actually blobs of cream) coming out of the funnel. Each bowl of soup would be topped with a steam engine at the last minute.

We had to cut the croutons by hand, and it took ages. It was almost impossible to make them look like steam engines – most resembled lumpy elephants or billowing clouds, but we got half a dozen good ones in the end. Once we had the contract, we told ourselves, we would have metal cutters made.

Cooking the lunch was not the only test the Sherwoods put us through. They wanted to view our premises and see a catered dinner in action. I was proud of our Sebastian Street premises, and of course we had them gleaming more brightly than ever for the inspection. But we had a problem: almost nothing would be happening at the time they had elected to come. The food for the one event we were doing that evening would have left already, and the prep for the following day would be over and done. I couldn't bear the idea of the Sherwoods walking round a silent and empty kitchen.

So we faked it. We got half a dozen cooks to stay on, and decided on a route for me to follow with the visitors in tow. As we entered the first kitchen one chef immediately set about stuffing a boned duck while, just as we got to him, his colleague started wrapping an already stuffed duck in muslin and painting it with melted butter. When we got to the next work bench a cook was putting the finishing touches to a huge platter of colourful grilled yellow and red peppers with black olives, while someone else turned on the Magimix to whizz fresh pesto, and a third cook was feeding dough through a pasta machine. As we walked into the hot kitchen, two cooks immediately picked up a huge salmon and lowered it into a fish kettle, adding white wine, slices of lemon and bunches of herbs, while another started tossing almonds in her frying pan. And so on through the three kitchens. The minute the Sherwoods left, the salmon went back into the fridge. We'd pre-sold the ballotines of duck and the pepper and olive salad to Leith's Restaurant for the first course trolley, and the pesto and pasta was stored for next day's staff lunch.

When this performance was over, I drove the Sherwoods in one of our vans to see a catering event in action, where Mrs Henderson and Declan, well-primed, duly sang the praises of the wonderful company they worked for.

I've no idea if it was the steam engine croutons, the staged activity in the kitchen or the catering event that swung it for us, but we got the contract. Needless to say we never made the locomotive croutons: the train waiters only had fifty-five minutes to serve and clear a three-course lunch in a moving train – carefully placing individual croutons into each soup cup and adding the smoke blobs was obviously out of the question. So the first course was a hot watercress and spinach soup, ladled from a silver soup tureen by one waiter, while another followed, offering regular croutons and soured cream.

The main course we finally decided on was a pink and white fish terrine. I had an antique cylindrical copper mould with a curved hinged lid, with removable discs at each end. By half filling the mould with the pink trout mixture, piping a length of the white pike mousse (speckled green with chopped parsley and tarragon) down the middle, and topping up with more pink mixture, the resulting mousse would be perfectly cylindrical with a core of white and green in the middle.

For some reason I wanted round rather than rectangular slices, which was fine when experimenting with my one and only mould and selling the idea to the train bosses. But now I needed twenty such circular moulds, catering suppliers had never heard of them, and antique ones would cost too much – if we could even track any down.

Eventually we found the solution. If you three-quarters filled an empty one-pound baked-bean can with the pink trout mouse, froze the white fish mixture into rigid sticks and pushed them into the middle of the still-soft pink mixture in the tins, then gave them time for the middle to thaw before cooking in a *bain marie*, it worked a treat. Only one problem: we hardly ever used tins of anything, and the few we did were catering size and too big for our purpose.

Never say die: I brought the empty cans from home. The staff must have thought I lived on tinned food, but the truth was worse. They were cat-food tins. Benedicat's dinner came in just the right size cans, and he got through seven of them a week, so I sterilised them and removed the labels at home. You never knew – one of our cooks might have had a friend working on a gossip column. Imagine a *Londoner's Diary* headline, 'Orient Express lunches cooked in cat-food cans.'

The first lunch was very nearly a fiasco. I was making the terrine, a classic quenelle mixture which requires a lot of double cream to be beaten into raw sieved fish and egg white. The trick is to keep the mixture very cold. If it warms up it will curdle – 'split' in chef-speak.

Which is exactly what happened. All the rehearsals for this dish had been done in small quantities, but this time I combined the minced pink trout flesh and egg white for two hundred people in our biggest industrial mixer and slowly added the cream. The process took too long, nothing was chilled enough, and the mixture warmed up and split.

By now it was six o'clock in the evening and the cooks were due to leave. None of us had a clue how to rescue it. I rang Albert Roux. You can't, he said. Start again from scratch, keep everything really cold and do it in small quantities.

The pink trout came from a fish farm outside Oxford. They were closed by that hour, but I managed to raise the owner, who went out to his ponds and killed a dozen huge fish for us. His son drove the sixty miles to London and delivered the order at nine o'clock that night. Two of the cooks stayed on to help me. By the time we had re-made the pink mixture (successfully this time), filled the tins, put the frozen white mix into them, given them time to thaw (if we had cooked them with a frozen middle the outside layer would be overcooked before the core was defrosted), cooked them, cooled them in iced water (we had no blast-chiller in those days) and finally got them into the fridges, it was four a.m. But they were perfect.

All the same, it was a relief when the season was over and the menu changed.

Winning the Orient Express contract took us from being thought of as a few young women with a modest little business, to being regarded as serious professional caterers. When, in 1985, the contract for the new Queen Elizabeth II Conference Centre, in the heart of Westminster and to be the biggest in the country, went out for tender, the catering consultant running the process rang me.

'We're really keen to consider enterprising new caterers who care about good food, not just the usual big companies. Why haven't you tendered for the contract? It's perfect for you.'

'We thought about it,' I told her, 'but it would take us from twenty-five employees to over fifty in a single jump, and half our eggs would be in a new and untried basket. If it were to fail, it would bring down the company. We'd be betting the farm.'

Nevertheless, we agreed to have another look, and they agreed that they were not, as the tender documents implied, bound to have a regeneration system, which would mean most of the food cooked in advance and reheated, something I would never agree to.

To our astonishment we got the contract. There was a committee to convince, but the man who really made the decision was Brigadier Roy Kendrick, the centre's director. And then he let us re-design the enormous kitchens, which contained a fifteen foot-long bank of deep fryers, evidently intended to fry chips by the truckload, but no brat-pans, steamers, combination ovens, vacuum packer, or blast-chiller. Indeed, apart from acres of stainless steel workbenches, there was almost no kit suitable for cooking good food from scratch.

The Brigadier also allowed us far more office space than they'd intended. Our offices, I remember, were furnished with magnificent oak desks, specially commissioned by the Property Services Agency. Apparently, the number needed for this huge building had been calculated on its square footage and the assumption that the premises were exclusively for offices. Since one whole floor was exhibition space and entrance lobby and another mostly reception and dining rooms, there were a great deal of extra desks, paid for by the tax payer, hidden away in some government store in Milton Keynes. We gladly relieved them of half a dozen or so.

I hired the head chef, Alan Brazier, from the Portman Hotel. He had excellent references and I liked him at once. He nodded in agreement as I took him through Leith's cookbooks, explaining that we never, ever, used inferior ingredients, that we made everything ourselves, that all decoration had to be relevant – watercress with a mixed grill because its bitter flavour counteracts the fatty richness of the meat; tarragon only if the sauce is a tarragon one; radishes if they are young, fresh and delicious, not just for their colour; chocolate curls on the dessert only if it's a chocolate dessert and made with the best chocolate, and so on and on, including dire warnings about never ever carving radishes into hand grenades, shredding spring onion tops into brushes or carving swans out of apples.

And then, on our very first job, a lunch for a medical conference paying extremely little, I walked into the kitchen to find that the trifle had been made with a bought-in cake mix, packet jelly, some gluey fruit pie filling from a can, powdered custard, and cream out of a spray can. The cheese-boards was rubbery orange cheddar from a block and assorted cheese biscuits, instead of our standard oatcakes and water biscuits. And Kevin, the second chef, who had followed Alan from his previous kitchen, was carving turnips into chry-santhemums and dying them purple for elaborate table decorations.

For the second, and last, time in my catering career I lost my temper. I swept poor Kevin's painstakingly achieved flower carvings into the bin. The contents of the cheeseboards and the trifle bowls followed. I sent out for cheese and biscuits from Paxton and Whitfield in Jermyn Street, and got the whole kitchen hurriedly making expensive fruit salad.

When the lunch was over, calmer now, I sat down with Alan and Kevin.

'Okay, you guys. What happened? How come

you produced that horrible food when I have been banging on about good food for a fortnight?'

Alan said, 'At the start of every job I have ever had the boss has gone on about good food, buying the best and so on. Just like you. But at the end of the first month when the cost of the food means the gross profit is too low, it's a whole other story.'

'Did I ever say one single word about food costs? Did we ever even discuss the GP?'

'Okay, I believe you now. I'm really sorry.'

I apologised too. They would both have been justified in walking out: humiliating head chefs in front of their juniors is not the way to command loyalty. But they both stayed.

Nine years later Alan Brazier had become our executive chef for the whole group. He was evangelical about the 'Leith's way', telling new chefs the cheese and trifle story, insisting they'd better believe we meant it about good ingredients, no unnecessary tat, simplicity rather than elaboration, etc. And Kevin eventually followed Alan as the QEII Centre's head chef. A year or two later he came with me and Sally Procter, the co-principal of Leith's School of Food and Wine, and JBR from Leith's restaurant, to New York to run a Leith's Restaurant week in the Barbizon Hotel and do Leith's cookery demonstrations in Bloomingdale's department store.

A couple of years into the QEII contract, I got my comeuppance for bawling them out in front of the whole brigade. I walked into a busy kitchen in January and saw a mountain of fresh mint sprigs with four or five cooks standing round the table, carefully pinching out the top spriglet of leaves from each stalk and binning the rest.

I was outraged, but kept my voice polite.

'Chef,' I said, 'it is January. That mint must have cost a fortune, and ninety per cent of it is going in the bin.'

'We need six hundred mint sprigs for the banquet tonight. To go on the Crème de Menthe mousse.'

'But why not put a single leaf on each, not the top sprig!'

'Because you always say that if we are scaling up a recipe the quality should be as good as for four people. If it was a party for four, we'd use top sprigs. So, we need six hundred stalks of mint to get six hundred top sprigs.'

Touché.

There is no doubt that the QEII was initially too big a leap for us, although the first seriously big job, the EU Summit, went like a dream. We turned the top floor into a seafood restaurant with a centrepiece consisting of a real rowboat filled with crushed ice, nets, shells, seaweed and fish. Over four days we served forty-two thousand meals, all fresh and made on site.

But hard on the heels of this success, came near disaster.

Imagination, the creative agency set up by the extraordinary Gary Withers, booked a three-day event for the Ford Motor Company's UK-wide dealers. Imagination could transform anything into anything, and for this they turned the Centre's vast, boring exhibition space into a New York night club and booked Victor Borge, the famous Danish pianist-comedian, for the after-dinner entertainment. The car dealers arrived by their hundreds, in two batches a day, one lot to be given lunch, the other dinner – though the illusion of a club's late-night dinner was to be as real at midday as at night. Because the guests had to travel for hours from all over the country, and get home again at a reasonable hour, the first 'dinner' was at noon and the second at four in the afternoon. We had an hour to turn the room round between services and wash up everything. Almost all the staff were from agencies, many young and untrained, and we knew none of them. We barely knew our own staff.

I'm sure only a very few guests noticed anything wrong, but I remember the event with anguish. The kitchen managed to cope, just, although Kevin put himself out of action by slicing his fingers instead of the rare beef fillet. Then half the customers wanted their beef well done and Alan ended up cooking the slices on the shelves of the hot-cupboards.

The service was an undignified scramble. I remember Robert Kelso, the managing director of Leith's Good Food, hastily drying plates before putting them down in front of the VIP table, including our client, Gary Withers.

Most of our problems arose from a lack of time

for training or briefing – waiters served from the wrong side, were unable to answer questions, forgot things, and got lost – the building is famously difficult to navigate. One young waitress, bending low to serve the vegetables, got her dangly earrings caught in the customer's hair. With the platter of veg in one hand and the serving spoons in the other she could do nothing about it and I had to untangle her. Needless to say, the Leith's dress code for staff did not permit dangly earrings, but there had been no time for the usual staff inspection.

Nothing improved. Gary had insisted that there be no waiting staff present during the Victor Borge performance, which meant that a bunch of student waiters were imprisoned for an hour in the dispense-bar, where they got stuck into the wine. One of them, drunk as a skunk, had to be evicted after he'd sat himself down at the VIP table and tried to join the party.

That was Day One. We still had two more to go. I wasn't surprised to be summoned to Brigadier Kendrick's office at eight a.m. the next morning. Gary was there, looking like thunder, intending to sack us and call in more experienced caterers – and stick us with the bill. I did the only thing I could: apologise, admit our complete incompetence and promise to do everything I could to get the next two days right. We'd already arranged to hire more equipment so we wouldn't have the washing-up scramble, begged the agencies to send us some competent senior staff as well as the young ones, and we'd booked the agency staff in hours early to give them waiting lessons. And the cooks had been in since five a.m. to get ahead. Roy Kendrick interceded on our behalf and Gary relented. And the next two days were fine. Very fine.

Checking facts for this book, I asked Alan for his help. He wrote to me of this event:

I found you wanting to kill someone. With tears in your eyes you said, 'Alan that's it, we have now lost the contract.' I remember giving you a big hug, saying that won't happen, we are too good, we will bounce back and we did, big time.

They were good times Prue, staff worked hard but we allowed them to also enjoy and have fun. That my dear lady, was down to you, yes the boss, who everyone respected – well, once they got to understand what we stood for, simple and the best. I can't remember that much that I did not enjoy.

We did get much better at everything. We quickly earned a reputation for treating conference delegates like proper people, not as units to be fed rubber chicken with rice and bought-in ersatz mousse, or white-bread sandwiches with minimum filling. At the time, most London head chefs gave their attention to the expensive party banquets, not to conference lunches on a budget. But I have always thought a plate of good sausage and mash, or even a bowl of spag bol, properly made, a better option than finger food. Canapés and sandwiches can cost less in ingredients but they are labour intensive, and I would rather see money spent on the quality of the food.

Our service became better too. We began to build up a loyal team of casual staff for big events and to train everyone well. We wanted waiting staff to be proud to wear a Leith's apron. But we were still learning.

One day I was entering the Centre as a young man came dashing through the lobby, his face dark with fury. He yanked his Leith's pass off his jacket and threw it on a table. I managed, with difficulty, to catch him.

'Hey, what's up. Are you working for Leith's?'

'No, I'm bloody not. The bastards have just thrown me out.'

I made him sit down and tell me why. He pulled out a sheet of paper. It was our waiting-staff dress code. 'Look at this. I have every single thing they demanded, and I had to buy the trousers specially, and it cost all the money I have, and now they tell me I'm not dressed right.'

His hair was in gelled spikes – but short, as decreed on his piece of paper. His shirt was crumpled, but clean and white, as demanded. His trousers were jeans, but they *were* black. And although his shoes were heavy bovver boots, they were black and polished. He had done exactly as asked, but we had not been specific enough.

I did a deal with him. We agreed that we would employ him for a week, he would go down the road and buy another pair of trousers and a pair of ordinary shoes, the cost of which we would lend him and deduct from his wages. He would wash his hair and iron his shirt upstairs – waiters often needed an iron and we had one.

He became a regular, and after a year or two joined the staff as a barman. He worked for us for years, and I was grateful for the lesson: if you want instructions to be followed, they have to be crystal clear.

Another lesson was harder to master: if you don't like someone, don't employ them. I did not like our general manager, Melvin, but he had great experience, he was a smart and goodlooking blond Swede, and he came with terrific references. But he was cold. Not unfriendly exactly, just very contained. When he disagreed with you he didn't say so, but you could see his jaw clenching and unclenching. And he was obstinate as hell.

One day, when the Centre had been open for three weeks, I was walking through the basement when I noticed the unmistakable odour of rotting garbage. I followed my nose, the stink getting fouler and fouler, until I discovered its source. Bags and bags of rotting food waste, flies everywhere, burst bags spewing out chicken carcases crawling with maggots.

I took the lift straight up to Melvin's office.

'The rubbish room cannot have been cleared for weeks. What's going on?'

'It's not our job. The Centre's porters, not ours, are meant to do it.'

'But, Melvin, it's *our* rubbish!'

Melvin's jaw was clenching. 'The agreement says we are responsible for putting it there. They are responsible for moving it onto the apron at the loading bay for the bin men to collect.'

'But that is not happening.'

He shrugged, jaw working overtime. 'Not our problem.'

Deep breath. Stay calm. 'It *is* our problem. What do you think your staff think of you if they're ordered to add more rubbish bags to piles of already rotting garbage? There are maggots down there! If Brigadier Kendrick smells it he'll assume it's our fault. And we're meant to work *with* the Centre staff, not draw battle lines.'

I couldn't convince him, so I resorted to ordering him to get the rubbish moved there and then and sort out whose job it was afterwards.

Thirty minutes later he was still at his desk.

'Have you had the rubbish cleared?'

'No. The kitchen porters have left for the day. Tomorrow, I'll get the Centre . . .'

I turned on my heel and went down to the rubbish room. There were – I counted – forty-two bin bags of putrid rubbish. I re-bagged every one, sealed them and humped them onto the apron

313

outside the back door. The operation took me about three hours. I was wearing smart little black patent summer sandals with heels and within minutes they were slimy and wet from squelching through liquefying mess. I ended up doing the job barefoot, tramping through the maggots and slime.

When the room was empty I hosed walls and floor down with hot water and bleach. I took a kind of unholy satisfaction in doing the job more than properly. Then I washed and disinfected my feet and shoes and went upstairs for a shower. And resolved to get rid of Melvin.

That incident served me better than I could ever have guessed. I had acted instinctively, and in a fine fury. But if I had planned it, it could not have done me more good. Word got out that the boss, usually to be seen swanning around in business suits or evening clothes, had rolled up her sleeves and spent hours clearing rotting garbage.

A lot of catering consists of cleaning. If the boss can still pick up a broom, scrub out a van, or sterilise a fridge, it does his or her reputation a power of good. Years later, when we had just got the contract for the public catering in Hyde Park, a press photographer took a shot of me scrubbing bird mess off the stone picnic tables prior to opening. He offered to do a more conventional shot of me looking decorative with the lake behind me, but I figured the scrubbing would send a better message – about hygiene, hard work, enthusiasm, etc, rather than smug satisfaction.

Melvin's successor, Patrick Harbour, was a massive improvement. He eventually became managing director for the whole of Leith's group of companies. He had worked for the King and Queen of Jordan as their food and beverage manager, he had a passion for good food, and he was, and is, a thoroughly nice guy.

Patrick was great in all the obvious ways: honest, hardworking, imaginative, etc. But he also achieved something that I had absolutely failed to do – he got the office staff to go home on time. It worried me that they would often stay late into the evening, claiming they needed the time to work on events when the cooks had gone home and the phones stopped ringing. But Patrick's wife had a senior job with British Airways and her job meant Patrick sometimes *had* to leave work at five-thirty to collect their child from the nursery. And, since the boss left early, and patently managed his job within the allotted hours, the others followed suit.

The QEII Centre opened a few months before the marriage of Prince Andrew to Sarah Ferguson in July 1986, and all the rooms overlooking Westminster Abbey were sold to private parties wanting to watch the arrival and departure of the wedding couple, and the royal, rich or famous guests. I booked one of the rooms myself and invited a clutch of VIPs who I thought would be good for business. It was a great day, and for the first time I began to think we would get the hang of this conference and big-event business.

That contract got us more publicity than we deserved because I was young and female and never backward in coming forward into the limelight. Maybe due to my actress-mother's genes, my instinct is always to talk to the press rather than hide from them. The *Evening Standard* carried a large photo of me sitting on the lawn outside the QEII building, brandishing a teapot in one hand and a tea tray in the other and grinning from ear to ear.

I don't like my reputation for egotism or for bossiness and would prefer to be self-effacing like my son and accommodating like my daughter, who must have modelled themselves on their father. But my personality has, undeniably, been a factor, if a small one, in my success. I am the only person I know who *likes* having her photograph taken. I don't often like the results – too vain for that – but I love the dedicated attention of the photographer.

The Queen Elizabeth II Centre was officially opened by Her Majesty about a year after its actual opening. You would have thought that that would have been enough time to iron out all the teething problems and for the event to go like clockwork, but the well-known royal gremlins that ensure a rocky ride were at work as always.

I've always hired people who do things better than I do, which largely accounts for the success of the company. I am utterly untrained as a waiter and I'm naturally clumsy. When I was a teenager,

I knocked over a drinks tray, and my mother, trying to make a joke of it in front of her guests, said, 'It's just like having a horse in the house.' It hurt, but it was true.

So I had every intention of having our head waiter give the Queen her tea, but Roy Kendrick decided it should be my job.

I thought I'd better get this right, so I rang the Palace and spoke to an equerry.

'Can you tell me how Her Majesty takes her tea?'

'Oh, she'll have just what everyone else does. If it's a plastic cup, she'll have that, if it's . . .'

'No, I mean does she take milk and sugar? What *kind* of tea?'

'Just offer her whatever everyone else is having.'

'Look, *everyone* always has a preference of how they like their tea. Strong. Weak. Black. Sugar. No sugar. How does she usually have it?'

'I don't think I can tell you that.'

Did he think it was a state secret?

'Look,' I said, 'I will know very soon, because I'm about to serve her some. It would just help me to be quick and efficient about it if you would tell me what she has at home . . .'

'If you insist. The butler brings a tray and on it there should be a teapot, hot water jug, milk jug, cream jug . . .'

'Cream jug?'

'Yes, you see in Scotland tea is often taken with cream. And then there should be a sugar bowl, and a dish of lemon slices.'

I gave up.

A solid silver tray with all that stuff on it weighs a ton. I was so nervous I took a Valium and got our faithful Mrs Henderson to give me a lesson, but I still had to dig my elbow into my hip to stop my arm dropping off and only half fill the jugs so I could hold the tray up at all.

When the Queen finally arrived at the end of a long receiving line she looked decidedly grumpy, as well she might. She had just been on a two-hour trip round a lot of boring offices and conference areas. And the Cabinet Minister doing the honours had got a list with the guests in reverse order and it wasn't until he was half way down the line that someone had the courage to tell him he was getting the names wrong. The Queen nobly insisted on starting again.

She must have been gasping for a cuppa.

'Black or White, ma'am?' I said, remembering to say Mam to rhyme with Jam.

'Black, please.'

I picked up a lemon slice with a cocktail stick, put it in the cup and started to pour tea into it.

'No lemon, thank you.'

What to do? I only had one cup. So I fished the lemon out with the stick. But where to put it? No little saucer for these eventualities. I put it, splat, down on the white tray cloth. Not a pretty sight. I then topped up Her Majesty's cuppa with water, thinking that people who like black tea usually like it weak.

'No water,' she said.

Too late. Now the poor woman had weak lemony tea when she wanted strong black tea.

The Duke of Edinburgh fared rather better. When we'd rung his office his equerry had said, 'Lapsang Souchong. With milk. Tea in first. No sugar.'

Thank you, sir.

My enthusiasm for contracts led me to some deals I should never have touched with a barge-pole. The most notable were for the public parks. I'd been impressed by the Tavern on the Green in the middle of New York's Central Park, then an excellent and fashionable place, full at lunch and dinner and serving good, if not wonderful, food. Why not in Hyde Park?

The Department of the Environment decided to pull down the Serpentine Restaurant on the road that runs from north to south of the park and rebuild it. Though an attractive building by the architect Patrick Gwynne, it had been shoddily constructed in the Sixties and had not been well maintained. It had to go.

Every caterer in the country wanted to get the contract for the new building. Of course they did. Imagine: a new lakeside restaurant, with a car-park, in the middle of rolling greenery smack in the centre of London?

In the meantime, the Parks Department needed to arrange temporary catering while the old restaurant was being demolished and then re-built. Most caterers were more wary of that. The caterer would be responsible for building the new temporary Serpentine Restaurant, which wouldn't be on the road or have a car-park, and there would be no guarantee that the winning caterer would get the long-term contract in the final building.

I figured if we did a good job in the three-year gap, we would learn a lot and be in poll position to claim the plum. And anyway, the deal included the big Dell Restaurant at the other end of the Serpentine Lake, and several ice-cream and snack kiosks dotted round the park. Surely those would be profitable?

Rayne disagreed. 'You've never done popular catering. What makes you think the British public is ready for a plate of seafood and a glass of Chardonnay?' He did his best to dissuade me, as did others. Annie Herriott, head of our Events and Parties division asked, 'How can I sell Leith's parties at the caviar-and-champagne end if we're also selling slimy burgers and Mr Whippy to the general public?'

I rang up Rocco Forte, who had the current contract.

'Prue, if the sun is shining you will be overrun with more customers than you can handle. If it's raining you'll have a restaurant full of staff and not one customer. Either way, it's a nightmare.'

But I wouldn't listen. We were not going to sell junk. We would sell the best sandwiches, the best salads, real coffee, Italian ice cream. Rayne used to say that in a disagreement he might as well give in at the start, since he'd have to in the end, and once the die was cast, he was wonderful, leading negotiations with the Parks Department and erecting our tented building.

We quickly gained the contract for Kensington Gardens as well as Hyde Park and I was thrilled.

Our contract required us to have the restaurants and kiosks open from eight a.m. to sunset and the Serpentine Restaurant open in the evenings too, regardless of season or weather. The only people in the parks early in the morning are joggers and dog walkers and they don't want breakfast.

Our posh little lunch-and-tea room at the Kensington Palace Orangery was a listed building and we were not allowed to put kitchens in it. The food came from our Bondway depot and from the kitchens at the Serpentine and was put together behind a screen.

Rocco was right. On wet days no one came and we had expensive, and morose, staff hanging around wishing they were elsewhere. And we had not reckoned on the ice-cream mafia. We had the exclusive right to sell ice cream but the Mr Whippy vans would just come in and trade right next to ours. The park police, summoned, would get rid of them and an hour later they would be back. One of our managers, remonstrating, got beaten up.

The Parks officials were as unhelpful as possible.

They would fail to open the public loos and we'd have queues of mums trailing children through our restaurants to use ours. They would not allow taxis to drop customers off at our Serpentine Restaurant, so few ventured there if it was even slightly overcast. They had provided a lamp-lighted path to the restaurant, but for the whole of the first year the lights came on in the day and went off at night, and no amount of badgering, pleading, shouting and threatening could get the timer changed.

If our loos backed up, a frequent occurrence, we had to call Park Maintenance, who would send a couple of chaps in suits with a clipboard when what we needed was a plumber.

We weren't allowed to kill the rats that infested the back of the Dell, but I did, illegally, put down rat poison, and sadly managed to dispatch six rare ornamental ducks. That did nothing to improve relations with the park authorities.

The pigeons dive-bombed the customers' trays and the sparrows would wait until we opened the doors of the Serpentine restaurant and fly in with the staff. We hired a falconer with a hawk on Tuesdays and Fridays to keep the birds away but they quickly learned to resume operations on the other days.

Most importantly, as soon as the old Serpentine was down and the area re-grassed, but before the new building could be started, a public movement to prevent any new restaurant at all was started.

The campaign succeeded and the new restaurant was never built.

But blaming others is easy. In truth, we were not very good at park catering. I'd hired a plausible but useless manager, who spent his time devising business plans of the sort he'd learnt at business school, but little in training or watching the staff. Students on summer jobs need a lot of watching. One of them, trusted with putting the ice-cream money in the safe, failed to lock it, and the week's entire takings were stolen. The careless student, I'm sorry to say, was my schoolboy son Daniel.

It wasn't only money. Booze and food disappeared daily, the expensive cappuccino machines and ice-cream makers were not being properly maintained so failed repeatedly, the menus varied wildly on the whim of successive chefs. In short we didn't know what we were doing.

Our nadir was the Pavarotti concert in the summer of 1991. Half a million people were expected. The Dell restaurant was right next to the concert site and we looked forward to bumper sales. We ordered tons of food and drink, worked night and day, hired platoons of staff, arranged for boats to ferry customers across to the Serpentine Restaurant on the other side of the lake for posh after-concert dinners.

Then the concert organisers erected eight-foot high fences round the area, effectively barring customers from the Dell Restaurant.

And it rained. Not gentle English rain but

Noah-scale floods. The audience with seats sat in pools of water on their plastic chairs (you couldn't tip the water out because the seats were linked together in rows), the rest sat on sodden grass. But the rain was warm and once we settled for an under-water concert, it was wonderful.

Pavarotti, water streaming down his face, wrung out his famous white hanky. He was then at the top of his game, and that great voice filled the park to a background of steady downpour. His last aria, naturally, was 'Nessun Dorma' and the crowd went wild. Princess Diana came on stage at the end, her hair in dripping ringlets, as happy as the rest of us.

But our plans for making a fortune were out the window. We threw away mountains of food and lost all the money we'd made that season.

We had bad weather for two out of our three years in the park. When our contract was up we were asked to re-tender, but with the new Serpentine Restaurant project cancelled, we decided to cut our losses.

The venture was a total failure and we lost a fortune. Rayne never, ever, said I told you so.

I left the park with a mixture of relief and disappointment. I knew in my soul that good catering was possible in a public space, and my successors have proved it triumphantly. The old Serpentine swimming clubhouse is now refurbished as a much better cafe than we had in our tent. Oliver Peyton now runs the stylish new-build restaurant in St James's Park. It can be done, but it's tough.

If we were struggling in the parks, our reputation as good conference and banqueting caterers was spreading, eventually leading, in 1994, to one of the best contracts we ever landed, the Edinburgh International Conference Centre. We had already catered for the Prime Ministers' Conference held at Edinburgh's Meadowbank Sports Centre, where we'd fed the international delegates, their staff, and the world's press. We had craned in twenty containerised kitchens, as well as dry goods and equipment stores, refrigeration units, offices, and changing rooms for the staff. We turned the running track that ran under the stadium into dining rooms.

The day before the conference began, the chief environmental officer, horrified to learn that we were cooking from scratch (the authority preferred the reliability and safety of bought-in factory-frozen dishes, regenerated on site) turned up on an inspection.

He was amazed to see live lobsters poaching, cooks gutting fresh salmon and making fish stock from the bones, chickens and ducks being boned. Happily, he was so bowled over by the organisation, efficiency and cleanliness of the operation that he came back with all his officers in tow – to show them, he said, how outside catering should be done.

Despite this approval, I hadn't expected us to win the conference centre contract in the face of Scots mistrust of the English. But Hans Rissmann, the CEO who would make the decision, was a civilised German who had managed some of the world's biggest and best hotels and took no notice of Anglo-Scots feuds or squeals of outrage from our Scottish rivals. He wanted excellence, and he didn't care where it came from. I remember him telling me and Patrick Harbour, by then our group managing director, that the reason he hired us was little to do with our presentation, our menus or our prices. It was because he could see hunger and excitement in our eyes.

As is usual when kitchens are designed by catering consultants rather than actual caterers, those at the Edinburgh Conference Centre were full of kit we didn't need. Once again we set about making alterations to provide for a fresh food operation, which we did with great success. I would like to claim the credit for this, but the truth is that caterers do best with a good client, and Hans was exceptional. Encouraging and enthusiastic, he understood the high-end food business backwards. He is hard driving, demanding and never leaves a fault unchecked. As I write this, sixteen years later, Leith's is still there and so is Hans.

Conferences and big events are what make the big money in catering. Leith's Restaurant and the cooking school brought us invaluable publicity and renown, but not much profit. The school was a steady but not spectacular earner; the restaurant would make a hefty sum one year and almost nothing the next. One year, in the recession of the early Eighties, it made a profit of exactly £4,000, while American Express creamed off £12,000 in commission on credit cards!

The great thing about an exclusive contract in a venue that doesn't belong to you is that you are not responsible for the costs of the buildings and you don't have to do any marketing. The client repairs the lift and changes the carpets, and delivers the diners to you on a plate. If the partnership works, you can do very, very well.

Success, of course, rests on the deal you do. Too tough and you lose money, too cushy and the client will come to resent your large profit. I learnt this lesson at the Institute of Chartered Accountants (the ICA), where they had a grand Livery Hall and an office block full of hungry staff. The incumbent caterers had what must have seemed to them a deal to die for. They ran the restaurant in the basement, the livery dinners for hundreds, and all the office catering (teas, coffees, canapés, lunches) on what was known as a 'cost-plus' contract. This meant the ICA had to meet all the expenses and underwrite any losses, pay for any capital investment and fork out a management fee on top.

The Institute had no idea that their caterers were also getting kickbacks (sanitised by the word *over-riders* in the trade) from all their suppliers. This is the pernicious, and still common, practice of charging the client the full cost (often inflated) for materials, ingredients, etc, and then getting a percentage re-imbursement from the butcher, baker and candlestick-maker at the end of the month.

For the catering company it was win-win all the way, yet their employees were as unhappy as the client. The kitchens and restaurant badly needed updating and refurbishing, but the ICA was reluctant to invest in something which was losing them £60,000 a year; and, since the caterers *couldn't* lose money, there was little incentive for them to do a decent job. The restaurant food, old-fashioned, heavy and unimaginative, was slopped out of stainless steel containers from a hot counter, as you might expect in a prison. The average number of lunchtime customers was eleven.

The Livery Hall banquets made money and the chef took more trouble with these, but it's a miracle the customers weren't poisoned. I have seldom seen such filthy kitchens – there was a thick crust of mouse droppings round the edges of the floor.

We proposed a deal under which the ICA would refurbish the restaurant and open it to the general public (previously it had been members only). We would share the costs and the profits from the whole venture – restaurant, banqueting, staff meals – fifty-fifty with the Institute. We would keep open books and share any discounts openly negotiated with suppliers, etc.

It worked a treat. The restaurant was packed, and far from losing £60,000, it made twice that in the first year, netting the ICA and Leith's £60,000 each.

We were the ICA's blue-eyed boys for a good three years, but when the five-year contract came up for renewal, the ICA's council had largely changed and the Master was a smart woman who took one look at the accounts and said, 'Why are the caterers getting half the profits? Surely we can get good cooks for less than that?' She had no knowledge of the disastrous situation we had inherited, and had no idea that we were the people who had turned huge losses into big profits. She just saw us as overpaid. Which, by then, we were.

With a packed restaurant, parties in the evenings, the bar becoming a happy-hour haunt for the City, and the Livery Hall hired out more frequently, the profits had grown ever bigger and we were getting half of them. I had made a fatal error: what I *should* have done was reduce our take over the years, but, happy with our performance and more than happy with our profit, I didn't even think of it. So we lost the contract.

By now we were into public catering in a big way: the Natural History Museum, Hampton Court Palace, the Design Museum, the British Library, the Design Centre in Islington and others. I don't think we did any of them particularly well, though we had great moments. One day I opened a letter handwritten on blue paper. It was a 'fan' letter, congratulating me on the excellence of the catering at Hampton Court Palace tearoom, the freshness of the scones, the pretty china, tea in a teapot, nice waitresses, etc.

At the bottom were the words, 'Not for publication'.

That made me look closely at the address and signature. The letter was from Deborah, the Duchess of Devonshire.

Amazing. Not only was she one England's most famous and beloved aristocrats but – more importantly to me – she had masterminded the best public catering of any 'visitor attraction' in the country, the restaurants and farm shop at Chatsworth, the Devonshires' vast ancestral seat in Derbyshire.

Grateful, I responded to her note, and she sweetly invited me and our general manager of Leith's at Hampton Court to come to Chatsworth and meet her team. We were shown round by her manager, then, to our surprise and delight, given lunch by the Duchess and her husband Andrew, the Duke of Devonshire, in their private drawing room.

I will not forget it. Not because we were being served by a butler in white gloves and eating off eighteenth-century Meissen; not because we were surrounded by Canalettos and Rembrandts on the wall, and the famous Eworth portrait of Henry VIII on an easel by our side, nor because we were looking out on the magnificent Capability Brown parkland. No. I remember the occasion mostly for a conversation between their Graces, Debo and Andrew.

The Duke, distinctly grumpy: 'Debo, this place is freezing. What's the matter with this thing?'

I follow his gaze to the heater, circa 1950, with a single radiant electric bar in front of a curved reflective metal sheet. Its flex, brown and twisted, snaked across the priceless Aubusson to a distant wall.

The Duchess: 'But Andrew, it's your fault. You wouldn't let me buy the two-bar one.'

CHAPTER 15

STAR TURN

Packing it in

Under Chef Alex Floyd's reign, Leith's Restaurant food got lighter and the portions smaller in line with the public mood. But year after year we failed to gain a Michelin star.

I'm a fan of Michelin. I never believe chefs who say they don't want a star – it's the one accolade recognised by their peers, and the one most trusted by customers. Chefs may not want two stars because it might mean food priced at a level their customers can't afford, and they may not want three because that will make them a special-occasion-only place for the mega-rich. But one star? Everyone wants a star.

By the end of the Eighties Leith's had been one of London's top restaurants for twenty odd years and we had plenty of other accolades, but still no Michelin star. One day I rang the *Michelin Guide*.

I'd heard that Michelin disliked starter and dessert trolleys, that serving exclusively British cheeses was a no-no, that we should be writing our menu in French. I wanted to hear from the horse's mouth whether, since we would not change our style, I should give up now.

The editor, Derek Brown, came on the phone. Would I like him and his chief inspector to come and see me?

I could not believe it. I hadn't thought he would take my call, let alone make such an offer.

I asked Alex and Nick to join us and we sat nervously waiting for a lecture about the trolleys or the lack of classic French food.

The great man consulted his file. They had visited us seven times in the last year he said. All the inspection reports were good, but there were problems.

'Take bread for example. On the first two visits it was excellent, obviously home-made, interesting selection, served warm. Then, on the third inspection it was bought-in, part-cooked baguettes. Perfectly okay, and properly baked on site, but disappointing. Then the next time it was home-made again, good flavour but heavy, undercooked, soggy. Then next time it was the par-baked stuff again, but cold and undercooked. And since then it's been excellent again. No choice, but really good seeded loaf, thickly cut.'

As he spoke I followed the trail with dismay, Yes, that's when we lost a great baker and resorted to buying bread. Then we had that young girl who thought she was a baker but was a disaster. Then we were on part-baked again and it was the waiter's job to do the finishing, and they'd forget and sometimes it would go out half-baked. And then, at last, we hired a pastry chef who could bake.

It was shaming, but worse followed. 'The other repeated problem is with the first-course trolley.'

'But our customers love our trolleys. It's what makes us different.'

'I agree and our inspectors love them too. The problem is not with the selection. It's with the dressing. According to one of our inspectors you are using the same olive oil and vinegar on all the salads. He guesses Spanish olive oil and balsamic vinegar. Very good for the grilled peppers and the leeks vinaigrette, but too heavy for the seafood salad and the halibut carpaccio. And anyway, if the customers are expected to have a spoonful of several salads, would it not be a good idea to do the dressings with different oils, different vinegars, maybe different flavourings?'

Of course he was right. We had a great bucket of vinaigrette in the fridge and when all the salads and starters were out on the trolley, the larder chef would go round with bucket and ladle and give each one a splash. What a missed opportunity.

A year later, we got our Michelin star.

In 1990 I turned fifty, and with Rayne heading for seventy we decided to sell the business. I wanted to spend more of my life at home in Chastleton, and had high hopes of finally doing a bit of travelling with Rayne. And I wanted to write fiction, not cookbooks.

If I don't write my novel now I never will, I thought, and if I don't stop writing cookery books I never will either.

By now the company was making a lot of money. Leith's Restaurant had its Michelin star; Leith's School was the biggest and best of the private cookery schools; we had prestigious catering contracts all over the country; we had given up the loss-making parks venture, and we employed nearly five hundred people.

But selling turned out to be more difficult than we thought. After a year of uncertainty for the staff, we withdrew the company from the market. And then, suddenly, in 1993 we had an offer from Accor, the French hotel company. They wanted the catering company and the school, but not the restaurant. That suited me fine – I thought I might have withdrawal symptoms if I didn't have any business at all to run, and the deal for the rest of the group was terrific.

They would pay what we asked, half right away and the balance after three years, provided we met our profit targets. I would remain with the company until then, nominally as joint managing Director, but really for my goodwill and contacts. They would appoint a French MD to actually run the company.

We would spearhead Accor's entry into the UK, and they would provide the capital to expand and exploit the Leith's name more vigorously than we had been able to do. All our businesses and all our staff would stay as they were. In spite of the prospect of a new Accor man at the top, our directors understood my and Rayne's desire to sell up, and they were excited at the opportunities for expansion.

Too good to be true? Too right it was. I'd not reckoned on the controlling nature of the French. We'd naively imagined they would leave us alone to get on with it, but they immediately rented a large and very expensive new head office in Victoria, and installed eleven staff to control the finances of the company. Until then our finances had been controlled by Rayne, working half a day a week in our 'head office', which consisted of three small rooms over the restaurant. Unsurprisingly, that first year under Accor we made the first loss in the company's thirty-two-year history.

Accor's devotion to bureaucracy was mind-blowing and our managers complained bitterly. One said, 'When you were the boss and I wanted to replace a freezer, I'd ask you, you'd say yes and I'd have bought it by lunchtime. Now the upward process of request and the downward process of consent takes six weeks.'

But bureaucracy was not the most grave of our problems. We'd thought the French, being famously gastronomic, would want quality food. I suspect that Gerard, our new French MD, was on a bonus that was based on turnover rather than profit. He was already paid a good salary, and could probably make the same again if he increased sales substantially. But I could not question this because his bonus was paid by Accor's Paris head office.

If true, it would explain how he could sign a catering deal with Sumitomo Bank for about half what I would have charged. Unless we were to feed their staff on cheap burgers, frozen pizza and reconstituted chips, we could not make a profit. We lost money on that, and on four other new contracts, but turnover went up and so, I imagine, did Gerard's pay.

Rayne, trained as a lawyer and wise to boot, had stipulated that if Accor sold the company within the earn-out period, we would be paid in full, regardless of results.

And, thank the Lord, the giant British company, Compass, bought Accor's worldwide catering division, Eurest (of which Leith's was now the UK bit) a year later, which meant we got paid in full.

But a second sale was unsettling for the Leith's managers. They had started out full of hope, and determined to be loyal to their Accor masters, but losing money is dispiriting and working for people who countenanced frozen onion bhajis even more so.

Telling them that we now belonged to Compass was tough. Compass had long been the biggest catering company in the country, but was not thought of as the best. Indeed, small companies like mine, while sometimes envying their profits, were scornful of their standards. I had solemnly promised our directors that I would not sell to Compass. I could do this with confidence because, though I much liked their urbane chairman, Francis Mackay, he had previously offered us exactly half what Accor paid for us. I knew we would never sell to them.

Now, there we were, sold to them anyway. Bruised and battered from the Accor experience, the Leith's senior people nonetheless again put their hopes and their weight behind the new regime. Francis was now chairman of the new bigger Compass and we all attended his first UK conference. He set out an inspiring plan for the future – over-riders and 'buying' contracts were to be a thing of the past. Our reputation was to be built on quality, not size. Innovation and enterprise would be encouraged. Decisions, as far as possible, would be devolved to the separate businesses. Leith's was welcomed into the Compass fold as an example of best practice. Francis had us eating out of the palm of his hand.

Also, the best of the Accor directors, Alain Dupuis, who had done such a fair deal to buy us originally and whom both Rayne and I liked enormously, left Accor to stay with Eurest as its chairman. He also joined the Leith's board.

At first everything looked rosy and the Compass regime was a huge improvement. We got out of the loss-making contracts as fast as we could, we abandoned the Victoria offices, and we went back to more or less running our own business. Our French MD went back to Paris and Patrick Harbour resumed his previous managing director role.

All seemed well – until Compass decided to amalgamate our Events and Parties business with Payne and Gunter, a caterer they already owned, with the result that we promptly lost two of our most important contracts, J.P. Morgan and the Orient Express. Johnny Moss, our demanding but supportive client at J.P. Morgan, didn't want to deal with Compass, and Nick Varian at Orient Express felt Payne and Gunter's kitchens were too far away from their Battersea sidings and feared we'd literally miss the train if the traffic was bad.

It is almost impossible for a big corporation to retain staff who are accustomed to a small one. They resent being told what to do, they prefer the systems they have carefully set up over the years, they are passionately loyal to the standards and ethics of their previous owners.

As times got tough, Compass found that adopting our way of doing things was too difficult, and put pressure on us to adopt theirs. But life was still bearable until Leith's was put under the control of a director whom I shall call Tom James. Tom was brilliant at two things: controlling costs and blarney. His cockney accent and barrow-boy confidence charmed the socks off potential clients, who thought they'd found a rough diamond. But to his staff he was disloyal, abusive, given to poking his managers in the chest and saying, 'Just do it.'

A few examples: one of the divisions Tom was in charge of did the catering at Ascot Racecourse, and since the client was far from pleased, they were in danger of losing the contract. Tom rang Patrick Harbour.

'Get your arse down to Ascot,' he barked. 'I've decided Leith's is to be part of our tender pitch. You can't do the presentation because you don't know what's in it, but you'd better be there to answer questions and schmooze them.'

Patrick was aghast. He protested that Leith's could not possibly agree to a contract that he had not even seen, and since he'd had no part in preparing it he'd be unable to answer questions anyway.

Tom was furious. As far as he was concerned Patrick should have been on his knees with gratitude for being given the contract. It was in the bag. All he needed to do was turn up and smile.

Patrick had no option. He sat cringing through a presentation with menu proposals that he found boring and vulgar, and costs that he considered unachievable. He knew he was promising the impossible and being dragged into the over-rider scam. Gradually he realised that what Tom was proposing was little more than changing the name over the door to Leith's because Leith's had a 'posh' reputation. Happily the client, the beady

Angus Crichton-Miller, saw through Tom's ploy and hired another caterer altogether.

Tom was the absolute antithesis of everything Leith's stood for. One day Patrick was in a meeting and Tom rang the switchboard.

'I'm so sorry, Mr James, but Patrick is in a meeting with a client. I'll get him to ring you as soon as he's free.'

'Fuck that. Get him now.'

'Is it an emergency, Mr James? I'm not allowed to interrupt client meetings.'

Tom exploded. 'I'm his fucking boss. When I say jump, he jumps. I don't care if he's talking to the Queen of England. Get him.' The poor girl called Patrick out of his meeting.

All our directors except Caroline and Nick left. Compass wasn't interested in Leith's School of Food and Wine which they had bought as part of the package, so they sold it to Caroline, and her backer, Christopher Bland, then the chairman of both the BBC and British Telecom. He left Caroline to get on and run the school. And Nick was alright because we'd not sold Leith's Restaurant.

I should in fairness say that I don't think Compass was all bad. Far from it. In many ways it was an excellent company, the darling of the City, making good profits. They were completely honourable in their dealings with me and Rayne, and they were tremendously supportive of me personally, and of my later charitable ventures.

Though I would question the wisdom of putting the Leith's name on all their current contracts, some of them are run better by Compass than they ever were in my time. And Leith's has continued to expand and do well.

But it is almost impossible for takeovers to be harmonious until all the bosses of the taken-over company have left. After that it's easier for loyalty to the new owners to develop.

When giving a lecture at the Royal Society of Arts about small ambitious companies, I used my experience with first Accor and then Compass to illustrate this point. Feeling a bit guilty, I sent a copy to Alain Dupuis (ex-Accor and by then Compass) with a note of apologetic self-justification. He faxed it back with a hand-written scribble accusing me, correctly, of biting the hand that fed me. That hurt, not just because there was truth in it, but because he was one of the good guys.

I found I really liked not having the group to run any more, and decided to sell the restaurant too. I suggested to Caroline that she and Christopher buy it, which they did. They ran it for a few years and then sold it on. It is now called the Notting Hill Brasserie, and is still excellent.

I had always admired Elizabeth David, though I found her uneasy company. She could be unkind about other writers and cooks and I wondered whether she slagged me off too when I was out of the room. But she was the best food writer in the country.

After her death and before I sold Leith's School, I went to the auction of her things, intending to pick up a few wooden spoons to give to each of the Leith's teachers as mementos of her and of me.

But the nine wooden spoons went for a massive five hundred pounds so I wandered round hoping to find something else. I decided to bid for the contents of a drawer which was being sold as a job lot. E.D. never threw anything away, and among the free samples, packets of cake candles and other rubbish, there were some peelers and corkscrews, pastry brushes and measuring spoons.

And then I noticed that the table upon which the drawer sat had a sale ticket too, and my heart gave a lurch: this must be the famous table at which she'd written and cooked for many, many years. She used to write at one end and cook at the other, and sometimes clear a space to have 'an omelette and a glass of wine' with friends. I'd eaten lunch with her there.

At the auction I sat in the front row with Jill Norman, Elizabeth's oldest and best friend as well as her editor (and by then her executor and publisher). I think I got the box of bits and pieces for ten pounds. Bidding for the table was brisk, and I paid a thousand pounds for it. I was outbid on the pine dresser, which went to Clarissa Dickson Wright.

When I got the box of junk home, I found all Elizabeth David's knives at the bottom. How could the auctioneers have missed them? They are wonderful – old and worn, characterful and varied. A bone-handled carving knife and fork; a small paring knife, the wooden handle worn smooth with use; a thin boning knife sharpened to a curve, and a couple of knives with split handles that had been repaired in the now-banned-as-unhygienic traditional method of binding them tightly in stout string.

I could have given a knife to each of the teachers, but it seemed a shame to break up the collection so I had a glass-fronted wooden case made for them and gave them to the school. Caroline hung it on the wall above the entrance to the main kitchen, and I gave the each teacher something from the E.D. box, a peeler, pastry brush, cutter or some such. The school moved to Chiswick a few years ago and the knife collection went too.

As to the table, my husband greeted its arrival with, 'Good God, you paid a thousand pounds for *this*? You could have got a better one for fifty down the New Kings Road.'

'But darling, you don't understand, this is *Elizabeth David's* table. It is priceless. It's sacred.'

'And I suppose these are sacred toast crumbs in all the cracks?'

The table has wide pine planks three centimetres thick, and is pale from years of scraping and scrubbing. We put it in the bay window of the kitchen in Chastleton and for years the whole family ate almost every meal off it.

But it was not perfect. It had huge square legs that the unwary bashed their knees on, and was not quite wide enough for the space. I decided I'd insert another plank so we could seat ten, and have the legs moved in a bit to avoid more yelps of pain. Everyone I mentioned this plan to let out cries of 'Sacrilege' and 'You will destroy its value.' But I decided Elizabeth wouldn't mind, and sentiment should not take precedent over sense.

But I could not find – not anywhere – a three centimetre-thick old pine plank. I tried every wood merchant, architectural salvage place, the internet, everywhere. So the table was saved.

And then Jill Norman rang up. She had always wanted the table, and if I would sell it her husband was proposing to give it to her for her sixtieth birthday. So I did.

At about the time Rayne and I sold the business, I met a young woman at the Royal Society of Arts (RSA), Peta Fawagi, a consultant who had been counselling businessmen about coping with redundancy and retirement. It had struck her as extraordinary that these senior managers and directors, who spend all their business life thinking about the priorities for their business, about succession planning, risk management, and strategy, were absolutely unprepared for their own futures. Redundancy came like a bolt from the blue and they were unable to cope. They had no support system outside of office friends, and weren't plugged in to the local community the way women were through their children and charity work. These men had no hobbies, except perhaps for golf, which they played with colleagues now no longer there.

Peta decided to set up her own business, called Life Strategies. And she wanted me to be a client. 'You're perfect,' she said. 'You are selling your business, you've just become Chair of the RSA. You are re-inventing yourself.'

'But, Peta, I don't need you. I've done all that.'

'But everyone can do with counselling. I could really help you.'

'Counselling! I do *not* need counselling.'

She went on and on, and in the end won the argument when she said, 'Look Prue, you're my mate. I need a woman to put in my brochure.'

I agreed to six one-hour sessions.

Peta later told me that at the first session I'd sat with my arms folded, breathing hostility and discomfort. But by session two, I was hooked. Talking nonstop about yourself is a very pleasurable ego trip. Besides, she was good.

I found myself telling her that I wanted to write a novel but was nervous about it. Maybe I didn't have the skills.

'What would you say to someone who wanted to be a cook but thought they might not have the skills?'

'I'd tell them to go on a course.'

'So why don't you go on a novel-writing course?'

We talked about all the things I was doing, and the things I wanted to do but couldn't because I was too busy. Among these were holidays with each of my children alone, walking trips with my long-neglected girlfriends, starting a catering college in South Africa, learning to sing.

Peta made me bring a list of all my current activities to the next session. We went through them and she watched my reactions as I talked about them. If I grimaced she put a line through it. If I extolled it, she put a tick beside it.

'Just resign from the ones I've crossed out,' she said. So out went all the committees that were talking shops or that I'd joined because I didn't like to say no.

And then she made me block off a fortnight every two months for myself.

Within five years of the sessions with Peta, I had done all those things: taken the writing course and had my first novel published, gone ahead with the South African Prue Leith Chef's Academy, walked with friends, and had holidays for two with Daniel and Li-Da. I'd even taken singing lessons, though those were a resounding failure.

I will always be grateful for the one-on-one holidays. Boarding school, adolescence and their being away at university had inevitably meant a loss of closeness with the children. I wanted to have each of them briefly to myself. I was particularly keen to close the gap a bit with Daniel who, as he grew up, had become increasingly uncommunicative – at least to me. I think I embarrassed him with my extrovert enthusiasms and my tendency to have an opinion on everything.

So Daniel (now called Danny by all his friends but resolutely Daniel by his parents) and I went together to Hong Kong at the time of the handover, which was a fascinating time to be there.

But the most memorable event, for me, was in Beijing. When a friend, Victor Chu, heard we were going to see the Forbidden City, he absolutely insisted I meet the Chinese Minister of Culture and the Minister of Education. I tried to insist that I was not important enough and I'd be wasting their time, but Victor was adamant. He'd made all the arrangements, and I realised he'd lose face if I cancelled. I found myself, unsuitably dressed in casual clothes (I'd come for a holiday, not a VIP meeting), collected in a limo and driven to an ostentatious building with a red carpet laid down the stairs.

A posse of uniformed men scuttled about opening doors and ushering me into the building, where a further reception committee greeted me and took me into a spacious reception room with two heavy chairs separated by a low carved coffee table. On either side of these chairs were smaller, less important chairs, three on each side. I was ushered into one of the big ones, and offered tea. Very soon a group of three men and a woman appeared. The Minister of Education sat on the other side of

348

the low table. His two assistants sat on the far side of him and the woman, who produced a notebook, sat on the end. An interpreter stood behind and between us.

At this point I realised I was supposed to have an entourage to occupy the seats on my side. Damn I thought, I should at least have brought Daniel (I'd left him fast asleep in the hotel). It would have fascinated him and he could have given me some back-up.

What followed was pure farce. The Minister made a speech about the long association of China and Britain and the welcome handover of the historic region of Hong Kong, achieved in peace and harmony. He expressed the desire of his government to have friendly and productive relations with the West, and particularly Britain . . . on and on and on.

The woman at the end, head down, wrote in her book, presumably faithfully recording every boring word. At intervals the Minister would pause and the interpreter would say it all again to me in English. Meanwhile, I was frantically thinking about my reply.

To my astonishment it was easy. I just opened my mouth and out came the platitudes of the ages. I waffled on about the great Royal Society of the Arts, its belief in peaceful progress through the arts, industry and commerce, our international fellowship, our desire for cultural and intellectual co-operation, blah, blah, blah.

349

The poor woman wrote all this down too. Between us we were at it for forty minutes, after which we did a great deal of bowing and smiling and the meeting was over.

And then I did it all again (minus the red carpet I noticed . . . how quickly we get to like the trappings of power!) at the Ministry of Culture.

Did they, I wonder, look at each other in bafflement after my departure, asking, 'What was all that about then?' I, however, wouldn't have missed it for anything.

In 2001 Daniel and I had another holiday together, this time a riding safari in Botswana. On the first morning, when he was having difficulty controlling his horse I offered to swap.

'No, Mum. I'm fine.'

'But darling, I'm a better rider than you are.'

'Maybe, but you're too old to fall off.'

I was still scared of lions. My horse had claw scars on his rump from an attack while in camp. I was relieved to see that our leader gave lions a very wide berth.

One day, cantering along through the shallow swamps behind a fleeing herd of waterbuck, I looked up to find a dozen zebra had joined us to our right, while four or five giraffe loped along to the left. It was a magical moment. To be part of a herd that included waterbuck, zebra, giraffe, horses – and us – was just extraordinary. Maybe that's what swimming with dolphins feels like.

I asked our guide why the zebra and giraffe had joined us.

'Animals in the wild don't waste energy running for no reason. If they see us running they think we are fleeing danger, so they come too.'

One day I was in the bathroom behind my tent when I heard the by now familiar noise of cracking twigs as an elephant padded past. It always amazed me that elephants, who could toss our whole tent into the sky if they liked, would walk past, stepping carefully over guy ropes, their sides brushing the canvas walls, while we lay in bed only a foot or two away from them.

The elephant paused right next to me. I could have patted him through the canvas, but of course I just held my breath. I was conscious that this was a mad scene, me sitting stark naked on the loo, the elephant right outside. And then his great trunk came wavering over the wall (the bathroom section was open to the sky) and delicately latched onto the dripping shower head. I guess he preferred filtered water to that of the Okavango swamp.

Just as Daniel was closer to Rayne, I've always been closer to Li-Da. She is easier than Daniel, more tolerant and more openly affectionate. We went to Cambodia together and came back with a two-ton stone Buddha, now installed comfortably at the end of an English rose tunnel.

Then, a few years ago, Li-Da and I went to Laos together. We were sent an itinerary for our hike in the mountains on the Chinese border. It included delicious picnics under waterfalls, getting up early to see how the locals call the birds, a 'home stay' in a picturesque mountain-top village with a traditional Lao welcome of a massage from the village women. Sounded great.

Of course it wasn't quite like that. When we finally met our guide he explained that the 'Five Day Walking Tour' included Day One spent on a ten-hour bumpy ride in an ancient combi, and Day Five to get to the ferry across the Mekong to cross to Thailand, which involved wading in the river, luggage carried on our heads. The three days in the middle did not include waterfalls or calling birds, and the 'home stay' visitors' house, said to boast a chemi-loo and mattresses, had blown down. The village chief kindly offered to put us up.

I'd not have missed it for worlds – and I'd not do it again for worlds either. We'd walked five hours uphill to get there. The chief's house, on stilts like all the others, was much the biggest and seemed to be the council chamber, meeting place and communal kitchen. There were two fires in the middle of the floor, one for meals and one for animal feed, but no chimney. The smoke just finds its way, none too well, through the grass roof. Two of the chief's many wives were plucking what looked like kingfishers and canaries, the feathers of iridescent blue and lemon yellow going straight into the fire. The people live on a diet of sticky rice and whatever they can trap: birds, squirrels, rats. They draw the line at cats, which – thank heavens – are sacred to the Buddha. Food waste, of which there is very little, goes through gaps in the floorboards to the chickens and pigs under the houses.

As soon as word got round that we'd brought beer and plenty of food, the room filled up, mostly with men. Our guides cooked huge quantities of the sort of fare the villagers would be lucky to see once a year on a feast day: chicken and vegetable soup, green curry with pork and vegetables, sticky rice and mango. The men sat round on their hunkers eating and drinking until there was no more of anything. The women crouched similarly, but in an outer row, each with a toddler on her back and a baby on her front. When offered anything they shook their heads, smiling and shy.

The men, greatly animated, debated some great matter at the tops of their voices. The women squatted silently and the children slept. It was bitterly cold. Li-Da, our guides and I lay fully dressed in a row on the floor. When, hours later, the chief stomped out, followed by all the men and older boys (they were vacating the house to make space for us) the women immediately unhooked their babies and settled down where they were, wrapped in the clothes they wore.

In the night I wanted a pee. I crept over sleeping bodies and climbed down the rickety wooden ladder in the dark, to step onto what I took to be the ground. It was a water buffalo. It scrambled up and stumbled off, as alarmed as I.

We talk of the peace of the mountains. I have seldom had a less peaceful night. First the men drinking and yelling until midnight, my encounter with the water buffalo which set all the village dogs barking and then, at three a.m., a two-hour crowing competition between rival cockerels, the chief among them under our house. By five, the noise of children, dogs, chickens, cows, pigs, and men all clamouring for the women to feed them, was quite something.

I was struck by the cleanliness of the villages high in the mountains. In the valleys the people live like the poor the world over, surrounded by litter and garbage, and sometimes raw sewage. The men watch porn or football on satellite TV, listen to pop on their mobile phones or shine up their Chinese motorbikes while the women go to work in the paddy fields.

But so-called civilisation has not reached the hilltop villages. Many hill tribeswomen, who wear long, full skirts, still go bare-breasted and bare-foot. Some of the older ones have silver coins sewn into their headdresses. There are no plastic bags, no smelly drains, no garbage.

It took me a while to work it out. And then I realised it all depends on the ratio of pigs to other creatures, including humans. The mountain villages teem with animals, but the pigs outnumber the rest. And the pigs eat everything: all the garbage, plus the bovine, canine and human waste. It is a little disconcerting to have a large pig follow you into the bushes and stand expectantly a few metres away, hoping for a warm dinner.

It was spring when we were in Laos, and my lasting mental snapshot is of the piglets and puppies, almost exactly the same size, playing together. The puppies were doing that puppy-jump on all fours that means 'come and play', while the piglets sniffed and rootled at the puppies as if assessing their edibility. Dogs being dogs and pigs being pigs from infancy.

CHAPTER 16

THE GREAT BRITISH SANDWICH

. . . and other tales from the boardroom

As Leith's School reputation spread, we were increasingly asked if we would franchise the business to set up a Leith's School in Japan, Australia, America, South Africa. I would always say no because the applicants didn't have the money to pay for our involvement to police the Leith's name.

So when I had a letter asking me to meet a food teacher, Judi Dyason, with a view to setting up a school in Johannesburg, I was expecting the usual story. But Judi's partners turned out to be a consortium of game lodge and small town-house hotel owners, led by the South African entrepreneur Tiny Barnetson, who wanted a college to improve the quality of graduates for the industry: South African state catering colleges were underfunded, students watched too many demonstrations, did too much work on computers and blackboards, and did not cook enough.

I was keen, but Caroline had enough on her plate and turned the opportunity down. So I went ahead, using the Prue Leith (rather than Leith's) name, which I still owned.

The Prue Leith Chef's Academy is in Centurion, near Pretoria, in a large single-storey house surrounded by gardens. There are professional kitchens, a public restaurant, great teachers and about a hundred students.

Determined not to be an all-white school, we raised funds for bursaries, scholarships and student loans for poor black students. A house across the road was converted into a student residence where they could stay very cheaply.

But philanthropy backfired. Young people brought up in the old ANC culture of refusing to pay rent to the local authority as a protest against apartheid, do not think honouring debts is important. Not one of those early students paid their rent or paid back their loans, whether to the Academy, the bank or their sponsors. And none honoured their commitment to work for the restaurants that had paid their fees on condition that they work for them later.

This had the sad effect that fund-raising for future students became almost impossible. Today the Academy's black students are mostly from the new middle class.

Tiny Barnetson held that knowledge is best gained by hands-on practice, with students working in a real live restaurant under the pressure that entails. The result has been a hugely successful catering college. Once I saw an ad in the Jobs Vacant column of a catering magazine: 'Only Leith's graduates need apply'. And then I really knew what 'puffed up with pride' felt like.

Long before I sold my business I was involved in other organisations, some voluntarily, some paid. My first directorship was with British Transport Hotels (BTH), which ran the hotels and the train catering divisions of British Rail. The thirty-odd hotels included the staggeringly grand Gleneagles, the Welcome at Stratford, Turnberry in Ayrshire, all the station hotels (including the Adelphi in Liverpool built in 1914 for the transatlantic passengers) and lots more, right down to the tiny inn at the Kyle of Lochalsh.

There was a problem: though the hotels made a profit (just), this was siphoned off by the desperate parent, the railways, to help with the costs of track and trains, and to sink into the bottomless pit of freight. Year after year, BTH would budget to paint the outside of the Great Western at Paddington, or get rid of the ancient switchboard at the Adelphi, and every year we'd have to cancel the renovations because BR needed the money.

But still, I thought, we could do something about our magnificent but empty dining rooms. I suggested we introduce a brasserie-style lunchtime service, quick and modern, to appeal to a younger clientele. This was anathema to the old guard, who wrote their menus exclusively in French, cooked in the butter-and-cream tradition of Escoffier and looked down on any customer who ordered the house wine. At a meeting in the Adelphi I suggested a one-plate lunch with a glass of wine aimed at shoppers or workers wanting a quick break.

This provoked a chorus of protest: *They'll come in with shopping bags . . . and back-packs . . . we can't have carrier bags and back packs in the Adelphi . . .and drink Coca-Cola, and wine by the glass . . . and it will lead to low standards, women in trousers and men without a tie.*

And so on.

My one-plate lunch idea was stillborn. You need buy-in from the people who are going to deliver a new deal, and I didn't manage that.

I had more success with the Great Eastern Hotel in London. I persuaded them to adapt the style of l'Entrecôte in Paris, a no-choice steak menu. There was no booking, and guests were asked only two questions. *How do you like your steak?* and *Red or white wine?* They were then served a salad of lettuce, walnuts and stilton in a vinaigrette, then sirloin steak and chips, followed by apple pie and vanilla ice cream. End of story.

It was a thumping success and city types queued down the road to get in. I was given a Pullman silver tea set as a thank you, complete with a certificate proving it was a gift and not stolen off a train. I had it for years until, ironically, it was stolen from me – complete with certificate.

Eventually the hotels were sold. I was miserable at this decision but agreed to it. I was by then on the main BR board, and I knew that we would be forever raiding the hotels' coffers at a time when they needed increasingly serious investment.

The hotels, I reluctantly concluded, would do better, and could perhaps return to their former glory, in private hands. But the truth is we gave them away. Under pressure from Mrs Thatcher's privatising government, we sold them for an average of about a million pounds per hotel, which even then was highway robbery for the vendor (and a bargain for the buyer).

I mourned those hotels. I attribute my son Daniel's enthusiasm for nothing-but-the-best to his introduction to a toff's life at the age of ten. On a train trip round Scotland, he and his sister were treated like a little prince and princess by frock-coated waiters in the glorious Gleneagles dining room; were woken by a kilted piper outside their bedroom at Turnberry; could see the ferry to Skye out of the window at the Kyle of Lochalsh, and sat atop our luggage as it was wheeled into Edinburgh's Waverley station from the bowels of the North British Hotel on Princes Street. I remember almost every hotel with affection.

In 1980 Peter Parker, Chairman of British Rail, had put me on the main BR board. I was the only woman and the youngest board member and too scared to open my mouth. I sat silent round a huge boardroom table while the men talked about rolling stock and 'the road' (which is rail-speak for the track) and government funding. My first meeting went on for hours and my colleagues, all men, sneaked out one by one for a 'comfort break'. Finally I had to do likewise and I stood up quietly, only to have sixteen men rise politely to their feet to bow me out. So my first words at a major board meeting were, 'Please don't stand. You have to treat me like one of the chaps,' which they subsequently did.

When eventually I plucked up the courage to contribute, I asked if we ever talked about the passenger experience, and if not, could we? Peter flicked me a wink of approval. He wanted me there to worry about the customers, not the engineering or finances and other stuff the board knew all about anyway.

Early on I learnt how easy it is for a non-executive director to 'go native' and become blindly loyal to the organisation, rather than seeing things from the shareholder's and customer's point of view, which is the job of a NED. When I realised just how difficult it is to run a railway I began to think it was a miracle any train ran at all, let alone on time. The web of station, track, signalling and train operations, to say nothing of Head Office and government, was complicated beyond belief.

When I had been newly appointed to the main board, I was travelling in an observation car (wonderful fun, on the back of a train, looking through plate glass at the track streaming away) with some senior railwaymen. One asked me why we served instant coffee in horrible paper cups, and I was ready with my reply about the customers nicking the china ones, the difficulties of washing up in a buffet, the easier financial control of dispensed sleeves of cups, etc.

He listened politely then asked, 'How long have you been on the board?'

'Six weeks.'

'Six weeks! And nobbled already!'

He was right. The coffee *was* disgusting, and I was being overly defensive. Eventually we did improve it, *and* get better cups, though we couldn't go back to using china. Coffee sales had doubled since we installed the system of a measured dose of instant coffee in the bottom of each cup. The cups were countable, so we could hold the stewards responsible for the numbers of coffees used. Up till then the stewards had made half the coffees with their own coffee, and pocketed the profits.

I was definitely more useful to BR on the hospitality side than on engineering or finance. Train catering, once a glorious dining-car service on long journeys, had degenerated into a racket. I remember joking at a board, 'Why privatise the catering? It's privatised already. The stewards may not have paid for it, but they get the profits.'

Of course not all the stewards were dishonest, but scams were endemic. I received a letter from a woman who said that on the such-and-such line we did the best toasted bacon butties in the world, why could they not be served everywhere? Investigation revealed that BR didn't serve bacon butties on that line, but the steward did. He'd installed his own toaster, brought in good bacon, butter and bread, and was doing a roaring trade.

When we first introduced tills and insisted on receipts being issued, the stewards' reps told us, 'The tills will never work. They won't stand up to the bouncing and shaking. They'll be out of service in a flash.'

They were too. We installed sixty of them one weekend, and by Monday almost all of them were out of order. I don't know how many times you have to drop a till onto a station platform before it won't work any more, or how many times you hit it with a hammer, but miraculously they all suffered serious injury within a day or two.

But gradually we won the battle. In the teeth of opposition we broke the men-only tradition on the trains and hired young women who, properly trained, introduced a more customer-friendly style of service, and, I believe, jacked up the performance of their male colleagues.

Also, after a long struggle, we won an argument with the unions to introduce the narrow catering sales trolleys still in use today. The union claimed they constituted a safety hazard because they might be in the way in an emergency. The subtext was they preferred to lounge about in the buffet and make the customer do the walking.

At the time, station catering was not much better. Gloomy Fifties-style cafes doubled as waiting rooms and served 'tea and wad' – 'wad' meaning a soggy white bread sandwich. I went to see the sandwich production unit at Paddington station and asked why we only used white bread.

'It is Britain's favourite bread: Mother's Pride,' came the answer.

'And why Kraft cheese slices? Why not good English Cheddar?'

'Kraft is Britain's favourite cheese.'

'And why no seasoning in the sandwiches?'

'We used to put salt and pepper in them, but that stopped when we got the buttering machines. The seasoning used to be added by the girls who did the buttering. But they've gone now.'

On the morning I was there they were making three varieties of sandwich – cheese, tomato, and cheese-and-tomato. 'Why are the fillings so limited?' I enquired.

'Because our cheese sandwich is Britain's favourite sandwich, the best-selling sandwich in the country.'

I suspected this might be because there wasn't much else. I got the sandwich unit to make a batch of their standard sandwiches, plus new ones like bacon, lettuce and tomato (BLT, then a weird American invention), prawn with mayonnaise, egg and cress, and tuna and sweetcorn in both white and brown-bread versions. We offered them – quartered and on trays – free to the public on the Paddington station concourse (which, incidentally, is still charmingly called 'the lawn' by railwaymen – I guess in Brunel's day it must have been grass).

We monitored the order in which the rows of sandwiches disappeared. Brown bread with egg and cress was the winner, tuna and sweetcorn the runner-up. 'Britain's most popular sandwich' came second last. Last was the brown version of it.

So we started making deep-filled boxed sandwiches, and sales rocketed. For years afterwards the press would identify me as the lady who 'fixed the British Rail sandwich', which was a mighty exaggeration but gratifying.

After I'd been on the BR board for four years, Nicholas Ridley became Transport Secretary. He wanted to get rid of me and to appoint someone more in favour of privatisation of the railways than I was. I did not want to leave. I'd spent seven years, including my British Transport Hotels time, deeply involved in the improvement of the food and customer service. I was leading an initiative to put all the train and station staff through what they scorned as 'charm school', and I wanted to see it through. (It really worked. If employees are shown film of train staff refusing to help customers, of disabled passengers being shut in a pitch-dark guard's van for the journey; of filthy loos, and of buffets closed while stewards lounge about chatting in the first class seats, they begin to side with the passengers.)

I was also in the thick of a campaign to hold on to more women in railway management. We took equal numbers of male and female graduates from university, but most women did not last the course.

When I tried to find out why, I realised it was mostly due to the male managers' (largely unconscious) bias.

One young woman told me that she was frustrated, not by harassment or prejudice, but by old-fashioned good manners. When it was raining heavily, her avuncular boss would put a hand on her shoulder and say, 'It's horrible out there, lass. You stay in the warm and answer complaint letters. I'll send Jack out to deal with chaps on track.' No-one, she said, got promotion by dealing with the complaint letters.

So I did not want to leave the board. Although neither the 'charm school' initiative nor the Women in Management drive were strictly board jobs, I knew that I would have no authority if I was re-hired as an outside consultant; I *needed* to remain on the board. I asked for another year to finish the work, and Nicholas relented.

That appointment to the BR board was my ticket into non-executive director life. Peter Parker was a kind of informal mentor, giving me a nudge here and there all through my business life until he died.

The chairman of Safeway, Alastair Grant, was a customer at Leith's and, like Peter, he wanted a woman on his board. So, in 1989, I became a non-executive director. I don't know if I achieved much on the culture front at Safeway, but I did try. I instigated a survey of top bosses to find out if the female managers did their work as well as their male colleagues. The women scored four per cent better than the men. A second survey asked who they would recommend for promotion. The women were fifteen per cent *less likely* to be promoted than the men. When questioned about the inconsistency of this, the bosses' basic reason was that women were not 'committed' because they went home at five-thirty. I discussed this with one of the few senior women, who said, 'Par for the course. Men get promoted for taking eleven hours to do a job we do better in eight.'

More fun was getting Safeway to make a great sausage. Today most supermarkets do good sausages, but then they were made of the cheapest ingredients and they all tasted of dried onion powder. They exploded, then shrivelled, in the frying, leaked water, and the artificial skins stuck to the pan.

I sent Safeway excellent sausages from small manufacturers, but they were rejected because their kitchens didn't meet Safeway standards. I sent some I'd made myself with nothing but minced pork, salt, pepper, sage and twenty per cent breadcrumbs, in natural skins. Delicious, the meat buyer said, he'd get them copied. Months passed.

Finally I was sent a pack to try. They were disgusting, tasting exactly like all the others. Well, they said, no one would pay for an eighty per cent meat sausage, the British public adored the British sausage just as it was.

What saved the project was a speech given by the Chairman's wife, Judy Grant, after an annual board dinner. She said the wives of the board members had heard with delight about the imminent Prue Leith sausage two years before – and still nothing! How long could it take to make a sausage, for God's sake?

Stung by this, the Safeway machine suddenly burst into co-operation. I went to the sausage factory to meet Richard, its managing director. No board director had ever visited before, so I had to tour the spotless factory, meet the staff, and taste my way through dozens of sausages of every description which they made for restaurants, supermarkets, sausage companies, etc.

Finally we got to the latest version of my sausage. It was OK, but it still tasted of dried soup powder.

'Why the seasoning mix?' I asked.

'Everyone uses it. For consistency of flavour.'

'Why so much maize filler?'

'It keeps the price down.'

'Why the phosphates?'

'Because if the meat is frozen the liquid will run out when thawed.'

'Richard, this is just not my recipe. Could we please just make my sausage mix, here and now?'

'Well,' he said, 'we'd have to make sixty pounds of it because that's the smallest machine we have.'

'How about we mix it by hand?'

We used half fresh pork shoulder and half belly pork and minced them together, not too finely.

'Now, salt,' I said.

'Ah . . . we don't have any salt. Only the Dutch seasoning mix.'

'No plain salt at all, anywhere in the factory?'

'The canteen might have some.' They did.

'Black pepper?'

'No, the pepper comes in the seasoning mix.' He thought for a bit. 'But my wife, who works in reception, has a huge peppermill in her desk. She says it helps make the canteen food edible.'

'Sage?'

'No, afraid not. You see, it comes in the . . .'

'. . . Dutch seasoning mix?'

'Yes.'

By now Richard was warming to the challenge. 'I think those bushes we have outside reception are sage, aren't they?'

They were. Ornamental sage it's true, and dark purple, but the young leaves tasted fine. One of the butchers chopped them for us.

While we were stirring the mix, Richard suddenly said, 'Ah, I get it. This is butcher's sausage, like I used to make when I was a lad in a butcher's shop, thirty years ago.'

Within fifteen minutes we had made and pack-aged the sausages. Richard handed me a couple of packs to take home. 'Richard and Prue's Sausages' it said.

They went into the stores as Butcher's Sausage and sold at three times the price of our standard sausage. They won 'Sausage of the Year' and we had a celebratory press party at the Serpentine Restaurant in Hyde Park, which was still going strong at the time. We asked Dolly Parton to be the guest of honour and she posed for unforgettable pictures. Many papers carried one of her attempting to lick a sausage placed in her cleavage.

We sold a lot of Butcher's Sausages, and pretty soon every other supermarket was making good quality bangers from good quality meat.

My next non-executive job was with the Leeds Permanent Building Society. Mike Blackburn was the CEO and Malcolm Barr the chairman, and one day they asked me to dinner in my own restaurant and suggested I join their board.

I discovered afterwards this was due to a bit of sisterhood help: I had joined an all-women dining club set up by a bunch of women in business who liked to talk to other women in the same boat. There were only twenty-five of us and we took it in turns to give the others dinner. There were no subscriptions, few rules (no politicians and no actresses was one) and the purpose was to relax and chat. One of our members was the Building Society Commissioner, Rosalind Gilmore, who made it her business to badger all the big building society chairmen into appointing women to their boards. I don't think the Leeds chairman would have agreed, but Mike, the CEO was already on the lookout for a woman board member, and he prevailed.

I confess to taking the job out of simple curiosity.

I had never been into a building society, I knew nothing whatever about the financial industry, and I still added up on my fingers. But I thought it would be fun to learn about something so alien to me.

I never did get to understand the financial overnight deals and swaps and derivatives and so on, the means by which money-men make more money from the money already in their coffers. But in those days I didn't need to. For the most part, building societies carried on a very simple trade that a child could grasp: they borrowed from A and lent to B, and they charged more to B than they paid to A.

My first AGM at the Leeds was a revelation. The hall was packed with shareholders, many of them our own staff. On the platform was a line-up of grey suits, with me on the end. The chairman introduced us, going down the line, singing the praises of each member of his board: this non-executive was Mrs Thatcher's speech writer, this one was chairman of a large plc, this one owned the biggest shoe-shop chain in Britain, this one was a professional accountant, senior partner in the firm of X, this one was head of his family firm, the biggest brick-makers in the North, this the former personnel director of ICI, and so on.

When he got to me his introduction went something like this:

'And now you see our newest recruit, and I'm sure you are surprised to see that she is a lady.

But don't worry. She is Prue Leith, and I can assure you that she is not a feminist and will not be burning her bra or anything ridiculous like that. Indeed, she is very nice, and I am sure you can agree with me that she is very good-looking.'

I found myself looking at a woman in the front row, whom I did not know at the time but who turned out to be the most senior female executive in the company. She caught my eye and just rolled her eyes to heaven and sank slightly down in her seat.

When Mike Blackburn left us to become CEO of the much larger Halifax, and we were eventually taken over by them, I was one of the five Leeds directors – two non-execs and three executives – who went onto the new Halifax board.

I cannot say I really enjoyed the Halifax. I liked and admired my boardroom colleagues, but I began to feel out of my depth when we decided to float the business on the stock exchange. I wanted us to continue to behave like a building society, borrowing and lending, and was frightened by the more complicated world of banking we were rapidly getting into.

So I was relieved when my time was up. I left just before the Halifax merged with the Bank of Scotland, and two great financial institutions, the Bank of Scotland and the Halifax Building Society, were destroyed. There but for the grace of God . . .

While I was still on the Safeway board, the

chairman mentioned that he was going fishing on the Spey with the famous Gordon Baxter of jam and pickled beetroot fame.

'Really?' I said. 'Gordon has been inviting me for ten years and I've always managed to wriggle out of it.'

'Wriggle *out* of it? Out of fishing on the Spey? On the Ballindolloch beat? In September? Are you *mad*?'

I realised then that turning down a supper at Buckingham Palace cooked by Gordon Ramsay, wines by Lafite Rothschild, and sitting next to George Cloony, would have been a lesser idiocy.

So the next year I accepted Gordon's invitation. And, taught by the famous (at least to Scottish fishermen) Commander Wilson, I caught a fish on my first afternoon in the Junction Pool and, like the fish, I was hooked.

Since then salmon fishing has been something of an obsession. There is no logic to it. It wastes hours – weeks – of time, it costs a fortune, mostly you have to release the fish, and it's cruel.

I once went to fish the Aa river in Norway with Jamie. We arrived to find the lodge full of men with tellingly battered waders and jackets. Two of them, a Norwegian and a Swede, looked vaguely familiar.

Jamie rumbled them first. One was Sweden's champion fly-fisherman, and the other was Norway's. We'd seen their pictures in the Robinson Bailey catalogue. It was rather like going for a golfing weekend and finding you're sharing the gaff with Jack Nicklaus and Tiger Woods.

Next day our guide appeared, and he turned out to be Norway's champion fly-tier, who supplemented his income by teaching casting. But it was the first week of the season and the water, five feet too high, came off the mountain in a whitewater torrent. Everyone agreed that no fish were to be had, so Jamie and I had a relaxed day, no danger of catching anything, and learning to cast with a heavy sinking line and a fly on the end of it big and shiny enough to double as a Christmas decoration.

Our new friend the fly-tier proceeded to sell us his newly invented, electric-hued flies. 'What are they called?' I asked. He said he hadn't named them yet, but if I caught a fish in this water, he'd not only eat his hat, he'd name them after me.

After supper everyone except Mikael Frodin, Sweden's champ, went to bed. But I couldn't resist a few more casts and went down to the river bank in jeans and sneakers. No point in waders since I wasn't going into the water.

Suddenly I had a fish on the line and it was a whopper, fighting like the devil. I yelled at Mikael across the river but he couldn't hear me above the noise of the rapids above us and the weir below. I had to keep the line short because if I'd let the fish run it would have gone over the weir, so soon my arm was aching and I was too out of breath to yell at Mikael any more. But finally he noticed

I had a fish, and he came across the river with a net to help me land it. A perfect fresh, silver, yard-long hen fish weighing twenty-four pounds.

That poor fish was weighed, measured, photographed, and generally inspected by the half the village, drawn by news of the first fish of the season.

It dawned on me that all the photographs were going to be of Mikael with *my* fish. So, in jeans and trainers, I jumped in the river to get in the picture. I was so excited I didn't feel the freezing water. Someone asked me how long it had taken me to land the fish. 'Five minutes,' I said. 'Maybe seven.' It was twenty-five, said Mikael.

That's what pleasure does for you. It also explains the whisky bottle on my sideboard with *Presented for the first fish on the AA of 1997* on it. I confess to topping up the bottle rather than ever having to throw it away. And framed in my loo is a huge green salmon fly with silver stripes called the Green Prudence. Oh, the glory!!

About the time the Leeds Permanent was being taken over by the Halifax, in 1995, I was asked to join the Whitbread board. I'm sure they asked me for the usual reason – they needed a woman to prevent questions at the AGM about exclusively male line-ups on the platform. I didn't mind, so long as I was treated like everyone else when I got there.

Whitbread is Britain's oldest company with a two hundred and seventy-year history of brewing, pubs, hotels and restaurants. In my time we had franchises to run Marriott hotels, Pizza Hut and TGI Friday's in the UK, bought Costa Coffee and, for a while, we owned Café Rouge, David Lloyd Leisure, and a nursery group. Our most successful enterprise was the budget hotel chain Travel Inn, soon to become Premier Travel Inns, run (along with our Marriott hotels) by the remarkable hotelier Alan Parker. Within days of nine-eleven when *all* our American hotel custom disappeared overnight (sixty per cent of the Marriott business) he had cut our costs to the bone. He squished the hotels into groups of two or three, appointed the best manager to run each group, and made the others redundant. It was brutal, but essential. Other companies, less able to make the tough decisions, floundered.

I've only twice been picked out for comment in the financial press. Once, shamingly, when I unwittingly bought some shares in a 'closed period' for which I was publicly reprimanded by the Financial Regulator. But I am proud of the other mention: I was called 'the scourge of the Remuneration Committee' because I had managed to persuade the Whitbread Remuneration Committee to restrict senior management to the same percentage rise as the rest of the staff. I'd argued how mad, and bad, it was that top executives often got annual pay increases, including bonuses of perhaps thirty per cent while the shop floor worker would be getting only a two per cent rise. Which means, of course, that the gap between rich and poor gets ever wider. Not good for staff relations, or, I argued, for a harmonious society.

I managed to repeat the trick in 2001 when I joined the Woolworths Board and chaired the Remuneration Committee. We were in truly dire straits so persuasion was easier.

The slow demise of Woolies is a heartbreaking story and, with hindsight, inevitable. Kingfisher, in hiving off Woolworths, kept the big town-centre freeholds of a hundred and sixty-seven stores, for which we now had to pay crippling rents. Many of our smaller stores were very profitable but it was not enough. For the five years I was on the board, the chairman, Gerald Corbett, and the CEO, Trevor Bish-Jones, worked their socks off. But competition from out of town stores with parking lots was brutal and our traditional strongholds of music, children's toys and household goods were taken over by the supermarkets. I remember when the first Harry Potter video came out, we sold more than anyone else, but we lost money on every one because we were trying to hang on to a customer base by matching the price in Tesco's, whose buying power was better than ours and who could afford to forgo profit to woo those customers in.

We were still good at decorations and celebrations but there were not enough festivals to keep us in profit. We sold a lot of fancy dress. One year our most popular outfit was not the Halloween pumpkin or the Christmas Rudolf, but the French Maid's saucy get-up. A lot cheaper than in the sex shops of Soho, I guess.

I think Woolies' fate was symbolised by the often-asked market research question:

What do you feel about Woolworths? Answer: wonderful; British institution; would be terrible to see it go; essential part of the High Street, etc.

When did you last shop in a Woolworths? Oh, years ago. I never go now. Tesco is so much more convenient.

CHAPTER 17

EDUCATION, EDUCATION, EDUCATION

Tell me and I forget . . .

let me do and I understand

When in 1995 the Royal Society of Arts (RSA) asked me to chair the Council, though daunted, I agreed. Years before, I'd accepted an invitation to a fellowship because I was impressed that the RSA, one of the oldest learned institutions in the UK (it was set up in 1754) had a broad outlook – unlike the other great institutions: the Royal Society is concerned with Science; the Royal Academy of Arts is strictly about fine art; the Royal Society of Medicine about medical matters, etc. The RSA is dedicated to the 'encouragement of Arts, Manufactures and Commerce', which covers just about everything. Its thirty thousand fellows come from commerce, industry, public service and voluntary sectors. In essence the charity is there to try to figure out what bits of society need fixing and then do something about it – a think-and-*do* tank rather than an academic affair.

Originally set up by the drawing master, Thomas Shipley, to encourage good design and good practice by the awarding of 'premiums' or prizes, the RSA has had a hand in setting up the Royal Academy, the National Trust, the Royal National Lifeboat Institution, the London School of Economics, and much else. They also held the first public exhibition of paintings, the first typing exams, the first cooking exams.

In 1793 Captain Bligh of the *Bounty* fame, won the RSA Gold Medal in response to an RSA challenge to find a way to better feed the slaves in the sugar plantations. He carried 2,000 breadfruit trees from the South Seas to the Caribbean and planted them. When I held his letter to the RSA claiming his prize (he had to wait two years for another Captain to report back that 1,700 of his trees were successfully thriving) I found my hands shaking and the hairs on the back of my head standing up. I could not believe that I was holding a piece of paper that had been held by Bligh, over two hundred years ago.

I like the story of the chimney brush best. Appalled that desperately poor Victorian chimney sweeps were forced to send their children up inaccessible chimneys in the choking dark, the RSA offered a prize for a solution to end the practice. But the invention of the winning brush (extendable and articulated) had a disastrous unintended consequence: the chimney sweeps could not afford them, and the sweeps were in danger of losing their trade to richer men who could. So the women members of the RSA (the Society admitted women from the start) set up a fund to buy the brushes for the sweeps.

I confess to having plotted my rise in the RSA like a politician, though I was less after position than access to the debate about education. I was fired up about the hopelessness of British schooling for those students who are not academic. The prevailing attitude was that the brain is more important than the heart or the hands. I felt, and still do, that schooling should equip everyone for life, and we need cooks and engineers, who actually *make* things, as much as professors who think and politicians who direct.

But what hope did I have of getting a hearing with anyone in the government? None. No one would listen to someone whose qualifications amounted to the twenty-five yards swimming certificate, a pony club badge and a cookery diploma.

But everyone respected the RSA. If I could just get on to the education committee, and influence them, then we could influence the department. I asked my friend Heather Brigstock, who had been High Mistress of St Paul's Girls' school and was now in the House of Lords, how to get on the education committee.

'Easiest way would be to get on the main council. All committees have council members on them.'

'For God's sake, Heather, the Council is stuffed with the great and the good, people like you. Grandees in every seat. How will I ever get on Council?'

'Consider it done,' she said. And indeed it was. Heather championed me and I was duly elected.

Pretty soon I was on the education committee, chaired by the wonderful Sir Peter Baldwin, ex-government mandarin and all-round force for good. At my first meeting a neuroscientist showed us recent research on how the brain works. How distress and anxiety and even discomfort close it down, preventing learning. He gave the example of how difficult it is to read the departures screen when you only have seconds to catch your train. In flight or fight mode you cannot absorb information.

All these mental and psychological barriers to learning seemed to me so easy to get rid of. If classrooms are cold, seats uncomfortable, loud bells ring, doors bang, teachers shout, kids fight, the loos are a no-go area and the food is stuffed full of sugar and additives, is it any wonder children don't learn? They spend a lot of their time uncomfortable, bored or anxious. Of course they hate school.

I was glad to see A levels gradually losing their grip on the educational psyche. Of course they are great for maybe fifteen per cent of children, but most of us learn better by doing than by academic theory. I like Confucius's dictum: *Tell me and I forget. Show me and I remember. Let me do and I understand.*

I went hammer and tongs at my job as RSA chairman, spending perhaps two days a week, sometimes more, at the Society's house in John Adam Street. I found the mix of bright, innovative people stimulating and exciting. Chairing a lot of lectures and attending others on the arts, science, political policy and much else, after a career of intensely practical concerns like menus, fish suppliers and garbage collections, was bliss.

I think the RSA programme that I am proudest of, and with which I was most deeply involved, was the Focus on Food project.

Few schools were interested in cooking in the Eighties and Nineties. Heads keen to prove how academic their school was did not teach the subject at all. And when the curriculum was overhauled in the Eighties there was a proposal to kill cooking in all schools. The food teachers only managed to keep it as an option at all by positioning it as part of design and technology, calling it food technology and shifting the emphasis towards the manufacture of food. The word 'cooking' disappeared, though good food teachers would still slip in some cooking under the guise of recipe development, or nutrition or taste-testing for manufacture.

It incensed me. One teacher proudly recounted the project she was doing with her class.

'We are studying biscuits', she said. 'It's a ten-week project.'

'Ten weeks! They must be master bakers by the end of that!'

'Oh, no. But it is very thorough.' She then went on to explain that in the first nine lessons the class established what a biscuit was, walked round Tesco to see the variety of biscuits, compared packaging and designed their own, compared recipes from different countries, studied the nutritional content of different biscuits, wrote a marketing plan for their new biscuit and costed the ingredients, labour and etc. And, she said with enormous pride, 'And then, the last lesson, we made a biscuit.'

'Was it good?'

She looked embarrassed. 'To be honest, no. By then we had discovered that sugar, fat and salt are bad for you so we made a water biscuit, and it was not a success.'

Grrrr. She probably put the whole class off cooking for life. All over the country children were going home with designs for pizza toppings rather than with the real thing. And too many schools who were teaching cooking were making chocolate chip cookies.

Christopher Lucas, the director of the RSA when I was offered the Chair, was my great ally in getting food education into the RSA's sights. Cooking, he said, involves everything we are supposed to care about: arts, manufacturing and science.

In 1997, fired up by Christopher, I organised two lectures on the same evening. The food campaigner, Suzi Leather, told us that in the rush for convenience we were throwing the baby out with the bath water: we were losing cooking skills and food knowledge, increasingly eating cheap junk and endangering our health. And that, in losing the habit of cooking and eating with our children we were losing the prime opportunity for family bonding.

Matthew Fort, the *Guardian* columnist and food writer, said that our lack of interest in good food was a disaster for the economy: undiscerning customers meant poor restaurants which did not attract tourists, jobs in the industry went to foreign workers because we scorned cooking and waiting, and our lack of interest did not encourage farmers so most really good food came from abroad.

(Interestingly, a lot has happened in the UK since then but Suzi's fears have been realised while Matthew's hopes have started to come true. While the poor eat ever more junk and the nation cooks less and less, restaurant and pub food has got infinitely better, it is now fashionable to be a cook and, though most farmers are having a tough time, at least an increasing number are running farm shops, making cheese, growing organically and selling directly at farmers' markets.)

While the lectures were going on in the Great Room, I had three well-known chefs giving a class of ten-year-olds from Primrose Hill Primary their first cooking lesson downstairs. They made supper for the two-hundred-strong lecture audience.

The event was a success and led directly to the

establishment of Focus on Food. Anita Cormac and Roger Standen, members of the RSA who ran an educational charity at Dean Clough in Halifax, were chosen to run the project. Our budget for the first year was £350,000 which was to cover teaching materials and help for school teachers, an academic study of the attitudes of children to food, and the building and operating of a Cooking Bus (actually a pantechnicon lorry, the sides of which expanded to provide a state-of-the-art teaching kitchen complete with full-size sinks, cookers and cupboards round the sides, and tables in the middle which could be lowered or raised according to the age of the pupils). The Bus, staffed by two teachers and a driver-cum-assistant would travel round schools, teaching children to cook and training teachers.

We were all very excited, but we had yet to raise the money. Then one day I had a call from Stuart Hampson, a member of Council and Chairman of the John Lewis group, which includes the Waitrose food shops.

'We would like Waitrose to sponsor Focus on Food.'

'Wonderful. Which bit?'

'All of it.'

And they did, for nine years. Gradually other sponsors funded more buses and Focus on Food spread all over the UK, becoming a real force in education.

★   ★   ★

For me, about the only downside of the RSA was our illustrious president, Prince Philip. Of course we were immensely proud of his involvement with the Society – he was president for fifty-nine years, and he was good at it – knowledgeable, intelligent and involved. But he wasn't easy to deal with and he frightened the socks off me. On his visits to the Society's house for official functions (presentation of RSA medals, or his annual lecture, or a formal dinner) I would head the reception committee standing at the entrance, wearing the Chairman's badge of office. I would greet him and offer him the President's badge. Without fail he would tell me that it was the wrong one and I was wearing his. And I was no good at curtseying. Once, the then Duchess of Devonshire was with me, and she, at over eighty, swept him the deepest, most graceful curtsey, head down, skirts on the floor, like a ballerina. It was beautiful to see. Meanwhile, I, her junior by thirty years, could barely manage a bob.

Prince Philip could be blunt to the point of rudeness. Once he came to give the actress Judi Dench the Society's Benjamin Franklin medal. We'd had the usual pantomime about the badges downstairs. I took him into the drawing room, where Judi and her daughter Finty and their friends, plus Council members were waiting to be presented to him. Seeing the photographers, he said, irritated, 'Why have we got *two* photographers? You know I hate photographers.'

I knew nothing about the photographers, but, trying to lighten his mood, I joked, 'Maybe one is back-up in case the other's useless?'

This irritated him further, 'What rot,' he said loudly and turned away, ignoring the line-up he was supposed to meet, and instead talking to other guests. I apologised to Judi and to the photographers and hissed at a waiter to get him a drink.

What gave him the right to be gratuitously rude? I was pretty cross so while HRH, now restored to good humour, was dutifully doing the rounds of chat to the pre-dinner crowd in the library, I investigated the matter of the photographers. One was hired by the RSA with the agreement of Prince Philip's office. The second one was hired by the Palace to follow HRH around and take pictures for a book.

Later, at dinner, I could not resist telling him the extra photographer was his, not ours.

'Nonsense,' he said, 'I don't have a photographer.'

'He says he's taking pictures for some official record of your life,' I said.

'Oh that. Well, he's not my photographer.'

I guess 'sorry' is not in his vocabulary.

But he can be delightful company. Never given to platitudes, his conversation is always interesting. Like all the Royals, he talks for half the dinner to the person on his right, then turns to the person on his left, so, while the royal attention is on you, there is time for a decent conversation and he's always well-informed and outspoken. But still, I always found it something of a relief when the royal back was turned.

I never saw Prince Philip anything but charming to, and interested in, children or junior staff, but he is famous for having a go at people who, I guess, he thinks can look after themselves. And there does seem to be something about my character that attracts hostility. Perhaps it is my voice. I sound either laid back, middle-class and bored, or clipped and bossy, though I don't *feel* any of that.

I don't want to portray myself as a victim, but once or twice I have sparked unbelievable behaviour from usually civilised people.

Many years before, in 1974, we'd been asked by the actress Janet Suzman (who had known both Nan and my mother for years and was a friend) to dinner. I was roundly attacked by the then very famous vicar of the church of Bow Bells. He was well known in the City for his lunchtime lecture series and his tremendous good work in the East End. I was pregnant at the time but not yet married – we were waiting for Nan and Rayne's divorce to come through. The vicar was at the other end of the table from me. Suddenly he raised his voice. 'I hear you are having a baby out of wedlock. How can you countenance bringing a bastard into the world?'

I'd no idea how to answer that but he didn't want an answer, he wanted to deliver a lecture about the sinfulness of pre-marital sex and the

389

effrontery of not being ashamed of the result. My protestations that the baby was long wanted and would be deeply loved just provoked him further. I ended up running out of the room to cry in the loo.

The next morning I received a great bouquet of flowers. I softened immediately. Poor fellow, I thought, he'd probably had a glass too many and got carried away and now he's feeling guilty for being so unchristian. But the flowers were from Janet.

Some years later, Rayne and I went to dinner with Jim and Shirley Sherwood at their beautiful house in Oxfordshire. Shown into the drawing room, I was introduced to the ex-Duchess of Marlborough, sitting in a blue gown on a blue sofa. I smiled at her and said, 'You look wonderful. A symphony in blue!'

'Do you always make personal remarks?' she snapped.

I made a hasty retreat. But at dinner I found myself opposite her, with Jim sitting at the end of the table between the two of us. I talked for a while to the man on my left, and then, when he turned to speak to his other neighbour, I found myself isolated, with Jim still talking to the Duchess. I kept my eyes on my food for a bit and then looked vaguely up, thinking I might join their conversation, but not wanting to intrude. She caught my eye, but far from including me, she barked, '*And* you listen to other people's conversation, do you?'

I remember my face burning as with shame, as if I had been caught out doing something atrocious. But there was an embarrassed silence at our end of the table and then my neighbour to my left rescued me. As we left, Jim followed us to our car and apologised for not jumping to my defence. But, poor man, he could hardly take on his aristocratic guest under his own roof.

One day in 1994, a year before I became Chairman, I was in the back of a taxi going round Trafalgar Square and I noticed, for the umpteenth time, that the monumental plinth on the northwest Corner, was still unoccupied. I thought, why on earth doesn't Westminster Council put back whoever was once there? So I pulled out a pad and wrote a letter to the *Evening Standard* asking just that.

Well, of course I should have done my research. The paper received a flood of replies explaining that there never had been a statue on the plinth, not since it had been laid out in 1840. It had been intended for William IV but he'd died before it could be completed and he was so unpopular that no one wanted to pay for it. Ever since, numerous attempts to fill the plinth had been thwarted. Everyone's hero was someone else's enemy, or considered unsuitable for so prominent a position.

Of course, that just spurred me on: there had to be a way. Then I thought: why not ask the public what they want? I appealed to newspapers and radio stations for suggestions and they came flooding in: the footballer Gazza; Pooh Bear; the Queen Mum leading Red Rum; Mrs Thatcher on a tank; Nelson Mandela. The most frequently proposed idea was for a giant pigeon.

And then the debate widened. Why did it have to be an equestrian statue, or a hero? Why not a group sculpture, an abstract theme, a modern installation? I was beginning to feel out of my depth. So I persuaded the RSA to take it on. Michaela Crimmin, the RSA Head of Arts knew how to manage committees and how to get the arts establishment on side.

She said I had to have a feasibility study done. If we don't, she said, we'll never get official support and we'll never get any funding. So we applied to the Arts Council and they came up with £7,000. Then my education into the way this stuff works began: you pay a professional to tell you, in a report, what you have just told them. They couch it in the language public bodies, councils, prospective funders like. You apply to these people for more money, to conduct public consultation, to assess the risks, to sound out the interested parties (the Victorian Society, the Georgian Society, the Fine Arts Commission, English Heritage, the Westminster Public Art Advisory Committee, London First, the Department of Culture, the National Gallery, the Residents' Association of Trafalgar Square, the Armed Forces, the Public Services Association, Uncle Tom Cobley and all).

To me this all looked like a waste of public money, but it got us taken seriously and now we knew where we stood: the Palace never sanctions statues of Royals while they are still living; any sculpture favoured by one of the Armed Forces would never be agreed by the others; political heroes were unwelcome in Trafalgar Square – they belonged in Parliament Square, and almost any suggestion by any institution would be howled down by some other body.

We formed a committee. It included Sandy Nairne, then director of programmes at the Tate; James Lingwood, director of the arts company Artangel, Mick Brundle from Arup Associates, the architectural and engineering firm which had agreed to advise, pro bono, on the technical erection of the works of art – not an easy business, the plinth is seventeen feet long and twenty-four feet high and it is itself a listed monument so you cannot drill holes in it. And sculptures had to be robust enough to survive revellers, protesters and hooligans without causing them any harm.

James Lingwood had a brilliant idea – why not use the plinth for 'contemporary temporary' exhibitions of a variety of works? That way anyone with violent objections could comfort themselves with the thought that the hated work would not be there forever, and it would give a fair crack to every desire: for contemporary installations, for conceptual works of art, for modern statues and sculptures.

But first we had to find the artists and next we had to get planning permission. Sandy led a small committee to select the first three artists and Rachel Whiteread, Bill Woodrow and Mark Wallinger were chosen. Mick Brundle, who knew his way round the labyrinthine procedure for planning permission, led our submission to Westminster Council. For this, we needed the world and his wife on side. I think I presented our plans to thirteen different bodies. All of them gradually came round except the Royal Fine Art Commission, chaired by Baron St John of Fawsley, better known as Norman St John-Stevas. We needed the Commission's approval, or at least we needed them not to object, because English Heritage, who could veto the scheme, set great store by the Commission's view and Westminster Council would not move without endorsement from English Heritage.

I knew the eccentric Norman slightly, but he would not take my calls. I did get to speak to the Secretary to the Commission, Francis Golding, who agreed that the Commission's brochure stated that anyone with a proposal should consult them as soon as possible. Yes, he said, I know, but Lord St John refuses to discuss the plinth. He believes it should stay empty.

I went to see Peter Palumbo, the great developer and friend of Norman's and asked him to intercede. Peter was immediately enthusiastic and picked up the phone. I could hear Norman's response from across the desk.

'Horreur, horreur, horreur!' he cried.

Palumbo put the phone down. 'Sorry,' he said, 'but he won't see you. He's adamant.'

So I got an appointment with Virginia Bottomley, Secretary of State at the Department of National Heritage in her offices a stone's throw from the plinth. She liked the plan. Emboldened, I told her my problem with Norman. 'The gossip is', I said, 'that he wants the plinth to stay empty until the Queen Mum dies and then he'll get a statue of her with her favourite horse on it. He won't even hear our proposal.'

I asked her if she'd invite him to a meeting 'to discuss the RSA's plans' in a drawing-room in the Canadian High Commission which directly overlooked the plinth. The High Commissioner had already agreed to be there, and I could put our case. She agreed and I left in high hopes. Norman could hardly refuse the Minister of Culture, could he?

Yes, he could. Adamant as ever, he managed to dodge every date we tried.

Soon I got a letter from the Commission baldly announcing that the commissioners had discussed the RSA's ideas for the plinth and unanimously decided against them.

I was livid, and countered that as we had not been given a chance to outline our proposals or show them any plans, and we had as yet made no formal application, they were in no position to judge the matter. We urgently needed a meeting.

Could we be included on the agenda of a commissioners' meeting so that we could have a fair hearing?

I think Francis was keen to see fair play, if his chairman was not, and eventually I received an invitation to lunch with the commissioners, 'to discuss any matters of mutual interest to the Commission and the RSA'. Thank you very much, I replied, but I wanted to address the meeting, specifically about the plinth project. Could I please have an hour on the agenda, bring the RSA Director, Penny Egan with me, and could the commissioners please be sent the proposal and plans in advance?

Francis must have persuaded Norman because in the end they agreed. On the day, Penny and I turned up at noon armed with a half-hour presentation to be followed by half an hour of discussion.

We sat downstairs and waited. And waited. At one point Francis appeared and, patently embarrassed, said he was very sorry but the meeting was overrunning. I asked if the commissioners had been sent the papers we'd submitted in advance? He was afraid not, Lord St John had vetoed it.

We were admitted at ten to one. Norman did not introduce any of his commissioners – there were about a dozen – nor did he introduce Penny. His introduction to me went something like this:

'Well, you all know Prue Leith, the well-known cookery lady. I am sure it will surprise you to find that a cook is somehow concerning herself with the arts. But there we are. Prue, I'm sorry but we really only have ten minutes before lunch so I think we must dispense with your presentation. We all know the RSA plan is to put various modern installations on the plinth. Perhaps we should let the commissioners air their views.'

It was hopeless. Norman gave what air-time there was to a sculptor (whom we had been unwise enough not to consult or invite to be one of the artists featured). She objected, she said, on artistic grounds: modern sculptors of any worth would refuse to have their works displayed on a plinth, that out of date symbol of superiority and authority.

Penny and I left, further fired up to defeat the old fox. We wrote to Francis, saying we had been given an unsatisfactory hearing and asking him to make sure that before the commissioners voted on the matter at their next meeting, they receive the information we had sent. And then we set about lobbying the individual commissioners.

We quickly realised that there was much more support for us than had been expressed in front of Norman, and that when it came to a vote, we'd probably have a majority.

But, as always, we under-estimated our Norman. By the time of their decision meeting, we were in regular contact with three commissioners who supported our proposals. One of them rang us to relay the result straight after the meeting. The majority of the commissioners were in favour of our scheme, a few were neutral. Only Norman was dead against, but, in deference to their chairman whom they did not want to embarrass, the decision was to take no stance, for or against, the initiative. We were jubilant. That was good enough for us.

But then a letter came declaring that the Commission had unanimously voted *against* the scheme. You had to admire the man. He certainly did not give up easily.

But now my dander was most definitely up, and I wrote to him saying that I knew how the votes had gone and that I would like to see the minutes of the meeting. I never got them, but the Commission suddenly dropped their objections, which meant English Heritage raised no objections and Westminster finally gave us permission to go ahead with the first three works. It had been a five-year war, but we'd won it.

The first occupant of the plinth was a life-size white Christ figure with a barbed-wire crown of thorns, *Ecce Homo* by Mark Wallinger. Erected just before Christmas 1999, it looked tiny and vulnerable standing on the edge of the twenty-four foot massive plinth and was instantly admired by critics and public alike.

Chris Smith, Secretary of State for what was now the Department of Culture, Media and Sport, asked John Mortimer, the playwright, to review the scheme. Happily, he approved, and since then works by some of the country's most celebrated artists have had their moment of glory on the plinth. It was empty for a hundred and fifty-five years. I hope the current scheme lasts as long.

(There was an amusing addendum to this saga. A few weeks after we'd got planning permission, I saw Norman at a party given by the American Ambassador. Oh God, I thought, this is going to be tricky, but he dashed over, velvet cloak waving exotically, greeted me like a long-lost friend and asked me to join his committee judging new buildings for the Royal Fine Art Commission's annual Building of the Year Award. I was so astonished I agreed, and it was great fun. We hopped around the country in a private plane, saw some wonderful buildings and were very civil to each other. I never mentioned the fourth plinth and neither did he. But I did think I was supping with the devil.)

One incident at the RSA amused me a lot. The Society had decided to have a portrait of the Queen painted to celebrate her fifty years as first our President and then, after her accession, our Patron. We consulted with the Palace and agreed on a young painter called Justin Mortimer, whose work I'd seen in the National Portrait Gallery. I remember being a bit nervous that, though the Palace had OK'd the choice of painter, the RSA Council might not. So I edited the pack of photographs he'd sent us of his work, removing the more outré pictures of torture and bondage and showing them only the conventional portraits. The Council approved.

I had also asked Justin to paint my Daniel and Li-Da, then in their late teens, in a joint portrait. One day I went to his studio to see how he was getting on with this. The painting was almost done and I was thrilled with it.

He said, 'I've finished the Queen too. Do you want to see it?'

Of course I did and he pulled off a sheet from a large painting on an easel. It was a very good likeness of her Majesty, but my heart stopped. He had chopped off her head, which was floating away to one side of her neck. I could just see the headlines. 'Off with her head!' And 'RSA decapitates Her Majesty.'

I rushed back to look at the contract with Justin and saw to my relief that if either the Palace or the RSA was not happy we could oblige him to try again or we could reject the picture. But it was a good painting and we felt its unconventional take on the Queen befitted our modern image of the Society rather well. I decided to try it out on Prince Philip, so when he was next in the building I held a large tranny up to the light for him to see. He garrumphed a bit but said he did not think the Queen would object, and if the Palace art experts approved that would be fine.

Later, when I was no longer chairman, and the Society decided to have a portrait of Prince Philip as well, it upset him rather more. The painting was sponsored by Bernard Matthews of turkey fame and Prince Philip is portrayed with an elongated, distinctly old, bare neck, like a turkey's. HRH let it be known that neither portrait should hang in the main entrance hall.

I imagine the temptation to use the opportunity to make it into the papers with a newsworthy portrait of a Royal would be irresistible. And they are very good paintings.

CHAPTER 18

LOSING RAYNE

Journey's end

I found the last decade of Rayne's life hard. I was in my fifties, energetic and up for everything. He was in his seventies and, though not ill, was growing grumpy.

He became increasingly didactic, impatient of argument, and unwilling to engage in the sort of conversational sparring over current affairs, politics, books, art, sport, that he had always loved and been so good at. Indeed, good conversation became impossible. Up until the early Nineties, he'd always been the best person in the world to talk to, interested in others' views, trenchant and funny in his own.

Of course I wished I could have the old Rayne back, but there were occasional moments of such irritation and despair that the thought of widowhood seemed preferable to what I was going through.

His secretary, the devoted Miss Joshua, said, 'He's closing down his systems,' as if he was a *Star Wars* robot. But I think she was right. He became, as old people so often do, repetitive, devoted to routine, unwilling to go out.

He just couldn't be bothered with anything, which maddened me. He'd rather kick a cupboard door shut than bother to get it fixed. He, who had always been punctilious about maintenance, refused to have the house painted, or re-wired, or re-plumbed, all of which it increasingly needed.

Nonetheless, if we were alone, he was relaxed and affectionate and I loved being with him. He lived the life he liked, one of reading, writing and sleeping (and of course secretly smoking) in his study, with television and meals downstairs. He would sink into bed at night sighing, 'Best moment of the day,' and put an arm round me, cosy and content.

He wouldn't travel any more – indeed he'd not liked it for years, and I remember how thrilled Li-Da was that he turned up in Glasgow for her graduation in 1995. I think it was one of the last plane journeys he made.

My last attempt at a big outing was on the night of the Millennium when I talked Rayne into booking a suite at the Marriott Hotel in County Hall on the Thames, looking across the river at the Houses of Parliament. The plan was that friends and family would drift in for a drink, Rayne and I would have a room-service supper and then, fizz in hand, watch the promised 'river of fire' that was to streak up the Thames. But Rayne was too ill and we had to cancel. Instead we had dinner for two by the fire. Rayne went to bed early and I sat up with the telly and the rest of the champagne watching fireworks from all over the world. But the much vaunted river of fire we were to see on the Thames failed to ignite.

I'd always known that marrying someone so much older than I would mean a difficult final lap together. I told myself then, and I know now, that it was a more than fair price for the happiness he'd given me. And once we'd sold the business, I could spend time at home writing novels, gardening, and cooking for family weekends while Rayne read, or slept, upstairs.

And because of my commitments as a non-exec board member and involvement with charitable causes, I had things to do, places to go, people to meet, and Rayne was always insistent that I continue my 'outside life'. I could go to London or away on working trips, or take occasional jaunts abroad knowing that our housekeeper, Lyn, one of the best women one could hope to know, would look after my husband better than I did.

When in February 2001 our ever-generous friends Jim and Shirley Sherwood asked me to join them on the inaugural Hiram Bingham train ride from Cusco to Machu Picchu in Peru, I couldn't resist. Leaving for Kennedy Airport from New York City one freezing winter morning, clutching a carton of coffee from Starbucks, I climbed into a yellow cab and failed to do up my seatbelt. My driver was Russian, didn't speak a word of English, did not know where Kennedy Airport was, and set off in the wrong direction. He drove through a red light and we were hit by a truck.

I was taken to Bellevue in downtown Manhattan, a state hospital serving the city's poorest. It is where the down-and-outs, drug addicts, ambulatory psychotics, and victims of crime are taken. Outside most wards sat an armed cop on a chair. It was like something out of a movie.

The nurses were hardened to the horrors of life. I was taken down to X-ray, where several waiting patients were handcuffed to policemen, who were a lot nicer to their charges than the nurses were. Getting on and off the gurney was so painful that I yelped aloud. Impatient at my slowness, two nurses just grabbed me by the arms, hauled me off the gurney and stood me in front of the X-ray machine, holding my arms above my head. I screamed and burst into tears. 'Shush yo' mouth,' said one of them. 'You ain't gonna die.'

On my first evening I was in agony. I rang the bell repeatedly but no one came. Eventually a large scowling woman stamped in and marched towards me.

'Oh Nurse, thank God, could you please . . .'

She glared at me. 'You planning on ringing that bell all night? We get no peace at the desk. What you think this is? A hotel?' And she yanked the bell out of its socket.

The staff shifts were organised along racial

lines. The day staff were mostly Puerto Ricans and were reasonable if not sympathetic. They were obviously the elite who talked to the doctors and filled in notes, and they didn't do anything unpleasant if they could help it. One day, unable to get out of bed and in the absence of a bowl to vomit into (and no response to appeals for one) I threw up on the floor. No one cleaned it up. I asked everyone who entered the ward but the reply was always a shake of the head or a 'Not my job.' The nursing shift changed at four p.m. but the Afro-Caribbean shift to midnight was worse, manned by a terrifying gang of women who kept us awake, all talking at a shout and screeching with laughter at the nurses' station. The leader of the gang (my tormentor who pulled out my bell) said my sick should have been cleaned up by the day shift and they were not going to do other people's dirty work. It wasn't until after midnight, when the kindly Filipinos came on, that the floor was cleaned. I spoke to the woman who did it. 'They leave everything for us. But we dare not complain. We need the jobs.'

I complained to Rayne on the phone, then regretted it, fearing it would be like ratting on a bully in the playground which only serves to bring more bullying.

Rayne rang me back. 'I got put through to some nurse on your ward and she actually said, "Listen to me, white boy. I in New York with your missus.

You in London. What you going to do to me, huh? You butt out, leave me do my job. Okay?"

Oh God, I thought, she's going to kill me. But he said, 'Anyway, I've now spoken to the administrator and he's going to move you.'

Much as I wanted to get out of Big Mouth's jurisdiction, I dreaded the physical movement of being loaded on and off a gurney again. In an effort to ingratiate myself with the nurse in the hopes of mitigating more pain, I said, 'I must be very lucky. I didn't know you had any private rooms in this hospital.'

'We don't. You goin' to a padded cell.' She cackled and slapped her thighs with merriment.

It wasn't padded or a cell but it was mighty secure. It was a room used either for criminals for their protection from rival gangs, or for shot policemen who might be finished off by their enemies, posing as visitors. It was in fact a nice big room, with a wide window giving me a view of the Empire State Building. Security consisted of a passage with first one, then another, heavy, bullet-proof doors, like the doors to a safe, which locked automatically. It was wonderful – I was insulated from the noise of the ward; there were no desperate women in neighbouring beds talking to themselves or crying, *and* there was a private bathroom which I could get to after a day or two.

An American lawyer friend, outraged at my lack of interest in suing the taxi driver, insisted on sending me an ambulance-chasing lawyer who looked exactly like Danny de Vito. He got straight down to business.

'So tell me what happened. You got hit by a truck?'

'Well yes, but it wasn't the truck's fault.'

'Now, don't say that lady. We don't know yet.'

'But I do know. He couldn't help it. My driver went through a red light.'

'But you don't know that, you were in shock. We need to see if the truck was culpable. Could you swear on oath that you saw the red light? Which side of the road was it? Or was it overhead? How long had it been red?'

Of course he had me instantly confused. I ducked the question,

'Why don't we go for the taxi company?'

'No point. These cab companies, no flies on them. They aren't incorporated companies. Every cab driver is self-employed. He won't have any money, and if he did at the time of the accident, he won't have any now. Trust me. I bin round this block a few times. We gotta pin it on the truck company.'

'But they're innocent!'

'You English! What's the matter with you? You are the victim here.'

With lightning speed he had calculated my pain and suffering, loss of my holiday, flights, medical expenses and an extra week in New York as worth a quarter of a million dollars, of which, when we won the case, he would take a third. No wonder he was keen.

Maybe because I was too ill to argue, or even a little tempted by the thought of compensation, I agreed to let him represent me. He wrote an affidavit for me to sign and was disappointed when I wouldn't say the driver had not run the light.

'It's the difference between a fortune and peanuts,' he said. 'Are you absolutely sure it wasn't the van that jumped the light? Where was the light? Overhead? Which side? Can you really remember clearly?'

Once I could walk about I wanted my clothes. My suitcase, all packed for my holiday, and my coat, had been stolen from the cupboard on my previous ward. No one was the least surprised.

The hospital social worker arrived. She had a stock of clothes because many of the homeless were admitted in such threadbare garments that they could not be released into a New York winter like that – they'd be back with pneumonia in a flash. Which is how I came to check into one of Manhattan's finest hotels, the Mark (which the Sherwoods had kindly booked me into for the week I needed before being passed fit to fly), dressed in a nylon puffa-jacket several sizes too small over an orange fleece tracksuit several sizes too large, courtesy of New York Welfare.

I guess it is something of a miracle that Rayne saw his children grow up. When we married, one of the reasons he advanced for not having children was that he'd probably die while they were still little.

For the last ten years of his life he had to stop every few yards to get his breath back and pump some blood painfully through his clogged-up arteries into his legs. By the end he could barely walk at all and we had an oxygen cylinder and nebuliser. But he was not easy to gainsay. Twice, shoo'd out of the house with instructions to 'just go and stop fussing', I got as far as the station platform. Both times, about to board a train to London, I turned back, sure Rayne was too ill to leave without me, and both times we ended up in A and E.

Once I was to host a dinner with Patrick Lichfield for the British Food Trust at his house, Shugborough, a two-hour drive north of us. Rayne was wheezing badly, but was therefore more difficult and cross than usual and insisted I went. I rang home as soon as I arrived but he insisted he was fine, so I stayed for the dinner but told Patrick I wouldn't stay the night as planned. The Duchess of Devonshire, who was our President, was there, and we were schmoozing the local politicians and deep pockets for the charity. But I couldn't concentrate, and as soon as the main course was over I sneaked out to ring home again. This time there was no answer and I tried to believe Rayne had gone to bed and was safe asleep.

Somehow unable to convince myself of this, I left the party. I drove home as fast as I dared, ran upstairs, and found Rayne still fully dressed, slumped half on the bed, half on the floor, unconscious but breathing. I'm sure the ambulance got there very fast, but it felt like forever.

I got to know the dash to hospital all too well. Sometimes I didn't feel Rayne was ill enough to justify an ambulance and I would call the doctor, hoping for a visit. But since it was usually a weekend, which meant answering machines, call centres, locums and no bloody help at all, I'd invariably have to ring 999 anyway.

Whenever Rayne collapsed or couldn't breathe, the rattle as the ambulance went over the cattle-grid, the sight of flashing lights, the paramedics taking charge would leave me faint with relief. Then there would be the desperate pleading with them to take him to the Cheltenham General or Hornton in Banbury, but please not to the John Radcliffe in Oxford. Then I would follow behind the ambulance in my car, praying he would not be dead on arrival.

After a while we refused point blank to go to the John Radcliffe. It may have been one of the great teaching hospitals, but the nursing was dire, even in the BUPA-paid private rooms. The first time Rayne was an inpatient there, they didn't change his sheets for eleven days. They put his food tray down where he could not reach it, and anyway he was too weak to feed himself. His lips were cracked and dry, and when I held a beaker to his mouth he sucked desperately at it, obviously thirsty. When I complained the nurse said, 'He has

411

a jug of water by his bed. He can have as much water as he likes.'

'But he's too weak to pour it. And too shaky to hold the mug.'

She looked at her whiteboard on which were scrawled instructions for the patients.

'It doesn't say that on our board.'

'Come and look at him. See for yourself.'

But she was busy looking at her computer. 'It doesn't say that in his notes either.'

It took two days of badgering to get him a drip.

One New Year's Day he was admitted to the Radcliffe and Li-Da, who had been away in South Africa for a year, came with me to see him. Her first sight of her father was of him lying on his back, naked, tubes everywhere and a mask over his face, barely conscious. The big double doors to his room, which was dead opposite the main passage, were wide open. We closed the doors and I demanded a sheet, and eventually put his pyjamas on him. When I complained at the lack of consideration and dignity, the nurse said they had more urgent things to do than worry about closing doors.

I stood at the desk for a long time waiting for someone to look up and talk to me. Eventually a doctor did so, a look of irritation on his face.

'Could I speak to whoever is in charge of Mr Kruger? I'm his wife.'

He frowned. 'What do you want to know?'

'Well, he's just been admitted. Could you tell me how he is? What the problem is?'

'He's alcoholic, that's what the problem is.'

'Alcoholic? No. I'm talking of Mr Kruger in Room Six.'

'Yes, Kruger. He's got withdrawal symptoms. Alcoholic poisoning.'

'He's *not* alcoholic. He has two weak glasses of whisky every night, never less, never more. I have never seen him drunk in thirty years.'

'Mrs Kruger, your husband is alcoholic. He is blue. His hands are trembling. He is incoherent.'

'Could that not be because he's not getting enough oxygen? He has emphysema. He smokes, he doesn't drink. And the nebuliser makes his hands shake.'

'Well, we'll watch him, but he's in a very poor way, I should warn you.'

'Are you telling me he might die?'

'Yes, I am. At any time.'

When Li-Da and I were waiting for the lift, hanging on to each other and both fighting off tears, I felt a tap on my shoulder. It was the doctor. I thought he'd come to tell me that Rayne had died.

'Mrs Kruger.'

'Yes?'

'I am so, so sorry. I should not have spoken to you like that. And you are right, there is no alcohol in your husband's blood. I should not have jumped to conclusions.'

I don't think either of us said anything.

'It's not much of an excuse,' he said, 'but I've

been on duty over the New Year weekend and I've not been to bed for thirty-six hours.'

He said Rayne's condition was critical. 'We will do all we can for him, I promise.' He was as good as his word, and Rayne did not die.

Poor man. No wonder he'd lost his bedside manner. But why is it that hospitals are under-staffed on weekends and public holidays? If hotels and restaurants can roster staff to cope with evening service, weekends, Christmas lunch and New Year feasts, why can't hospitals?

But the next time Rayne was in the Radcliffe was as bad. One day I found him standing at the ward desk in his dressing gown, with bare legs and slippers, clutching his bag. He was trying to check himself out of the hospital. The three nurses at the desk had their heads down, deliberately ignoring him. He was swaying and shaking and I ran up to him and held him.

'Darling, what's going on?'

'Oh, thank God you are here. I want to go home.'

One of the nurses looked up. 'He is being very difficult. He won't go back to his room. He has a temperature of 103, look at him. He's shaking.'

I wanted to yell at them, 'Well, could you not have at least given him a chair to sit on?' But instead I said to Rayne, 'Darling, you cannot leave, you're too ill.'

I tried to lead him back into his room, but he said, his voice suddenly no longer wobbly, but loud and firm, 'I would rather die in the car park than stay another minute in this hospital.'

I knew he meant it, and I persuaded him to sit in his room while I commandeered a wheelchair. I took him downstairs, and from the car park I rang his consultant, who arranged for him to go to the Cheltenham General. We went straight there. It was two p.m. and the nurse helping him into bed and fixing his oxygen, put the bell lead into his hand and said, 'Mr Kruger, my name is Geraldine. I'm the senior nurse in charge this weekend and if you want anything, ask for me. Meanwhile, would you like a cup of tea?'

He nodded.

She looked at me. 'I'll bring a pot. You look like you could do with one too, Mrs Kruger.'

A few minutes later a catering manager arrived and apologised that lunch was over. 'But,' she said, 'we have a little kitchen on the ward and I could do you a sandwich? Or toast? Or cereal?'

Rayne waved away all suggestions, too ill to want food, but the young woman's smile was friendly as she leaned down to look into his face.

'Are you sure? How about jelly? With ice cream?' she said.

His face lit up like a child's. He smiled and put a thumb up. I could have cried.

I wrote to both hospitals afterwards, comparing the nurses' attitude, the cleanliness, the care, of the two hospitals. Chalk and cheese. No surprise then when the Radcliffe simply denied all charges and said it was my husband's fault for being difficult. No surprise either that Cheltenham got three stars (the highest score) and the John Radcliffe only one (the lowest) in the newly introduced star system.*

Those months, for all Rayne was fading fast, were good ones in many ways. Once he accepted that he was ill and that he needed me, he became less anxious to pretend he was fine, or to brush away all help. We spent the last few weeks on the first floor of the house, with a wheelchair to get him from our bedroom to the spare room which I had rigged up as a sitting room with a television. It reminded me of our early days together when we'd shared stolen time in my bedsit. Rayne became gentle and resigned, allowed me to nurse him and do the undignified things one has to for the very ill, without embarrassment. He was very loving and we'd spend happy stretches watching television or with me reading to him, or just tucked up cosily together.

When, a week before Christmas 2002, he got another lung infection it was back to the Cheltenham General. We brought him down in the open glass lift he'd finally agreed to after years of my badgering to install it. It was the first time the lift was used, and the only time he went in it. He was in a chair with two green-overalled paramedics and

* The star rating system did not last. There were such cries of 'unfair' from the poor scorers that the government lost courage and it was abandoned.

as I watched from the ground floor, I did think this might be for the first and last time.

He had a horrible time in A and E while four or five doctors and nursing staff struggled to get him breathing properly again. He thrashed about, resisting, frightened and desperately trying to keep hold of my hand. At one point he put my fingers in his mouth and sucked them like a child. But the medics pushed me out of the way – they had to.

I went and stood in the corner, praying, or whatever atheists do. Begging someone somewhere to make it all right. Someone did – but only temporarily.

On my morning visit a few days later I was surprised to see Rayne out of bed and sitting in a chair. He had an oxygen mask over his face, but his colour was less grey. He took it off when he saw me and for a few minutes I held his hand. We didn't talk much, but sat companionably, he occasionally removing the mask, and me gently putting it back after a few minutes. He hated the confinement and heat of it, but couldn't breathe without it. After an hour or so he told me to go away. I kissed him and said I'd be back at six. I got a smile of sorts and a weak wave as I left.

It was our year to do Christmas, and all the Leiths, plus a few friends, were coming. So, between hospital visits, I was preparing for it. I love Christmas, and that afternoon I set about hanging the Christmas decorations on the tree. I was cheerful: Rayne was noticeably better; maybe, after all, we'd get him home for Christmas.

I drove to the hospital, arriving about six and walked quite jauntily into the ward. The curtains were drawn round Rayne's bed and a nurse, walking swiftly down the ward, intercepted me before I got there. She turned me round and steered me into a side room. I knew the worst.

'He's dead?'

'Yes, I'm so sorry Mrs Kruger. He died fifteen minutes ago.'

I could hear myself wailing, 'No, no, no,' even though I knew it was true.

She told me they had done all they could: two doctors and three nurses tried for ten minutes to save him. Poor girl, she was only trying to comfort me, but I wanted to hear he'd died gently while having an afternoon nap. I had witnessed those medical fights for life, doctors being brutal to save him, he fighting like a tiger to be left alone.

I was distraught that I'd not been there. I remembered how he had hung onto my arm, sucked my fingers. How could I not have been at his side?

The nurse suggested I sit with his body. He wasn't yet laid out like an effigy on a tomb, face to ceiling, hands crossed piously across his chest. He still looked like Rayne, but now no longer struggling to breathe, no longer in pain. I spent maybe forty minutes, first guilt-ridden, then slowly realising that a perfect death is mostly a fiction, and that it did not matter. I ended up glad I'd not been there. I thought, selfishly, that if I had been, then my last memory of Rayne would be of him in extremis. That would have been hard to bear.

Gradually, a kind of calm settled on me. It was quiet in that little cubicle. Rayne lay, still warm, relaxed, half on his side, one eye open a tiny crack: I could see a sliver of iris. I talked to him and held his hand, stroked his cheek, kissed his forehead, finally just buried my face against his side.

If I were religious, I suppose what I was doing during that hour would be called praying. I was certainly letting the fact of his death and the fact of my coming widowhood take hold, and also feeling a profound gratitude. I'd been his lover or his wife for forty years. He'd been not only my lover and my husband, but also my mentor, guide, and business partner. Maybe my mother had been right that he'd also replaced the father I'd lost.

I felt sorrow, yes, but also peace. I knew I was about to be utterly miserable, I had no idea how I would cope – if I *could* cope – but I had none of the familiar panic at the thought of being without him. I just breathed in the comforting smell of him and thought, good-bye my darling. Goodbye. And thank you.

And then I took refuge in the purely practical. I started to clear his locker and found a packet of fags, which made me smile. I said, perhaps aloud, 'That's my boy, recalcitrant to the last.' I packed his bag, gave his cheek, his hand, his foot, a last touch as I left, then went to phone the children.

We had had so many crises and panics over the years that we all knew Rayne might die at any time, yet it still came as a shock. I could not get hold of Daniel – he was away being best man at a friend's wedding. I told Li-Da. We said very little. There was no need for more. She said she'd come at once, and she would track Daniel down.

My brother Jamie, with his wife Penny and their daughter, fetched me from the hospital and took me to my friend Jill Parker's house. Most of her family were there because Jill's husband Peter had died nine months before, and they were still clustering together for comfort. Li-Da drove down from London, bringing my brother's three sons with her. My son taxied across England, arriving at midnight.

I don't remember that evening as miserable. I remember it as sad, but companionable and loving too. There must have been a dozen of us for supper and we talked about Rayne, and about Peter Parker, in the good days.

Before bed, Li-Da, Daniel and I lay on the double bed in the Parkers' spare room. We hung on to each other, able to weep without trying to stop the tears. I was mourning my children's loss as well as my own. My heart went out most to Daniel, who had been so close to Rayne. He was the apple of his father's eye since the day, twenty-eight years before, when I'd come round to find him, new-born, in his father's arms, Rayne's face transfigured with joy and wonder. But I wept for Li-Da too. She'd always loved her dad, but they'd only come to really appreciate each other and enjoy each other's company in the last few years; she could have done with more of that.

After a while Daniel went into the attic room above us and Li-Da and I shared the double bed. I fell asleep, warm with her arms round me. And then, sometime in the night, I realised she'd gone. Worried about her, thinking she might be crying in the freezing garden so as not to disturb anyone, I lay awake wondering where to find her. I was just about to go in search of her when she came back and slipped into bed.

'Where have you been darling? Are you alright?'

'I'm okay. But I could hear Daniel crying. Through the ceiling. I've been with him.'

When we went home next day I opened Rayne's desk drawer where he had told me to look on his death. I found notes from him to Li-Da, Daniel and me. Mine was on a postcard and echoed the many notes he'd written to me over the years. I still have them in an antique porcelain box he'd given me.

I suppose when I am dead my children will find them and know just how much we loved each other: on this, my last card, Rayne had written, 'How can I say goodbye to her who has been the glory of my life? What expression of thanks can encompass all you have given me, done for me, been to me? No words, my darling girl. But my soul now reposes in you – to help you call on the courage I know you have to confront your new future with a level eye, and find happiness in it.'

How does anyone get through grief without children? Both of mine stayed with me for the five weeks between Rayne's death and his memorial service. And we all coped in different ways, typical of each of us.

I cooked giant family meals and attacked the house in a maniacal frenzy of curtain-buying, furniture-shifting, etc. And I organised Rayne's memorial.

Because I didn't want a tombstone that the children would feel guilty about not tending, I decided to floodlight the small island on the lake in our garden, something we'd talked of but never got round to. Two years before he died, Rayne had finished his eighth book, *All Under Heaven*, a history of China. He'd written it over the past thirty years, looking out of his top-floor study onto the little lake he'd designed, complete with red Chinese bridge and island with willow tree and pagoda. He barely ventured into the garden, but he knew every mood of sky, lake and landscape from that window.

Daniel disappeared into his father's study and read everything by and about his father and wrote a long and beautiful memorial essay. Li-Da looked after us all and made little Chinese candle-boats to set off in our lake when we scattered Rayne's ashes.

Rayne was an atheist; Li-Da and I are too, though she is superstitious. And Daniel is staunchly

Christian. Yet we had no trouble organising a ceremony. The vicar opened his remarks with, 'Those of you who knew Rayne at all well must be astonished to find yourself in church,' and then went on to explain that Rayne had no problem with the living doing what they needed to do.

Rayne had tried to decree, 'No ceremony, no gathering, nothing.' But he capitulated when I argued that since he'd be dead and didn't believe, it was a bit rich of him to interfere.

At the end of the service Daniel, Li-Da and I crept out of church and drove to the house, where we donned our wellies and trundled Li-Da's lamps down to the lake in wheelbarrows. Under a darkening sky we set most of them off, and they floated, serenely beautiful, across the water. We had a slug of whisky from a hipflask and took turns to scatter Rayne's ashes, mixed with dried delphinium flowers. They pattered on the still water with a pleasant, light-hearted sound, like crushed sea-shells, and the petals floated in a drift after the flotilla of lamps. Then we launched the rest of the candle-boats, shaped as lotus blossoms. Some of them keeled over and went up in flames, like Viking ships.

Then we switched on the new floodlights and went back to the house to join the party.

When I went to bed at about midnight Li-Da's candle-boats were burning steadily, looking like a little village on the edge of the gently floodlit lake.

I couldn't sleep. It was three a.m. when I saw the last light wink out.

CHAPTER 19

WIDOWHOOD

No time to think, no energy to feel

The bereaved quickly learn that they are an embarrassment. Your friends do not know what to do or say. They find it hard to follow their first instincts – to ring, to write, to visit – for fear of troubling you or embarrassing themselves.

'You must just ring up and invite yourself over if you're unhappy or lonely,' is no help at all. If you're either of those, ringing up is the last thing you'll do. And 'How are you?' (looking meaningfully into my eyes) upset me too. It was all I could do not to snap, 'How do you *think* I am?' or burst into tears. But the phrase that angered me most, and I heard it from many people, was a kindly, 'You'll find someone else, you know.'

In those first months I was a little mad. Once Rayne's memorial service was over, I went back to work like a demon. And a few weeks later, in February 2003, I set off for New York to see my Danny de Vito lookalike about the claim for the taxi accident of two years before. I have the typical

British attitude that accidents are just bad luck and suing people for causing them is not a nice thing to do. But here I was in New York, on my own, utterly miserable, and going to a crummy lawyer's office and an even crummier doctor's surgery in the Bronx, staying in a seedy hotel and eating takeaway pizza.

Back in England again, the loss of Rayne went on hurting, but gradually I stopped weeping on strangers' shoulders, reading Rayne's farewell letter compulsively every night, and saying yes to everything for fear of being alone. I must, though, have done more crying in that first six months than in my previous sixty-two years.

One day I was lying, eyes closed, on a bench on the terrace, feeling tearful, when Daniel came and sat down by me. 'Mum,' he said, 'you know, if you could accept Jesus, you wouldn't feel so bad.'

'But I don't. You can't make yourself believe in something.'

'If you would just open up to the idea, have faith, put your trust in God, you could, Mum. Let Him come in. Let go of your resistance.'

This made me cross. I sat up and barked at him, 'Resistance? Why would I resist such a great solution? Why believe that Rayne was dead-and-gone for ever if I could believe he was up there somewhere and I could be with him again?'

Daniel didn't react to my outburst. Just put an arm round me and said it would get better. For all of us. One day.

In the summer after Rayne's death, I took our now rather doddery dog, Mollie, to stay with friends in Cornwall. Early one morning, unable to sleep, I took her for a walk and came across a little church. It was old and beautiful and I spent half an hour studying the great slate slabs standing like giant tombstones all around the perimeter of the churchyard. They were engraved with the names, professions and dates of dead villagers, lists and lists of them in chiselled roman letters: PAULINE PENARTHUR, SEAMSTRESS 1600–1642; GLYN LANRITH, BOATMAN 1706–1756; GWEN TRELAWNEY, WIFE 1820–1885; JOHN HEGGARTY, COMPUTER PROGRAMMER 1969–2001.

I found this extraordinarily moving. The continuum of human endeavour, all our little lives, so unimportant in the great scheme of things but important enough for this small community to have recorded their dead for four hundred years.

Mollie followed me into the church and I sat in a pew, close to tears. I'm sick to death of being sad I thought. Why cannot Daniel be right? If only I could believe in God. And then I found myself talking aloud to Him, gently at first but, as I started to cry, more aggressively.

'If you exist, God, then come on, do your thing. I'm here. I'm willing, I'm doing my best to believe in you. Give me a sign or whatever you do.'

The little church was empty apart from Mollie at my feet, watching me anxiously and wagging her tail without conviction. I was by now in full flood, wailing and berating the Lord.

Suddenly I heard a sound behind me and turned. A woman was standing there with a bucket of blooms in her arms, obviously come to do the church flowers. Oh God, I thought, she'll think I'm a madwoman. Or she'll try to comfort me. I could not bear the thought of that.

But then, by mutual unspoken consent, we behaved like true Englishwomen. I walked smartly out of the church, nodding a, 'Good morning,' in as brisk a voice as I could manage. She nodded back and said, 'Lovely day!' And off I went, feeling foolish.

After a year of widowhood, I no longer howled with grief. Occasionally, in those first years, I'd pick up the car at the station and, alone and thinking of the empty house awaiting me, I would start to cry, sometimes wailing out loud. And then, one night when the rain was drumming on the car roof, I suddenly realised there was an element of pleasure in the howling: I was hamming it up, crying deliberately louder as the car ploughed through the puddles and the rain pelted down. What with the tears and the rain I could barely see. I stopped to find some tissues to deal with the misted-up windscreen and with me. I found myself smiling, mocking myself for being such a drama queen.

Gradually, I discovered some small benefits to widowhood, like being free to read at midnight or having sole dominion over the TV remote. Other widows sometimes told me of the pleasure of a silent night's sleep without a snorer at their side. But I missed Rayne's snoring and didn't sleep well without it. One night I let Mollie sleep in my room. She snored, and I slept like a log.

One of the things grief robs one of, along with happiness and sleep, is a sense of humour. One afternoon, a while after Rayne died, I was serving the lunch, very late, for Jamie's family and mine, but couldn't get them to come to the table. 'C'mon, everyone, this has got to stop,' I said. 'Rayne would never have stood for lunch at three in the afternoon.' And Daniel said, 'Listen, Mum, there isn't *much* of an upside, so don't knock it.' And we all laughed. Really *laughed*. I think that was when I first saw a chink in the gloom.

Because of my mother's senility, I had become increasingly anxious about my own mind. Maybe, like her, I would be away with the fairies by the time I was seventy-five? My friends would say that they too forgot what they were saying mid-stream, or couldn't remember people they'd met a month ago, it was normal. But I knew I was relying increasingly on my PA's efficiency rather than my memory. Francisca had been with me since 2000 and was, as she is today, utterly indispensable. Her reassuring theory was that I had too much to do, so of course I needed backup. Anyone would.

But I wasn't convinced, and for the past ten years or so I'd been going to the Memory Clinic in Bristol, run by Professor Gordon Wilcock. My plan was to be in the front of the queue if they discovered a drug that stopped memory loss. But I also went there for the reassurance, which I got year after year, that my brain was perfectly normal. Each year I would do the same apparently childish tests – joining up the dots, spotting the difference in pictures, remembering lists of objects, doing simple arithmetic – and some years I would do better than the year before.

I remember arguing that of course I did better. 'They're the same tests every year. I'm learning the answers.'

'But if your memory was bad, you wouldn't remember the questions, would you?'

But a few months after Rayne's death, something happened that had me scuttling back to Professor Wilcock in a panic.

I had been invited by Kate Rothschild and Marcus Agius (then chairman of Lazard's and shortly to be chairman of Barclays), to their new house in Belgravia for dinner. I was excited and delighted by the invitation. I hardly knew Kate, but much admired and liked Marcus and I guess I was flattered to be included in such illustrious company.

I was due to go to a charity event at St James's Palace that evening, so I asked Francisca to make sure my taxi came early, before the inevitable speeches, so I could slip away and be at the Agius's in time for dinner.

The charity event went on, it seemed, forever. I didn't know many people, and once I had shown my face to the organisers, I'd have liked to leave. I wandered around, occasionally looking at my watch, but it wasn't time to go yet. I was surprised when the speeches began because they were scheduled for seven-thirty and it was only just after seven. I stood by the big antique clock in the Queen Anne Room. In the middle of an interminable speech it suddenly chimed the hour and I was struck by the simultaneous loudness and musicality of the sound. I remember reading the clockmaker's name, but I neither noticed the time it told nor how many times it chimed.

After the speeches I wandered around a bit more, and saw that people were leaving. I thought perhaps St James's Palace was having two functions that evening and were hustling people out early.

Finally, tired of standing and very bored with the party, I left and began walking up to Piccadilly. Half way up St James Street, I called Radio Taxis and asked them to send my taxi early.

'That booking's been scrubbed. The driver waited half an hour at St James's Palace. We tried to call you but your phone was switched off.'

'But the taxi is not due until seven-thirty.'

'It was there at seven-thirty. The time now is eight forty-five.'

I had lost an hour and a quarter. Because my watch had stopped. It was unbelievable. In spite of my feet hurting and my back aching it hadn't occurred to me that I must have been at that party for hours. I had stood next to a clock striking eight o'clock but not registered the time. I had imagined the speeches were early rather than my watch late. I felt a sinking horror. I was losing my mind.

I rang Kate, jumped into another taxi, and got to the dinner as they were eating their first course. They had waited an hour for me, and the butler was pretty frosty, though my hosts were charming. 'My watch stopped' is not a proper excuse, and I felt terrible.

I poured out the story to Professor Wilcock.

'Mmm,' he said, 'your husband has recently died, hasn't he?'

I started to cry. He pushed a box of tissues towards me and explained that grief could affect concentration; I should not be alarmed.

I think the professor must have been right, because the next time I was tested my memory had miraculously improved.

If you work hard enough there is barely time to think and no energy left to feel. When Rayne died I was still on the board of Whitbread and Woolworths and a few smaller companies, and I was writing again. I also had several pro-bono jobs, chief of which was chairing the educational company 3Es, a spin-off of Kingshurst City

Technology College. Kingshurst was a state secondary school in Birmingham where I had been a governor since 1998.

I'd joined Kingshurst because, under the headship of Valerie Bragg, it had become a first-class school. Everyone did drama, music, sport and art. Nothing was too ambitious. They could learn Russian, Latin, Spanish. Almost all the sixth form went on to university. It was the first state school to follow the International Baccalaureate.

Shortly after I'd joined the board of governors we set up a commercial company to make extra money for the school. Ronald Somerville, the tireless Kingshurst chairman, twisted my arm to become the chair of this little company 3Es (after Blair's phrase 'Education, education, education' – though when the Tories got back into government I would say it was for Energy, Enterprise and Excellence.)

Valerie Bragg, still the Kingshurst principal, was now our CEO too and she never lacked ambition. The first local authority to put the management of one of their failing schools out to tender was Surrey. They had a school, Park Barn, in Guildford, that twenty years of fresh starts (new head teachers, changes of name, repeated licks of paint, extra funds) had failed to turn from a disaster into a decent school.

The first time I visited the school, half a dozen adolescent boys were on the roof of the hall with teachers pretending not to notice. Gangs ruled the lavatories and some of the girls had nothing to drink all day because they did not dare go in there.

There was minimal discipline. Children ran down the corridors, banged doors and yelled, with teachers shouting above the din to be heard. Sometimes a third of children were truanting or off shopping with mum. The staff were demotivated, just holding on for their pensions. Most of the good teachers were long gone.

Once again the indefatigable Ronald twisted my arm, this time to chair the school governing body while keeping my job as chair of 3Es. The first thing we did was hire a really good head. David Crossley had a brilliant record and liked a challenge. Making a good school is hard work but it is not rocket science. Any group of ordinary folk can tell you what is needed: a good head, good teaching, an exciting curriculum, extramural activities, discipline, encouragement, high expectations, commitment, suitable and properly maintained buildings.

After a year our five A★ to C results had risen to twenty-eight per cent; after five years to over sixty per cent, and after ten to eighty-five per cent. Kings College is now one of the best schools in the area and has tripled its intake.

Subsequently, 3Es won contracts to run or set up more state schools. Eventually we sold the company and Valerie went with it. By then 3Es was responsible for thirteen schools and had radically changed the lives of many thousands of children. I cannot say that my contribution to this story was vital, but I did have a tiny hand in it, and am proud of it.

Another voluntary job I spent much time on was the Hoxton Apprentice. I'd long wanted to open a restaurant that would train the most disadvantaged people – ex-offenders, drug addicts, homeless people, and young people who had somehow missed out on all the good things – to be waiters and cooks. I got my chance when I met Gordon D'Silva, the boss of a charity, Training for Life, who took up the idea. He got the local council to provide the building, a former Victorian school in Hoxton Square, while I raised support from the catering industry, particularly Compass. We set about proving that so-called no-hopers who openly said they were rubbish at everything, who appeared to have no ambition and no energy could, given encouragement, discipline and appreciation, end up with security, money, self-respect and a life worth living.

As I write, there are two more Apprentice restaurants. Two of our head chefs and the two managers are former trainees, and other ex-apprentices have gone on to work in some of the best restaurants in London.

And then there was Ashridge. Back in 1997, I'd had a letter from Sir Michael Angus, my chairman at Whitbread. Would I join his board at Ashridge, one of the oldest management colleges in the country? I'd never heard of it but I was impressed by the roll-call of captains of industry and academics on the board and, flattered, I agreed. Five years later I succeeded Michael as chair.

I was by no means a brilliant chair, but I worked hard and I can claim some credit for leading the hunt for the current, quite brilliant, Dean, Kai Peters.

The job every chairman hates is that of persuading someone to resign, or unceremoniously kicking them out. At the beginning of my career my husband, who chaired Leith's, used to do the dirty work for me. But in my non-executive 'afterlife' I had to do it myself and it was horrible. My advice to anyone offered a chairmanship is to find out how satisfied everyone is with the incumbent chief executive. I never learned this lesson and had successively to replace the chief executive or senior director at the Restaurateurs Association, the RSA, Ashridge, the environmental charity, Forum for the Future, and one of the head teachers at 3Es.

None was without stress, but in my experience square pegs in round holes generally know they don't fit and are relieved at the suggestion of divorce. Leslie Hannah, who was the dean of Ashridge when I took over as chair, was a respected historian and economist who had raised our academic reputation just by accepting the job. He was intrigued by the challenge of running a school that was also a business, but he found he didn't like it at all. He was sticking it out because he is an honourable man and he thought he shouldn't let us down. Jonathon Porritt, the charismatic social entrepreneur and green issues campaigner, knew better than anyone that his beloved Forum for the Future now needed a full-time chief executive. He was just too busy, too imaginative, too impatient to run the day-to-day any more.

But such a task can be perfectly horrible: I've held the poisoned chalice of chairing nomination and governance committees or being the 'senior non-executive director' for large companies, and had to persuade an unsuitable or out-of-date chairman that it's time to go, or, worse, tell him baldly that there is no other option. And when he's an old friend and an honourable guy it's worse. Sacking people is a lot easier if they've had their hands in the till or are all-round bad people. When they are good people but the company needs a different kind of leadership, it's tough.

Two years after Rayne's death, the greyness of grief had noticeably abated. I noticed with pleasure rather than resentment the carpet of yellow aconites under the trees, their myriad faces turned to the sun – and I knew that the worst was over. That feeling of there being no point in anything, that life is somehow flavour-free or lived through thick glass, came less often.

And then in early 2005, four years after my Manhattan accident, the court case finally came up and I agreed to go to New York again. Partly I felt guilty – ridiculously – that my Danny de Vito had been beavering away all this time, so far for no reward, badgering Bellevue hospital for records, the police for statements, and me to be more co-operative.

To my relief the case was settled 'on the court-room steps' and I was awarded $40,000 which was promptly paid fifty-fifty by the insurance companies for the taxi driver and the truck.

After Danny de Vito's cut there was still plenty left, and I spent some of it on a holiday for me and Ange at a glitzy Caribbean beach club with my friend Linda. I was not looking forward to it, beach holidays being so associated with Rayne. But in fact we had a merry and enjoyable week.

But seven p.m. remained a very bad time. Seven in the evening is when, for thirty years, Rayne and I telephoned each other if we were apart, or I'd see his face light up as I walked in from the train or, at weekends, we'd have a drink and talk trivia.

I remember once ringing my brother Jamie from a taxi, swallowing tears and saying, 'I need some brotherly love.'

'It must be seven o'clock,' he said at once.

Even today drinks time can be difficult. I don't often feel lonely but when I do, you can bet it's seven o'clock.

Jamie was, and is, a wonderful brother and I feel closer to him as I get older. David was my brother of choice when we were children and Jamie was an annoying little brat. But once we were grown up, the six-year difference between Jamie and me meant nothing. Once a successful, if not starry, actor, he gave up the theatre to be a house-husband to his highly successful writer and TV presenter wife and wrote a hilarious book about it, *Ironing John*.

The quality in Jamie I most admire, and am faintly jealous of, is that he really knows how to live. Once the children were at school, he took a job with a local company making wooden jigsaws, and worked hard and successfully at it. But it never filled his life as sometimes work fills mine. He wouldn't dream of forgoing tennis or fishing, or a round of golf or seeing a play, to spend the evening or weekend working. He is intelligent, interesting, talented and funny, but completely lacks self-importance or the desire to be in the limelight. The Leith house has always been full of friends, both theirs and their children's. Now it is full of in-laws and grandchildren. And there is always time for tennis, or sitting about drinking, eating and talking.

Jamie thinks my over-crammed schedule crazy. He'll say, '*Mafuta*,' (which, I regret to say, is Zulu for Fat One) 'why don't you just say NO? Pack it in? Stop accepting jobs? You can afford to stop, so stop.' I never have a proper answer.

Happily the Leiths live near me, and after Rayne died I stayed with them a lot. Sometimes I go off on salmon-fishing trips with Jamie. Penny is vegetarian so a fishing holiday would hardly delight her and it's great to be able to borrow my brother.

We've fished together for twenty years. At first we went a lot to Scotland, where I would catch salmon and he, in spite of a much longer and more elegant cast, would not. After years of this he went to Iceland and landed his first salmon. He texted me: *Broke the 15 year duck with an 8 pounder*

By way of a sixtieth birthday present I took him to Cuba in 2006, to fish for bone-fish, which you catch on a fly in the shallows. It's bliss fishing in your swimsuit in the sun, with mangrove islands, limitless blue sea and – in my case – the only humans in sight your brother and your Cuban guide, who comes complete with the secrets of bone-fishing, a little skiff, a picnic and a bottle of wine.

And then, on my seventieth, Jamie took me to Iceland to fish the Ranga river. The rest of the party were old friends, all men, delighted to have Jamie and me doing the cooking. To my horror the ingredients provided were orange-crumbed slabs of nameless fish, spuds, tinned sweetcorn and tomato ketchup.

Iceland, understandably, is not strong on fresh cilantro or organic courgette flowers. The freshest food in the supermarket was a packet of frozen peas. Nonetheless, I got going with a wonky frying pan, an oven with a door that didn't shut and one cheap, blunt knife. And everyone loved it, especially after the Hellmann's and the ketchup appeared. But then, I thought, they are men, more interested in the fishing and the beer than food.

Things improved once some of them started to catch fish. We had sashimi cut from the Icelandic char Jamie caught. The wasabi came from a tube. I returned to a pretence at gastronomy with a great fish soup that lasted for days and included various packets of soup-mix, onions, garlic from a tub, leftover frozen veg, tinned tomatoes and a lot of salmon. It was a long time since I had made aioli by hand, but I enjoyed it and the soup was surprisingly good. Or maybe we were just very hungry after twelve hours on the river.

That was the holiday I decided that twelve hours fishing is too much. I used to be the kind of fisherwoman who had to be on the river before breakfast and would be sneaking many a 'last cast' after time was called. Now, after three hours or so, I start to think of coffee and Danish. Or a large G and T, or a hot bath, accompanied by a glass of whisky.

But you do not get baths in fishing lodges in Iceland. If you have been standing in the rain all day you don't want to go home and stand in the shower. You want, if not bubbles and candles and champagne, at least a lie-down in hot water, glass in hand.

I sat in the corner of the shower, hot water raining down, planning a campaign to get fishing lodges in Iceland to convert to baths: they have free hot water from the hot springs, almost free electricity from the wind, and space galore. Why can't they make the bathrooms one square metre bigger?

I expounded all this to Jamie. 'Give it a rest, *Mafuta*. You're on holiday. No sorting out other people's problems.'

Next morning I was on a beat that is a geriatric fisherwoman's dream: no climbing to get to the river; car parked a few metres away so no need to lug the gear; easy wading; gravel bottom; rippling channel within easy reach of my cast; wind from behind, which makes me look twice the fisherwoman I am; weather overcast but warm (well, warm for Iceland).

Within twenty minutes I had a fish on the line. Chris, who was kindly being my ghillie, said he thought it was a nine-pounder. I privately thought, just you wait, it's a whopper. The fish pulled like a steam train.

And he kept it going for thirty-five minutes. I don't think I have ever had such an exciting half hour anywhere, never mind fishing. That fish wanted to tow me out to sea. When I ran out of line I plunged after him down the river. Whenever I pulled him in close and thought at last he was tiring, he would suddenly set off again and I would let him run with relief, at last able to drop my right hand down to my side for a few seconds, shaking out my arm to relieve the aching.

As the runs and reel-ins continued, Chris's estimate of the size of the beast increased. Eventually the fish jumped out of the water and for a flash I saw him. He was deep and thick rather than long and thin – more a rugger than a soccer

441

player, but he was huge: twenty pounds, I was sure.

Then, oh God, oh God, that awful suspicion that you've lost him; then, no, he's still there, just swimming towards you, then no, fuck, fuck, *fuck*. Nothing.

I reeled in a ball of woolly weed the size of a small melon. Chris suspects it was the weed that worked its way down the line to make a gag in the fish's mouth, and dislodge the hook. Who knows? I think I did everything by the book, but my overwhelming thought, following swiftly on the disappointment, was, hey, he deserved to win. I was cursing like a trooper, but I felt I should doff my cap to him. And that fish lives on in my memory, getting bigger every day. He's a twenty-five pounder now; next time I tell the story he'll be thirty pounds at least. One day he'll break all Icelandic records!

Rayne had assumed that on his death I would live in London. But I'd not much liked the London flat, and thought I'd sell it and live full time in the country.

But Daniel and Li-Da, to my surprise and joy, suggested we find a London house with three flats in it. I could downsize to a two-bedroom flat and they could have a flat each. I'd sell the unloved Colonnades apartment and they would sell the little house they shared in North Kensington – which we had bought them when Rayne found their clutter, mess, music and friends too high a price to pay for their company.

In 2004 we settled on a house in Notting Hill Gate. It was more expensive than a derelict house should be, but Notting Hill was becoming fashionable. It belonged to an orthodox rabbi, who wouldn't shake my hand, but who had no qualms about running what amounted to a doss house.

There were seventeen flatlets crammed into the five floors, most just a room with a cooker in the corner and a shower and loo behind a partition. The rabbi said with pride, 'You see I have not damaged the beautiful old cornices. They are intact.' So they were, because the walls did not reach the ceiling.

But we had to replace them anyway because the joists of the floors, as well as the windows, the ceiling and the roof, were all beyond repair. We ended by gutting the house, leaving only the four walls standing, and even they had to be rebuilt on the top floor. It would have been cheaper to demolish the house and start again, but the planners refused permission for this.

Then we discovered that the house was built on a tributary of the Westbourne and water ran only inches below the basement floor, and the house had no foundations. In spite of this it hadn't budged a millimetre in the last hundred and fifty years. But building regs required that we pour thirty tons of concrete under it.

The builder went bankrupt and the project ran

over-budget and took six months longer than planned, something I'm sure would never have happened with Rayne in charge. It was the first time I had done any property development without him. He had built my mews cottages, my restaurant, the staff flats, the various catering company premises and our house in the country. And he was an expert – he'd built huge blocks of flats and offices. Sometimes I wondered what on earth I'd taken on.

But I must have learned something from Rayne, because in the end we had a lovely house with a smart little garden which, I confess, looked a lot better once I gave up the battle with the foxes who dug up our lawn in search of bugs every time it rained. I substituted Astroturf and would receive plaudits on its perfectly mowed perfection.

Daniel lived below me and Li-Da above. I tried not to hang out of my window to see who my children, now thirty, were coming home with, and they only sometimes used my flat as a free shop. Daniel, particularly, would nick my washing up liquid, or more often, wine. All our flats were high-ceilinged, light and airy, and I loved having us all under the same roof again. I was there for a few days in the week and they would sometimes come down to Chastleton at weekends.

It was a widowhood few women are lucky enough to have.

CHAPTER 20

WHO IS THAT GIRL?

Gaining a daughter

One morning in late September, 2004, I could barely get out of bed. Two years before I'd had an operation to relieve sciatica, but now it seemed it had suddenly returned, big time. I crept to my GP and the nurse gave me a jab in the bum. But it didn't work and soon I was off to Cheltenham General in an ambulance. After a week they'd not found the reason for the pain and they sent me to Moreton Cottage Hospital, about three miles from my house. I got steadily worse, while the physio made my life hell.

I was soon on four-hourly doses of liquid morphine and daily doses of the physio. When I was high as a kite on medication the walking about was fine. But if the physio arrived half an hour before the next dose was due, it was torture. Once I simply refused to go another step, clinging onto a pillar in the courtyard, crying and begging for a wheelchair. She was well trained in dealing with recalcitrant patients and she was adamant. 'You must walk. Walk.'

I could not. I was making such a scene, weeping and pleading, that a passing doctor counter manded her and got me a wheelchair.

The difference between morphine and no morphine is amazing. During my drugged-up hours I dealt with my work (I was at the time trying to negotiate the sale of 3Es, the education company, to an Indian multimillionaire with a portfolio of schools in India and Dubai) and I wrote articles and dealt with board papers and correspondence. But when it was nearing the time for my next dose, I would be reduced to first groaning, then sobbing and finally howling, oblivious of the six or seven other women in the ward. But the nurses were not allowed to give me the medication until exactly four hours after the last dose. I learnt, when the nurse finally came with the little phial of morphine for me to suck, what it must be like to be a drug addict. I would have done anything to relieve that pain.

In fact I did do something. I got an unsuspecting friend to bring in a wash bag from home which I knew contained a big box of Tramadol pills, morphine-like painkillers. I secretly 'self-medicated' between each hospital dose. It worked a treat, though I've since discovered my topping-up scenario can cause respiratory depression, coma and death. Ah well.

After three weeks my doctor, Jill Barling, who had been unhappy with the Cheltenham General's diagnosis all along, sent me for an MRI scan.

Nothing. More tests and then another bumpy ride for a second MRI. Late that evening she hurried into the ward, looking anxious. 'You have an infection in your spine, between two vertebrae. If it spreads into your spinal cord – well, we cannot have that. You have to lie dead still, no movement at all. I'm sending you to the Nuffield Orthopaedic.'

The paramedics lifted me onto a board inch by inch and drove me at a snail's pace. I wanted to laugh: one minute I was forced to do agonising exercises and the next I had to lie like a statue.

The assumption was that I had MRSA, and I was put into an isolation ward at the Nuffield. Visitors had to go through sheep-dip to get to me, and the medics, unsure what my bug was, bombarded me with half a dozen different antibiotics, collectively designed to take out any nasties before infection paralysed me for good.

After a week, a lot better, I was back at Moreton Hospital, where I became happily institutionalised: I never wanted to leave my corner bed in a ward of OAPs, where the highlight of the day was the bed-time Ovaltine.

I'd even grown fond of the woman across the ward who talked companionably to herself, angrily to her possessions ('You just bloody stay there! Don't you *dare* fall off') and softly to God. After lights out she'd whisper the Lord's Prayer and 'God bless Maud and Don, all the nurses and all the patients, and thank You Lord that the one in the corner doesn't cry so much . . .'

The middle-aged nurses were lovely. Contrary to union advice, they'd help the paramedics lift a patient; they'd bring me a cuppa and a Marie biscuit in the middle of the night when I couldn't sleep. They'd gently lead the mad bloke, who made nightly attempts to escape through the solid wall next to my bed, back to his ward. They turned a blind eye to the wheelchair-bound septuagenarian I'd meet in the garden – she sneaking out for a fag, I to use my mobile phone.

They gave me a Zimmer frame. I loved it. I used the lower rungs as a footstool, hauled myself out of bed with it, leant on it to survey the view. Walking was a doddle.

I feared going home to a house with no Rayne. But eventually, after six weeks and three hospitals, I had to, and indeed it was grim. Not too bad when Francisca and my housekeeper Lyn were around in the day and I could potter about on my trusty Zimmer; for the first nights Lyn sweetly stayed with me. I was now taking multi-antibiotics by mouth – a fistful twice a day. Unsurprisingly they made me throw up, whereupon I had to repeat the dose. Eventually Dr Barling intervened and the hospital put a port above my heart into which we could inject the antibiotics, which would then bypass my gut. A district nurse came and taught me how to do it. That finally did the trick though it took another six weeks. We never did discover what the bug had been, but thankfully it was no more.

* * *

After a spell in a Tory think tank Daniel decided on a political career. He was a political journalist, policy wonk and, briefly, the Conservative candidate fighting Tony Blair for the Sedgefield seat in the 2005 election. He then became David Cameron's speech writer. When he wrote Cameron's third party conference speech in 2007, Daniel had been concerned that David was not going to use it because he'd not asked for the usual changes, additions and deletions. There goes my speech-writing career, he thought. But in fact David was spending the last hours before the big moment learning the speech word for word. That evening, Daniel took him a copy of the *Evening Standard* with the banner headline 'Speech of a Lifetime'. Cameron signed it with the message, 'Thank you, Danny.'

When Daniel fell in love with the beautiful Emma Ashcroft in 2001, the year before Rayne died, I, like many a doting mother before me, feared for my son's happiness. I could see that Emma was sparklingly attractive, almost magical, but she was no better than Daniel at putting the top back on a bottle, shutting the fridge door, emptying the rubbish, finding the car keys or paying a parking fine. I thought she would make a hopeless Tory wife. Also she was religious. Her evangelical bent, and her drawing Daniel into believing, scared me.

I thought my atheist husband would be worried too, but Rayne saw no problem. He liked Emma, and he could see at once that believing in God had made our beloved son happier. Daniel had been a bit lost after university. He'd split up with his long-time girlfriend, he couldn't decide whether he wanted to go into academe, journalism or politics, and he faced the world with a public-school stiff upper lip and an ironic eyebrow. Since the advent of Emma he was noticeably more relaxed.

So when Daniel told me they were going to marry, and he loved Emma more than life itself, of course I promised I would love her too. What I didn't know then, and would never have believed, was how easy that was to do. I now think I had been behaving like a possessive mother, and Emma was scared of me. The minute they were engaged she seemed to relax, and the happy, excited, outgoing Emma I now know, emerged. And I confess that she has greatly improved my son, making him more affectionate, and able to show his emotions in a way he could not before. I'd never felt unwelcome with him, but I was not as relaxed in his company as I was in Li-Da's. I was, I think, fearful of his disapproval. But Emma has somehow released his innate generosity and loving nature.

Before they married, Emma and Daniel had started Only Connect, a charity helping convicts and former prisoners go straight, and they worked together on it all the time Daniel was in politics. But in May 2008 Daniel decided to leave David

Cameron and work full time for Only Connect. The charity produces plays, sometimes in prisons with the inmates as cast members, or outside prison with ex-offenders. Participants join the Only Connect club as 'members' and are welcome any time. They get help with their problems, whether with drugs, drink, violence, housing, benefits, training, jobs, personal relationships or, usually, a mixture. Many members train with OC as youth workers and take plays and workshops into schools and youth clubs, trying to prevent the next generation from joining criminal gangs and getting into trouble.

Daniel and Emma's wedding, in October 2007, was wonderfully happy, by far the most enjoyable and genuine wedding I've ever been to. Emma came down the aisle surrounded by a bouncing, chattering, unrehearsed troupe of children, their clothes varying from Guards' uniforms and Little Lord Fauntleroy velvet to fairy dresses. Some of them, children of friends from their church or charity, were Afro-Caribbean and wore their hair in corn-rows and beads atop their white dresses and shiny black shoes. Emma's instructions had simply been, if you want to be a bridesmaid or a page-boy, turn up and wear your best.

The words of the hymns were up on big screens and we sang gospel, arms waving above our heads as in a pop concert. I'd have thought this would be embarrassing, but it was fun, happy and uplifting. Half way through the service, Daniel picked up a little boy who was hanging on his trousers and held him until it came to taking the wedding vows – at which point he turned round and handed him to me.

After the service we were all sent out for a glass of bubbly on the terrace while the photographs were taken. When we went back inside, the chairs were arranged round coffee tables, the altar end of the church was now a stage and the church choir had morphed into a pop group. We had sausages and mash, family style, and Daniel made a speech, bits of which I'll never forget. He said when he'd first seen Emma sparkling away in a red dress at the far end of a room, he'd said to a friend, 'Who is that girl?' and got the reply, 'Forget it Daniel, she's a Christian.'

He promised Emma that she would be his life's project. He teased the non-believers ('don't worry, we are coming to get you') and his family, complaining of the advice he'd had from us all. Li-Da, he said, had objected to the idea of a party in a church, saying, 'But you can't snog someone in a church.' He looked at the congregation-turned-audience, and said, 'Feel free. Snog anyone you like. Except my sister.'

If I am now delighted with my daughter-in-law and full of wonder at the calm, patient and humourful mother she has turned out to be, I am utterly devoted to her children – Malachi, born in January 2010, and Scarlett, twenty-one months younger. I am just as boring as every other grandmother, forever forcing strangers to admire pictures of them on my mobile phone.

In 2007 I applied for the chairmanship of the School Food Trust. The SFT was a small government quango set up after Jamie Oliver scared the hell out of the government when his school dinners programme hit the nation's TV screens and exposed just what some schools were giving children to eat.

I confess to having felt rather miffed that after forty years of badgering government about the very same issues that Jamie raised – children's diet, sales of junk food in schools, increasing obesity, lack of food education, and ever less cooking in schools – this mockney whipper-snapper telly star should get more action with one programme than I had in a lifetime.

But I quickly got over it and decided Jamie was a saint and saviour. Actually, he is one of the most genuine and likeable people I know, and the truth is that without his waking up the voters to the horrors of school food, the Labour government, like the Tories before them, would have been content to allow schools to go on making money from selling junk to children.

Such is the power of TV that, on the morning after the programme, Tony Blair allegedly rang Ruth Kelly, the Secretary of State for Education and said, 'I never want to see a programme like that again. Do something about it,' and Ruth Kelly replied, 'We'll have to change the law.' And they did. They set up a review body which first set food standards (basically specifying what *must not* be sold in schools) and then nutritional standards (specifying what nutrients school dinners *must* provide). The review body morphed into the School Food Trust to oversee the changes, encourage good practice and get more children eating school dinners.

About a year after I was appointed, we got a new Secretary of State, Ed Balls. I was horrified. I'd had a mini-tiff with him on TV a month or so before when Andrew Neil's lunchtime political programme had asked me in to talk about the School Food Trust. I arrived to find he already had a guest, the Treasury Minister, Ed Balls. It is a live show and I sat quietly while they showed a clip we'd filmed earlier, in a school in Hackney, where all the children were tucking into baked fish and couscous, followed by fruit salad and plain yogurt.

Andrew started his interview by pulling a Big Mac and a Coke out from under his desk and saying something like, 'So Prue, you are the Nanny State Food Czar. Are you telling me this should not be my lunch?'

Of course I had to grin. I said, 'No, Andrew, you are a grown up. Go ahead. Eat junk, ruin your health. My concern is, as you've just seen on the clip, with children.'

He turned to Ed Balls. 'Ed, what do you think?'

Ed, playing to the audience as all politicians do, said, 'Well, my daughter would never eat that stuff. Fish and couscous? She'd never touch it! She likes everything separate.'

I couldn't believe it. Here was a government minister not supporting what his government was proposing. It was monstrous.

I responded with something like, 'Are you saying that when ninety per cent of very poor parents, brought up on takeaways and chips in Hackney, have managed to get their kids eating "that stuff" as you call it, a privileged pair of top politicians' (he is married to Yvette Cooper, then Chief Secretary to the Treasury and now Shadow Foreign Secretary) 'cannot get their daughter to eat a healthy meal? What's up with you guys?'

We had an enjoyable spat, and I thought no more about it, until I was invited in to meet the new Secretary of State for Education and thus my new boss, Ed Balls! As we rode up in the lift to the top floor I told the chief executive of the School Food Trust, Judy Hargadon, the story, saying, 'I won't mention it. Maybe he won't recognise me.'

But to his credit Ed stretched out a hand and, grinning, said, 'Now, don't you start. My wife gave me hell when I got home, and next morning I got another bollocking from the Prime Minister.'

When I accepted the job as chair of the Trust, I said it was the most important job I'd ever done, but I never dreamed it could be so hard. I had this naive idea that we could do the job and wind ourselves down in three years: that all schools needed to do was teach children about food and how to cook; to stop children bringing food or drinks into school; ban vending machines; close the school gates at lunchtime; make the kitchens efficient and the dining rooms pleasant; provide delicious sit-down, knife and fork, healthy meals, and get the parents to refrain from rewarding their little darlings for eating up their greens with a Kit-Kat.

Q.E.D. Bingo, we could all go home.

My mistake was to assume that all teachers would accept that healthy children would concentrate better, feel happier, achieve more. But head teachers had other priorities and they genuinely did not think it was the business of schools to worry about the pupils' diets.

And, of course, I'd thought school cooks could cook. But some cooks had been hired in the turkey twizzler era, when all they had to do was open a bag. It astonished me that schools who would never dream of not updating the skills of their teachers, seemed to think that training catering staff was a luxury they could not afford.

I'd imagined that parents would be delighted that their children could get a healthy lunch, but persuading them that two pounds is good value was another thing. Especially if the local chippy offered all-the-chips-you-can-eat for a pound.

I was wrong on all counts, so those three years were tough going. Nevertheless, the Trust did, and continues to do, a great job in improving the approach in schools (learning about food, learning to cook, raising the quality of school dinners) and getting the numbers of children eating at school steadily rising.

Government funding was radically cut in 2011, but Judy turned the organisation into a new social enterprise and widened its remit to become the Children's School Trust as well as the School Food Trust. But the future scares me: schoolchildren only eat seventeen per cent of their food at school and the manufacturers have money to burn – probably more in a marketing budget for a single day for a single product than the Trust has available in a year. I'm now convinced we have to go on teaching children about food forever: how to cook, and how to eat.

CHAPTER 21

A SUDDEN INTEREST IN POETRY

Late love

In October 2006 I went to the Canaries to spend a weekend holding the hand of a friend and business colleague, Sir Ernest Hall. I had known him and his wife Sarah for years, mainly through the Royal Society of Arts for whom Ernest had provided free space and help when we were setting up an office, (and the RSA charity, Focus on Food) in the North of England. According to mutual friends, he was depressed by the double whammy of retirement from the business he had founded, and separation from Sarah.

Ernest had had an extraordinary life. Born in Bolton, he grew up in a working-class terraced house with no heating, with washing hanging in the yard and a privy out the back. Today, we would call it a slum, but it was then a close community of mill workers.

Somehow Ernest managed to get scholarships to the grammar school, then, determined to become a pianist, to the Royal Manchester College of Music.

458

But when he came back from National Service, and faced the realities of a career in music, with the near certainty of having to teach in order to live, he followed his parents into the mill, continuing to play the piano when he could. By then he had learned to type and so could get a job in the office rather than on the weaving floor.

With his innate enthusiasm he fell instantly in love with business and started the rapid climb to managing director. He moved the business from weaving to property development and, ultimately, to a profitable sale of the company, with the prospect of retiring in his late forties with a small fortune.

He didn't retire. With a partner, and his young son Jeremy, he bought the eighteen derelict Crossley carpet mills in Dean Clough in the centre of Halifax. With all the money they could muster, they built their 'Practical Utopia': a place where work and art could flourish side by side. Today most of the mills contain top-quality offices, and there is a hotel, a theatre, numerous galleries, artists' studios, workspaces for small enterprises and charities, two restaurants, a shop, and a courtyard with the old mill stream running through it. There are artworks everywhere.

Ernest met me at the airport. Since Rayne's death nearly four years before, and in the years that he was too ill for much more than affection, I'd been – if not exactly desire-free – certainly not looking for physical love. No sexual gratification could compensate for the embarrassment that undressing would have brought. My pale and unlovely body had barely seen the light of day, never mind a lover's gaze, for ten years, which was, I thought, as it should be.

But in less than three hours I realised that I had designs on my old friend.

We were driving along the coast road, the un-air-conditioned car warm, conversation sporadic and relaxed. But my attention was less on Ernest's commentary than on his body. How could I, an old-age pensioner, be transfixed by the sight of a bare brown arm? My eyes kept returning to the strong wrist, the pianist's fingers on the wheel, the hairs on his forearm glinting orange in the sun. I longed to put my hand on it, lace my fingers over his. That I managed to resist is testament to, or maybe an indictment of, my upbringing, in which nice young ladies did not make the first move. But I didn't have long to wait for him to make it, although it seemed like a lifetime.

After a second day of sightseeing, and dinner in a tapas bar, we were having a glass of wine in the Moroccan courtyard of Ernest's house. The tiled pool glinted through the potted palms and the air was soft and balmy. Ernest put his hand on my wrist and slid it up my sleeve and that was it.

I never even thought to be embarrassed. It was magic.

The trip had begun so inauspiciously. The airline had lost my luggage so all I had were the too-hot

460

clothes I'd arrived in and the white tee-shirt and cotton shorts Iberia's 'emergency pack' contained. I slept, swam, sunbathed and lunched in them. At night I wore an abandoned Kaftan belonging to Sarah. I had no make-up.

I was certainly not looking my best, but I wasn't looking for love. Then Nature, or Cupid, or maybe hormone replacement therapy – or more likely the combination of sun, wine and music – took a hand and it was all exactly as I remembered the last time I'd fallen in love: with my husband forty-plus years before. The talking all night, discovering just how lovely the night sky is, a sudden interest in reading and writing poetry, feeling sick, shaking, every sense alert, the whole world singing. There is not a cliché in the book that lovers don't feel at sixty just as much as at sixteen.

But the course of true love did not run smooth. The first time Ernest gave me cause for alarm was in the spring of 2007, six months after we'd fallen in love. We were on our way to Klagenfurt, one of those health clinics in the Alps where you're lucky to get a spelt biscuit to eat with your hay-flower tea. I thought we were off to a hotel spa where there would be romantic walks in the mountains, boating on the lake, lots of expensive pampering and plenty of lying about reading. I was wrong, but my problems were more to do with Ernest than with the spa.

The trip was a disaster from the start. I was

following Ernest through the departure gates at Heathrow, when he abruptly stopped in the middle of the stream of hurrying travellers to scramble in his shoulder bag for his passport. I caught the look of irritation on one man's face and reached for Ernest's arm to pull him out of the traffic flow. He rounded on me, flinging my hand off angrily.

'Will you stop nannying me!'

I was astonished. He'd never been rough with me. 'But darling, you're right in everyone's way.'

'They can walk round. I will stand where I like. Just stop interfering.'

A few minutes later he set off in the wrong direction.

'Darling, Gate 32 is this way . . .'

This time his irritation was more like rage. 'I know what I am doing. Do you think I can't find my way onto a plane?'

Now angry myself, I trooped after him, down an escalator in the wrong direction, anticipating the satisfaction of him saying, 'Sorry, darling, you were right.' No such luck. He eventually realised he'd gone wrong and simply plunged back the way we'd come with a cheerful, 'It's this way.'

Barely speaking, I left the matter of travel leadership to him. On arrival in Frankfurt where we were to change planes, I buried my head in my book, with the result that we missed our connection. He then tore a strip off the unfortunate woman behind the desk while I pretended he was nothing to do with me.

On our eventual arrival, we were taken on a tour of the spa hotel. Ernest was impatient with this, only interested in where he would find a piano on which to practise (he had a concert in a few weeks). The poor girl kept telling him that we would soon come to the dance studio which housed the piano. When we did, she said, smiling, 'This is the piano, and you can use it any time you like except eleven on Tuesday morning when there is a dance class.'

'Oh, that doesn't matter,' Ernest replied, 'I don't mind playing while a dance class goes on.'

And then I made, for the third time that day, the mistake of trying to help. I explained that she meant the dance class would need the piano.

'*Will* you stop interfering! Just stay out of it.'

I ducked out through the nearest door into the garden and burst into tears. I was totally unused to being shouted at. I grew up in a family where politeness ruled. I never heard my parents even raise their voices to each other. In my immediate family rows had been rare, and in my business life, differences were settled in civilised tones. Even a rude shopkeeper or angry driver makes me shake.

Once we got to our room my inability to let it go led to our first full-scale quarrel. Our shouting match ended with the first of several walk-outs. Blind with rage and tears, all I wanted was to get away, so I slammed out, dragging my suitcase behind me.

Half way down the hideous swirly carpet, I

realised I'd be going nowhere. It was nine o'clock at night, and I was up an Austrian mountain with no possibility of trains, planes, buses or taxis to whisk me away.

By the time I got to reception, I had calmed down a little. I asked for a separate room, saying I was exhausted and my partner snored. (Untrue. Ernest sleeps so sweetly sometimes you'd think he wasn't there.) My plan was to leave first thing in the morning.

Of course I spent the night tossing and churning, longing for a word from Ernest. I wrote him a letter protesting the unfairness of his behaviour, telling him I loved him, and suggesting we meet in the little front garden and talk about it. At dawn I put the letter under his door and parked myself in the garden.

He did not come. After two hours, unable to bear it any longer, I knocked on his door. He was sitting in a chair, writing. He handed me his answer to my letter, which he'd obviously written long before. He explained that he was working on his autobiography, indeed had been since four in the morning, and didn't have time to discuss anything. I must read his letter. I took it and left.

It amounted to a declaration that he was too busy with the important work of writing his book and composing music to bother with my histrionics. And that he was as he was, take it or leave it. And that he categorically refused to go on a plane with me again – we would have to travel separately. It was up to me. Not a word of apology, not an ounce of sympathy.

This 'Your choice' was to be a recurring theme, often with some mad condition attached. Every time we quarrelled in the next three and a half years – and we only ever quarrelled when he was in one of his crazy, over-excitable moods – he'd lay down his rules (we should not meet until after lunch; we should have separate bedrooms), and tell me to take it or leave it. Our quarrel ended when I rang him in tears, asking him to put his arms round me. Had I been able to leave the night before, I think I would have left Ernest for good. Back in London I'd have had the comfort of my children, and my friends who'd have helped me not to creep back. But up that wretched mountain, I was lonely and miserable, weak in the extreme.

By the next morning I realised how much I'd miss him. His arrival in my life had shown me just how bleak life without a mate had been. And, up till then, he'd been such a perfect mate: loving, interesting, fun, and always always there, even if only at the end of a phone in Lanzarote. I did not think: am I prepared to put up with this behaviour again? I just wanted the misery to be over and us to be back to where we were before.

After Klagenfurt, I soon found the price of Ernest's love was having to accept that his sudden eruptions of fury and occasional bouts of unkindness were part of him, as were the sudden plunges into despair and self-loathing. I did not know who the real Ernest was. The hateful egomaniac? The silent melancholic? Or the man I'd fallen so in love with?

It was Ernest's youngest daughter Viv, who explained bi-polar disorder to me. I was complaining to her about her father's changing moods when she said, 'Dad's bi-polar. Manic depressive. I am too. It's hereditary.'

She told me it was all about faulty receptors in the brain that sometimes took up too much serotonin, resulting in bouts of mania, or too little, which plunged the victim into despair.

'Look at the bi-polar website,' she said, 'You'll recognise the symptoms.'

I did. Ernest ticked ten out of ten of the boxes for mania and nine out of ten for depression.

I showed them to him. He brushed them aside. 'Oh, Viv! What does she know about it?'

'A lot. She's bi-polar herself.'

'That doesn't mean I am. Stop worrying. I'm fine.'

I had not yet experienced Ernest in deep depression, but he *had* told me that since his separation from Sarah and his retirement from Dean Clough he'd had frequent months-long periods contemplating suicide. He would, alone in Lanzarote, sit on the edge of his bed unable to move and convinced he was worthless. He longed to be asleep, not to be here, not to be Ernest Hall, then would force himself with the utmost effort to get up, wash, shave. Even toasting a slice of bread was beyond him. He would lose a stone in two months. Even his beloved Chopin couldn't ignite a spark of pleasure.

Slowly, with me pressing him, he began to accept the diagnosis. He was willing to admit to depression, and eventually agreed to taking Depakote to lessen the symptoms, but in all those three and a half years he never admitted to the mania. I think this is common with bi-polar. The patient will do nothing that might endanger the euphoria of the extreme highs, while being willing to do anything if it will alleviate the misery of the black hole.

We spent a good deal of time at Ernest's house in Lanzarote, most of it blissfully happy. It's only a four-hour hop from Gatwick, and even in January it's sunny enough to get a tan. Every time I entered the first white-walled courtyard, I'd feel that releasing of the mind and flood of wellbeing that beautiful places, bathed in sun, can bring. I loved it there.

In June of 2007, when we had been together eight months, Ernest, to my astonishment, gave me a Mercedes sports car. I'd never been much interested in cars, and was perfectly happy with my Subaru, a much-dented old workhorse. But the SL 500 made me begin to understand why people become obsessed with cars. I was relieved to hear that the car was not new: I'm too puritan to approve *that* much extravagance. It had been

Sarah's, but she wanted to change it so I got the Merc – which is a pretty good hand-me-down. That summer we drove round France in it.

It was the most romantic of holidays. The first night's B and B was a converted mill house, with rough lawns down to the river and willows overhanging the water. There was no one about and no answer on the phone. We found an unlocked side door, and inside was the nicest room, overlooking the mill pond, with a pile of clean sheets and towels on the big double bed. And the breakfast table laid for two. We concluded we were expected, if not greeted.

There was a piano downstairs and Ernest, who was setting to music some of the poems I'd been writing since we met, sat down to compose while I made up the bed.

Still no answer from our hosts, so, leaving a note on the piano, we set off in search of dinner. Nothing was open in the village except a grocery shop and a pizza takeaway. We had a picnic in the garden and sat talking as dusk fell and the stars came out.

It was concentrated happiness. But the next morning there was a small scudding cloud which maybe I should have seen as a warning. I asked Ernest where my poems were.

He went up like a roman candle. 'How would I know? I've not touched them!'

'But you had them last night. I gave them to you, remember?'

'I never touched them! Don't tell me I had them when I've had nothing to do with them!'

Deep breath. Keep calm. 'Darling, I'm not accusing you. I'm just asking you if you've seen them.'

'No, I have not. I know nothing about them.'

I found them downstairs, still on the piano. No apology. No admission of over-reacting.

But French sunshine, the pleasure of driving that car, Ernest being especially sweet (he would always be doubly loving after a blow-up) soon papered over the cracks. Mostly we were very happy. A friend in an email described us as, 'exuberant, skipping round the world like adolescent lovers'. Embarrassing, but accurate.

Typically Ernest was up for three months, then depressed for two. When he was down I felt protective and maternal. The only thing that comforted him at all, apart from the oblivion of sleep, was to lie in my arms like a child.

It was horrible for him and not much fun for me. But I never resented the 'downs' and maybe I contributed to them by not being brisker about the things bi-polar sufferers are advised to do: go on bracing walks, join a gym, keep a mood-diary, set tasks and targets and tick them off. I did try, but his misery would be too much for me and our good resolutions would soon be broken.

When he was depressed Ernest barely spoke. The contrast with his normal self was staggering: a man who lives for music, plays the piano for hours a day, loves the experimental and avant-garde in music as much as he loves Chopin or Mozart, would be unable to listen to a CD. Normally gregarious, he would not even telephone his children. Naturally generous, insisting on picking up every bill in a restaurant, he would suddenly think the price of a taxi would ruin him. All he wanted to do was sleep or, better still, die. His mind would dwell on ways he might kill himself. He would long for a plane carrying him to fall out of the sky.

In the spring of 2009, Ernest was so low I managed to persuade him, for the first time, that we should try to tackle the illness properly and check into the Causeway Retreat.

The brochure described an exclusive private island retreat in the Thames Estuary with designer décor, five-star accommodation, an outdoor heated pool, activities, and internet access. A place to relax and be pampered. Medically, the Causeway offered bespoke care from a team of consultant psychiatrist, nurses, psychotherapists, psychologists and complementary therapists.

Perfect. And I could come too. We booked a little cottage. It was expensive, but BUPA would pay about two thirds of Ernest's costs and I told myself that it would be a great holiday and worth the luxury hotel charges for me.

And so we set off, all cheerful, but our first sight of the place took my mind immediately to *Great*

Expectations when Pip is terrified by Magwitch on the Essex Marshes. We were looking at swirling mist, tidal flats and reeds bent by the wind. The island was a near-featureless, grey smudge far across the Blackwater Estuary. The Roman causeway was partly visible and partly not, disappearing in the mist and hard to discern in the mudflats each side. Broken marker posts and seaweed-slimed rocks marked the track intermittently, but by no means reliably.

But we made it to the island. No notices of welcome. Indeed no signs indicating Causeway Retreat anywhere. Just a redundant warning notice, reading **DANGER OF DEATH. OVERHEAD CABLE** attached to a pole which had long since lost its cable. By now Ernest was advocating instant about-turn, but I insisted we carry on. We advanced along a potholed track telling each other that this surely could not be our destination.

We drove around what looked like an out-of-season holiday camp fallen on hard times. Broken picket fences, once white, surrounded cottages whose windows were largely invisible behind the overgrown shrubs. Lawns were thick with thistles and nettles. It was two in the afternoon, but there was no-one anywhere. No reassuring sign pointing the way to 'Reception', no friendly face saying hello. Maybe we were trespassing? And no mobile signal to ring anyone up.

We drove deeper into the compound and found an abandoned yoga studio, several derelict buildings, an empty swimming pool surrounded by a sagging wire fence, a once magnificent walled garden, now neglected, a farmyard of rusting machinery. Then, finally, a lost avenue of trees led to a mock-Tudor manor house overlooking an abandoned pier, a lawn hosting a rabbit warren and a reedy pond.

Just as I was beginning to think Ernest was right and we should leave, we spotted a figure in the distance, clipboard in hand, corduroy trousers, long hair. Friendly. Yes, this is the Causeway Retreat. He's the head nurse. Yes, we are expected. Welcome.

Other nice people appeared and showed us our cottage. It was charming. Or would have been if you could see out of the windows, obscured by overgrown shrubs. If the front and back steps were not huge, uneven and lacking a handrail and the television worked; if the radiator had had a plug on it, or indeed a socket to put a plug into; if the carpet runner had been stuck down so you didn't risk your neck, and if you didn't pinch your bare feet on loose floor boards, or crack your head on the plate rack when getting up from the table . . . if . . . if . . . if . . . Yes, it would have been charming . . .

The place was short of staff and crammed with clients. The head therapist was away moving house; the consultant psychiatrist was in Australia; his locum came for one day a week and had to pack in sixteen patients in the few hours she had before

472

the tide would trap her on the island; the ther.
allotted to Ernest disappeared after three d
the yoga teacher, like the studio, did not exist. 1
CEO wisely never appeared at all.

But what staff there were, were lovely: game
covering up for management, trying to fix things
dealing sympathetically with the constant stream
of complaints, making promises they couldn't
possibly keep. The chef did his best, and the maintenance man provided me with tools to lop back
the jungle round our windows and clear some of
the broken trash out of the garden (they had not
had a gardener for five years); he also succeeded
on the second attempt to coax hot water out of
our boiler. The fitness trainer warned us of the
scary treadmill which jumped unbidden to full
speed, tried without success to get the sound
system to work, cheerily stuffed back the pipe
lagging that kept the draught out of the gaps
between walls and roof, and provided tennis
rackets for the lumpy court.

The clients were a collection of damaged souls
– some mad, some addicts, some suicidal. I loved
them. They were friendly and interesting: the
chap with a rage problem who had lost it in
the first-class cabin on a flight from South Africa
and shouted at his fellow passengers, all members
of the ANC government, calling them a bunch
of corrupt tyrants thieving from their coun-
trymen; the Chinese investment banker in
designer everything, addicted to sleeping pills

d amphetamines; the chap who couldn't stop
impulsively giving away money and was
surprised his wife left him when he gave a pros-
titute fifty grand – not for sex but out of kindness;
the 'pop star' who turned out to be a porn star.
They expelled her 'bodyguard' for hiding her
drug stash in a rabbit hole. Fair enough.

In our first week, due to the wrong tide timetable
being posted on the notice board, two cars had to
be abandoned when they put a wheel into sinking
sand. They were submerged by the tide before they
could be towed – drowned and useless – to land.
One of them belonged to a young nurse who had
no insurance.

But curiously, the place did make a difference
to Ernest, or rather his fellow inmates did. Between
them they convinced him of the need for both
medication and therapy.

It helped too that things were so good between
Ernest and me. Once we got some heat in the
cottage, and the TV to work, we holed up and had
an isolated and loving time. Three weeks of incar-
ceration together somehow cemented our love, and
one day Ernest proposed marriage.

At that moment I wanted nothing more. But my
practical nature would out.

'You have a wife already, remember?'

In spite of the impossibility of the offer, it did
make me consider what I really wanted. It
amounted to this: I wanted to yoke my life to
Ernest's, to one day be, for all intents and purposes,

married to him. But I needed to be sure I would not walk out on him. Which meant he had to go back on medication, and stay on it. If after, say, a year, he was stable and sane, then, I said, I'd want nothing more than to throw in my lot with his.

Ernest did sign up with a psychiatrist and a therapist, and went back on his drugs. And over the summer and autumn of 2009, the periods of depression duly diminished. We became more convinced of our love, and, it seemed, the possibility of happy-ever-after. We went to the music festival in Verbier and heard a young mezzo soprano, Catherine Hopper, in a master class. If Ernest ever finished the music for my love poems we would, we said, have her sing our 'Necklace of Songs' in a concert for family and friends.

From July to Christmas Ernest worked sporadically on the songs.

By the end of December his mood was happy and high. Too high – and Christmas 2009 was not a success. I had decided to sell the Mercedes to buy something more suitable for the potholes and mud of the country and Ernest got it into his head that I was trying to cheat him over it. He declared that he'd never *given* me the car, and it wasn't mine to sell. This in spite of having basked in my delight and astonishment at such a gift, and having transferred it into my name. If it was to be sold, he wanted the proceeds.

It was the first time I'd been the victim of his paranoia. He had sometimes complained to me of someone else's alleged duplicity or cunning, accusations he only made when not in his right mind. But telling myself he was ill did not lessen the hurt and bafflement. How could he think I'd cheat him?

I found the whole episode degrading and tacky, and was far more hurt by the charges of dishonesty and lack of generosity than by having to stump up for the car's replacement.

After a week he was suddenly back to his sunny, generous self. But that little bout of paranoia convinced me, if not Ernest, of the need for treatment for his mania as well as his depression.

One of our great pleasures at this time was the conversion of the falling-down old tithe barn at Chastleton into a house that we thought we might share in our old age. The barn is at the highest point of the farm lying to the north and west of the Glebe, which Rayne and I had bought a few years after buying the house. It was a derelict wooden building, clad in asbestos and rusting corrugated iron, but the beams and rafters inside were intact and quite breathtaking.

I had always intended to fix the barn, either as an investment or as my home in old age when I would need ground-floor living. But the insertion of Ernest into the picture doubled the pleasure of the enterprise. He has wonderful taste, with an eye not just for the beautiful and satisfying, but for the unusual and quirky. Also, it was dawning on me that I wouldn't be able to afford to live in the Glebe for ever. It cost far too much to run, and sooner or later I would have to sell it, or at least let it.

We spent a happy day at Architectural Heritage, a splendid reclamation yard, where Ernest ordered a beautiful centuries-old French stone trough, carved from a single block over five feet long and three feet wide. He also bought two pairs of ancient Indian dog-kennel gates, highly decorative, which I wanted as oriel windows for the two bedrooms tucked up under the roof at each end of the open barn.

Ernest's enormous black piano would grace the middle of the huge room, one end of which would contain the kitchen, the other my study, with plenty of room for sitting, music and dining spaces in between.

The barn had become our future home, and Ernest was more and more in the warp and weft of my life.

One day Ernest rang from Lanzarote to say he'd bought the property next door. 'It's amazing. The huge sitting room is an old camel barn. We've uncovered the old stone under the plaster and it's beautiful.'

'But what is it for?'

A concert theatre, he said. And two houses, one each side, for letting, and for artists to stay in when they came to give concerts.

477

'What? What concerts? Are you mad?'

The answer, of course, was probably yes, but not one he'd admit to.

He set about his new grand scheme for Camel House Concerts. He wanted to give the island a reputation for the best international music, and drove the new enterprise with his usual gusto. First he recruited an old friend, the renowned pianist Paul Crossley, and his partner John Brakband. Providentially, Paul and John had a holiday house on Lanzarote and they love the island as Ernest does. Paul became the artistic director and John the administrator of the venture.

For Ernest it meant a new lease of creative life. He sorely missed Dean Clough, and did not enjoy being alone in London while I ran around working. And though he liked coming with me to Orient Express Hotels (of which I had been a director since 2006) around the world, he certainly didn't want to settle for being my appendage. He needed to be the boss of something, and to be in the middle of an arts-based enterprise, surrounded by creative, interesting people. Camel House Concerts would mean a life spent mostly on his beloved Lanzarote doing the things he likes best: starting up ventures; converting old buildings; mixing art and business, listening to and playing great classical music.

Something similar held true for Paul Crossley. As the artistic director, albeit unpaid, of CHC, Paul would remain in the thick of the musical world, and could give the odd recital on an excellent piano without having to travel.

And John, a senior purser with a major airline, looked forward to something other than long-haul flights and hotel beds as a way of life.

I soon became as enthusiastic about the venture as they were. I was excited about meeting international artists, learning about music – and going back to my catering roots. I planned a champagne bar and Glyndebourne-style picnics in the gardens, and in the autumn of 2009 I gave notice as chair of the School Food Trust, and resigned from several committees and boards. Camel House Concerts, with half the year lived in Lanzarote, would replace them as a major part of my new life with Ernest.

By November Paul had signed up the pianists, singers and guitarist who would give the eighteen recitals to be held in 2010. Everyone he asked accepted with enthusiasm, and because the artists and agents knew and trusted Paul, they willingly agreed to come for a week's holiday, a rented car and a fraction of their usual fee.

John was tireless: gathering subscribers, getting the wine sponsored, booking flights, dealing with the artists' constantly changing requests, hiring their cars, designing the website in three languages. The four of us, John, Paul, Ernest and I became the informal committee of directors. Meanwhile, Ernest and Heidi redesigned the buildings, creating the concert hall, villas (which, when not used by the artists and their families, would become holiday lets), car park and gardens. And Sarah set about decorating the two houses.

By early autumn of 2009 all was on schedule and going wonderfully well. We left the September meeting in Lanzarote with a To Do list for each of us.

By February Ernest had at last completed our song cycle. He came to England in time for a few rehearsals with Catherine Hopper, who had agreed to sing them at our birthday party concert at the Glebe. Though I had spent my career organising other people's parties – everything from Elton John's Cave Man Party to formal balls for thousands, I had never given a big party myself. I'd had small family birthday dinners, we'd thrown a party for Leith's staff when I won Veuve Clicquot Business Woman of the Year, and there'd been a party on the publication of my first novel. And once, in my twenties, I'd had a barbecue with a friend in a forest – I remember dancing barefoot on the beech leaves, so happy I felt invincible. But I'd never had a full-on bash: no twenty-first birthday party, no engagement, wedding, or silver wedding party. So this was my big moment.

For me, it wasn't just a *birthday* party for the two of us. Privately I thought of it as a kind of celebration of Ernest and I getting together, almost a declaration. I'd told Ernest that I couldn't make promises until I knew that I wouldn't leave him, but now I felt we were all but there.

I don't believe anything will ever again be as perfect for me as that evening was. I'd braved the January sales to buy an Armani jacket at a ridiculously reduced price. It had just the right amount of cleavage, covered up my unlovely arms, and made me feel a million dollars.

Typically, I'd organised everything like a military campaign. I wanted the evening to be magical but not to look 'catered' or 'designed'. We sat on motley chairs from all over the house and ate at tables of every shape and size.

We had the concert before supper and Ernest was at his absolute best. He made a loving and funny speech about my inspiring his composition and then keeping his nose to the grindstone until he'd finished. We'd stolen the name 'A Necklace of Songs' from a love poem by Tagore which we'd printed at the beginning of the programme, Ernest's music was tender and passionate and Catherine's rich, pure voice suited it perfectly. I had a hard time staying dry-eyed.

Most of our guests, also in their sixties or seventies, had known both of us since long before we got together. They were, I think, touched and cheered rather than embarrassed, by this geriatric romance.

I'd had fun decorating the supper room, the food was simple and delicious, and my son Daniel and Ernest's daughter Viv made witty and affectionate speeches. It felt like a wedding.

Then we all trooped out to the terrace for fireworks on the lawn, with the floodlit lake, Chinese bridge and pagoda in the background. It was a clear, ice-cold night. I was anxious about the guests freezing out there, so I'd made shawls from a bolt of tightly woven orange wool. I'll never forget the sight of three Tory grandees – the Lords Howe, Chadlington and Heseltine – wrapped in blankets and gossiping in a group like old women.

To warm the guests' insides, the waiters offered Taylors 1985 port, which had been lying in the cellar for twenty-five years waiting for just such an occasion, or a ginger hot toddy of my own invention.

I called out across the lawn to the pyrotechnics man, 'You will be quick won't you? No longer than five minutes? It's freezing out here.'

'Madam,' he shouted back, 'you only paid for four minutes. So, believe me, four minutes is all you'll get.' It was a very good four minutes.

Hosts often say they don't enjoy their own parties. We enjoyed this one more than any either of us had ever been to.

Ten days later, everything came crashing down.

Ernest had gone back to Lanzarote as soon as the party was over to get on with the Camel House Concert arrangements. I had been a little anxious that, being so busy with composing and rehearsing for our concert, he'd neglected things he was supposed to do for the CHC such as get

482

a public performance licence, fix up bank accounts, make the payment for the transport of the piano and so on – things that only he, as the owner and paymaster, could do.

When I spoke to him, I suspected he was not doing any of these things. His mood was high, and he was enjoying running round the antique shops with Sarah, buying things for the two Camel House apartments, and adding to his building and garden plans.

I wasn't overly worried yet. John, Paul and I were to meet him in Lanzarote at the end of the month to iron out any last minute glitches. And after that we still had a good month before the first concert.

When we got there, Ernest was manic, irascible and unreasonable and brushed off all mention of the unfinished car park, the absence of signage, electricity, a platform for the piano, chairs and much besides.

As soon as Ernest and I were alone, I said, 'Darling, we're having our meeting in an hour. Paul and John are up to speed with everything they had to do. I need to sort the catering this week, but otherwise I am pretty well there. How about you? How is your To Do list coming along?'

He blew up at once, 'What list? I'm not answerable to Paul and John. It's none of their business.'

'Of course it is. They're on the committee. We're all answerable to each other.'

'No. I'm in charge. I will not be questioned by subordinates.'

I could feel anger ballooning. 'Subordinates! They're committee members. What is the point of having a committee if you're going to insist on ruling the roost?'

'Precisely. I never have agreed to a committee, and I won't have one.'

'Fine, no point in my being here then, is there?' I stomped off to his study, intent on getting a taxi straight back to the airport. I was shaking with a mixture of anger with him and distress at my own fury. No one else can trigger rage in me as Ernest can.

But I could not find a list of taxis anywhere, and my Spanish is non-existent.

John came to find me. I was by now in tears. He cajoled me back to some sense of the absurd and persuaded me to stay.

After lunch Ernest declared himself too busy for the meeting, and it was postponed until the next morning. I saw nothing of Ernest all afternoon and had a horrible night, awake and longing for some reconciliation but too angry and proud to do anything conciliatory. Ernest, oblivious, slept.

He woke at six. 'Shall I bring you a cup of tea?'

Grateful for the olive branch, I lay back and thought we might be alright after all. Ernest disappeared and promptly forgot about both tea and me.

At seven he found me making tea in the kitchen and, perhaps reminded of his offer, said, 'What are you doing here? I was going to make the tea.'

'That was an hour ago.'

Not a good start to the morning, and of course it triggered protest and denial.

Wisely, I changed the subject. Unwisely, I returned to yesterday's subject.

'Look darling, I have been emailing you and badgering you for weeks about where we are with the things you need to do. I know we have a month yet, but Paul and John are leaving in a couple of days and everything was supposed to be done by now and they are worried stiff—'

'What business is it of theirs to be worried? They are trying to get control of the concerts away from me. Camel House Concerts are *my* idea. It's my property, my building, my money. They have to understand who's the boss . . .'

That did it for me. Suddenly I was far more furious than he was.

'Those two, as you call them, have given hours and hours of their time to this project. And so have I. It may be your money, but you could not have done it without them. John has spent weeks on the website, and Paul has not taken one penny for getting all the artists, persuading them to perform for peanuts.'

'That is not true. He's a great musician, but he is hopeless at business. I could have got the artists for much less.'

'So why didn't you? Everything Paul and John have done was agreed by all of us. Everything. You cannot change it all now.'

'I can. Flexibility is my middle name. Their

idea of subscribers is ridiculous. I don't want subscribers. I can get much more money selling tickets at the door.'

He was impossible, changing tack, refusing to discuss anything, attack his only defence.

Beside myself with anger, I picked up a chopping board, intending to bang it down as hard as I could on the stainless steel surface. I think I could even have brained Ernest with it, but as I picked it up I saw it was badly cracked and for some reason I didn't want the thing to break. I put it down, gave Ernest a shove in the chest that made him stagger and, for the second time in twenty-four hours, slammed out, grabbed my bag and left.

Writing this now, I find the incident terrifying. Ernest later said that he had never seen such hatred as on my face at the moment I picked up the bread board. And it's true that, for those few seconds, I did truly hate him.

But is it not ludicrous too? Even hilarious? A seventy-year-old woman and an eighty-year-old man quarrelling like twenty-year-olds and then she marching off, pathetically pulling a little wheelie bag behind her. It's worse than a bad movie.

Once round the corner, I rang Paul and John, who rescued me and took me to the airport. They fed me white wine and coffee for hours as we waited for a flight, then hugged me goodbye.

I had a window seat. It was a beautiful morning, the sea and sky of competing blues, the countryside green with the early Canarian spring, palm fronds and euphorbias vibrant, little white houses shining in the sun. I was not just walking out on Ernest, but abandoning Lanzarote and my newly embraced future life. We had had a three-and-a-half year love affair. And it was over. I glued my face to the plane window, pressing a fistful of sodden tissues to my eyes.

Paul and John quit the next day too, unable to cope with Ernest's behaviour. Only Leopold, Ernest's beloved son, stayed on the island to look after his father and deal with the train-crash of Camel House Concerts.

Ernest remained manic for two months, believing he was invincible, quarrelling with everyone. He emailed me that he was back where he'd been for most of his life – creative, in charge, on top of the world. The CHC would give him a new successful venture, as long as he was in control. He would never be ill again, he knew it. He announced he had stopped taking his drugs.

He dismantled the website, deleted the German and Spanish translations, scuppered our plans for a music-lovers' club with events and picnics, decided not to bother with catering, and returned the subscriptions. Once the musicians knew Paul had gone, half of them quit or demanded their standard fees, which were too high for the fledgling Camel House to pay. But between Sarah (who returned to the island to help with the first concerts) and Leopold, something of the original plan was rescued and the first concerts were successfully staged.

By mid-March I was in Charleston, North Carolina, at an Orient Express board meeting and conference. I was lonely, raw and miserable. Out of the blue Ernest emailed me. *Would you like to come with me to see the Greig Museum in Norway?* There followed a detailed itinerary and suggestions for proceeding to Sarah's chateau for a family party, and then on to our previously planned Rhone trip. He had it all worked out and his tone was friendly and businesslike, but with no reference to what had happened. I replied:

> *I would love to be with you if you've returned to the land of the sane. But I can't just pretend nothing has happened and forgive and forget any more. Why get close to you again after two weeks of real unhappiness schooling myself to do without you, when, unless you accept that you are manic as well as depressive and start doing something about it, you will inevitably hurt me again? I would rather lose you altogether than have to go through this every three or four months.*

He then wrote me long emails explaining that he had no intention of going back to where we were, indeed he no longer wanted to live with a nag who tried to take control of his life, but rather he was proposing to see me just for odd holidays. *If you don't need me physically we have no future together.*

I found all this hugely hurtful, but as the months of our separation passed I toughened up. By the end of April I'd cleared my house and London flat of Ernest's possessions.

By then he had at last come down from Cloud Nine, but then he rapidly sank into the blackest of holes. His family insisted he come to England for treatment. Finally accepting that he was manic as well as depressive, Ernest agreed.

In May I emailed him:

Subject: Black Hole

Darling, please just drop me a line to say how you are? I still wake up and go to sleep worrying about you. Leopold told me a few weeks ago that you were very low. I hope you are out of it now, and have not gone back to two-month-long bouts.

Not knowing about you is horrible. I miss your other children, who never ring me now, as well as you. Is Sarah spending more time with you? Hope so, because she is very good for you.

'Our' barn is almost ready. One day, darling, I hope you will see it and we will be friends. But not yet, I am still too tender about the whole thing and I expect you are too. But one day, perhaps. X

He replied:

> *Darling, I am a very sick man and you are better without me . . . I will be lucky to survive much longer. The concerts were wonderful at the outset but are now coming to a grinding halt as you predicted. I feel horribly unwell. I deserve it all but my family don't which is terrifying. I do hope your grandson is lighting your life and you are enjoying him as I am sure you are. Please think well of me and think of our best times together. The party night was one of them. xx*

And then one sunny late May day, nearly three months after I'd left him, I was walking through Hyde Park feeling strong and forgiving. I knew Ernest was staying with his son Tommy. I scrolled down the names in my phone . . .

'Hullo, Ernest, it's me.'

Silence, then, 'Oh darling, how wonderful to hear your voice. I can't believe it.'

'It's such a lovely day. I thought, how about lunch in the park?'

So I sat in the new Serpentine Restaurant (a million times better than my version of fifteen years before) and waited for him, once again my heart thudding.

We had lunch in the sun, drank a bottle of Chenin Blanc and went home to bed. So much for my strength of character.

Since then, Ernest has been somewhat back in my life. But it is not the same. There is between us, unacknowledged by him and never mentioned by me, a channel of slippery rocks and treacherous undercurrents. I cannot love him as before, and I no longer want to be responsible for him. And to his great credit, Ernest has never wanted me to have to look after him and has repeatedly told me to 'kick him into touch'. When, back in Lanzarote, it became clear that he was in constant danger of falling (he has had a couple of bad falls in the last years, one of them requiring an operation to hoover up a haematoma on his brain), he promptly hired Linda, a professional carer. Long may she last.

He, Sarah and Leopold have successfully rescued the Camel House Concerts, albeit on a less ambitious scale. They are generally a sell out and continue to great acclaim. I have nothing to do with them any more.

I still love the man. And he still often delights and fascinates me. I love my (now very occasional) short breaks in Lanzarote, spending my mornings at his desk writing, with a view of the sea, while Ernest plays the piano or potters round his garden or – more often these days – watches television. And then lunch in the sunny Moroccan courtyard followed by a siesta. Then a little walk along the beach or clifftops before supper in a tapas bar up in the black-gravelled vineyards, or in a restaurant on the beach. And home for a DVD or a cosy early night. Very occasionally he comes to the

Cotswolds for a few days and, even more occasionally, we spend a week or ten days away together.

For all the horrors of his bi-polar condition, I would not have missed loving Ernest. Nor forget what fun he can be and how good to be with. Take shopping, for example: instead of, 'But you've already *got* a black jacket,' he'd say, 'Why not get the trousers and the skirt too?'

And if we were out on a jaunt, he *wanted* to trawl the galleries or stalls or antique shops in the hopes of a serious souvenir.

How many men *want* to take you out to dinner? If I came in exhausted from work, or we'd both arrived tired after a plane trip, he'd invariably say, 'How about the pub?' If there was nothing in the fridge, his response would always be, 'Carluccio's for breakfast?'

How many men suggest a play or a concert? How many men understand women's desire for a massage or pedicure or hairdo? Ernest not only understands, but likes them too. He loves clothes, far more than I do, and wears almost nothing but Issey Miyaki or Comme des Garçons, a hangover from the Seventies when he was in the weaving trade and wove exquisite cloth for top designers Above all, when well, Ernest knows how to live: interested in everything and everyone, enthusiastic and dynamic, happy to fall in with any suggestion, any change of plan. And never, ever, grumpy.

For sure, I will always be grateful for having had such a wonderful second chance at love.

CHAPTER 22

NOVEL ENDINGS

Or new beginnings?

I have been unfairly blessed: Happy childhood, great career, extraordinarily lucky in love. And even today, at seventy-two, I lead a privileged, indeed spoilt, life. I'm on the board of Orient Express, one of the world's most luxurious hotel companies with hotels in glamorous places all over the world. I live and work in London and the Cotswolds, neither exactly gastronomic deserts. And being a judge on the TV series *The Great British Menu*, eating exquisite food from Britain's finest chefs, must be the best job in television.

I agreed to be on *The Great British Menu* because I couldn't resist the ego trip. I adore being referred to, even as a joke, as 'the talent'. The talent! It hardly takes talent to be filmed spooning food into your mouth and saying what you think of it. But again, I'm actually too vain to watch myself on telly. One of the very few times I did, I was so appalled at the sight of one of my bottom teeth sticking up like a tombstone above the others, that I persuaded my dentist to saw it down.

And I love having people do my make-up and hair, fuss about how I look, fetch me in posh cars. I confess to finding a little bit of fame (I feel a lot of it would be really constricting) highly enjoyable. I like being stopped in the supermarket and being told how great the show is, or that I don't look a day older than sixty-five. Of course I know people say what they think you want to hear. Fine by me. It *is* what I want to hear.

Also, filming is like a day off. For what other job can you just turn up without any homework: no lines learnt, no research done, no food prepared – and just sit there with a couple of cronies, getting paid to eat great food and chatter?

For all that, my vanity slightly curtails my enjoyment of working in television. I cannot watch myself – I hate the way I look and the way I sound, and always have, even when I was young. Now, looking at pictures of myself in my twenties and thirties, I feel a pang of regret that I took no pleasure in my looks. I was convinced I was overweight and horse-faced. God, what I would give today to weigh ten stone and get into a size twelve!

By the Eighties I was a lot larger and once, as a guest on a cookery show, I found myself in a jokey cucumber-slicing competition with the much more famous Keith Floyd. I set about my cucumber with my usual competitiveness, hoping the camera would track my wafer-thin slices cascading evenly from the blade. But Keith just took a few chops at his cucumber, getting to the end in no time. The camera, far from following my professional knife action, was close up on our faces. Keith, chin up, eyes to camera, looked handsome and amused, while my head was down, tripling my chin, jowls bouncing with every chop.

I'm sometimes tempted to have another go at 're-shaping' with a surgeon's knife. But I've not got enough time left to waste it on weeks of pain, even for a good cause.

It surprises me that the BBC has not decreed me too venerable to be on telly. Perhaps I survive on *Great British Menu* because they like to be able to point to at least one septuagenarian female on the box.

Whether I really deserve to be sitting in judgement on great chefs and pontificating about food is debatable. I was never the chef at Leith's Restaurant; had I been, we would not have achieved our Michelin star. I have never been a fanatical foodie, bent on ever more invention, originality or perfection. I've been perfectly happy to nick ideas from other chefs, follow recipes, and leave innovation to better cooks.

But for the past seven years I've been putting fork to face for hours at a time and talking about every mouthful, competing with Matthew Fort's erudition and Oliver Peyton's taste buds. Between them, they know all the great chefs of today and yesterday – and probably of tomorrow. They understand the history of food, the origin of ingredients, the difference between *scorzonera* and salsify, and can distinguish between the flavours of mace and nutmeg. Matthew, damn it, can even tell how high up the mountain a Welsh lamb has been grazing, and Oliver can tell you it's Welsh! Sometimes I'm not even sure it's lamb.

I think entering the *GBM* competition is extraordinarily brave of chefs at the top of their game. When you're already famous, to face the possibility of defeat by someone younger and less well known takes courage. But of course courage (and confidence and self-belief) is what great chefs have in spades.

In the first series, poor Anthony Worrall Thompson, who at the time was all over our television screens, had made some highly original faggots, to my fellow judges' delight. Both were enthusiastically tucking in, but my plate smelt bitter, and being an old hand at examining students' food (I used to taste my way through ninety-six four-course meals cooked by students at Leith's School, remember) I immediately flipped my faggot over. The underside was burnt black. AWT looked exactly like a naughty schoolboy caught cheating. Another favourite memory is of the final banquet in the British Embassy in Paris. Richard Corrigan and Mark Hix, old mates and both highly competitive, were in the kitchen together. Out of sheer devilment, Richard nicked all Mark's very special perry (cider made with pears) destined for his dessert, and merrily poured it into the court bouillon for his fish. A fine display of kitchen abuse followed, but somehow the dinner was perfection and the pair of them, plus Tom Parker Bowles and most of the kitchen ended up at four a.m. eating tripe at the Boeuf sur le Toit in Les Halles. They did not look well when daylight broke.

I think the gifts I should thank the gods for are health, energy and optimism. Illness, or a glass-half-empty nature, cuts you off from so much satisfaction and happiness. My enthusiasm is a form of greed – I always want to go everywhere and do everything. Of course, one day desire will diminish, but right now I'm torn between wanting to see the parts of the world I have never visited and longing to stay at home, to see my children and enjoy my grandchildren. And like every mum I dream of my darling daughter finding the man of her dreams. Or maybe of my dreams. But I don't fret for her. She has a nature so resilient, optimistic and independent, she will be happy, I'm sure.

And I do long to give my garden more attention. I've always been a fair-weather gardener, and now that my knees don't care for weeding and my back objects to digging, I rather grandly instruct while the aptly named gardener, John Worthy, does the hard graft.

And then there is the irresistible appeal of fishing. I know old boys in their nineties who are still fishing. A heart attack in the middle of the Spey would be a great way to go.

But there is still a bit of the workaholic in me. There is an old joke which perfectly illustrates the popular, but false, image of the non-executive director: what is the difference between a non-exec and a supermarket trolley? Answer: not much. You fill them both up with food and drink, but the trolley has a mind of its own.

But the truth is that the responsibilities of board members are onerous and the job often arduous. Governance of public companies is extremely strict these days. When I joined the board of Orient Express Hotels, I had to get a lesson on New York stock exchange regulation, and test my financial literacy on line before I could join the company's audit committee.

Having said I was through with charitable causes, two years ago I joined the board of Slow Food UK, which promotes good, fair, clean food. Of its many educational programmes, Slow Food Baby is the one that interests me most. Research into the brain has made it abundantly clear that the nourishment babies get in the womb and in their first six months largely determines their diet for life.

I'm also trying to get a new project going to trial decent food in hospitals. The NHS sometimes behaves as if what we eat has no bearing on our health. Food in some hospitals is so dire that the patients go without or live on chips and chocolate brought in by their visitors. I suspect hospital food might be a harder nut to crack even than school food. But it is surely worth a try?

And, most importantly, I still have love stories in my head, demanding to be told. I don't really understand why writers write. Some will say they do it for the money, but I suspect they'd do it anyway. For me, it's like a disease, an itch, something I'm compelled to do. I have always written, whether private poems, journalism, cookery articles, business reports. But by far the most satisfying to me are the novels.

Right now I'm planning a trilogy of novels about a family in the restaurant trade that would allow me to trace the changes in food and restaurants from post-war spam to gastro pubs and Heston Blumenthal gastronomy – and provide me with three generations of characters to star in those love stories.

And since I'm no spring chicken, I had better get a move on. I feel as energetic and enthusiastic, or almost, as I ever did, but of course it can't last. While it does, though, I hope my PA, Francisca and Lyn, my housekeeper, will remain the twin pillars that prop the old girl up – she is the most fortunate of women to have them.

And of course I know with absolute certainty that my children, in that sickly phrase, will be *there for me*. I catch my daughter being patient and shepherding me about as I did my mother. Daniel increasingly assumes a *pater familias* role.

I seek their advice these days rather than give them mine.

Tempus fugit, no question. Maybe one day I will finally settle down to reading all those books and watching all the classic movies I've missed. Maybe.

One thing's for sure: if I do, I shall do so with relish.